85-1084

P9-DUT-769

Beyond Monetarism

BEYOND MONETARISM

Finding the Road to Stable Money

MARC A. MILES

Basic Books, Inc., Publishers

NEW YORK

Library of Congress Cataloging in Publication Data

Miles, Marc A., 1948–
  Beyond monetarism.

  Includes bibliographical references and index.
    1. Monetary policy—United States.   2. Federal
Reserve banks.   3. Chicago school of economics.
I. Title.
HG540.M54 1984   332.4'973   83-45254
ISBN 0-465-00663-9

TO

Erin

Averi

Todd

in the hope that the world

will be more predictable

when you have to buy a house

Contents

Contents

again on how reform of the "real" side of the economy could never effectively succeed without simultaneous reform of the monetary side. Monetarism could never work. It is a seriously flawed theory of policy. It had to be replaced by a policy that could bring about monetary stability.

While recent events certainly spurred the current writing effort, my feelings about the ineffectiveness of monetarism can be traced back as far as my undergraduate days at the University of Chicago in the late 1960s. My senior honors paper investigated whether Professor Karl Brunner's evidence that the Fed "dominates" the behavior of the money supply over the half business cycle also held over shorter periods of time. As a faithful Chicago undergraduate, imbued with the spirit of monetarism, I was sure that it would. Yet I was introduced to a young Chicago professor who would serve as my advisor, and who insisted that no such evidence would be found. That advisor was Arthur Laffer, and he turned out to be right.

These initial doubts were reinforced by my graduate education at Chicago. Studying macroeconomics, or "money" as they called it at Chicago, further opened my mind to the limitations and failings of conventional theory. While microeconomics was a nicely self-contained theory whose parts fit neatly together, macro theory seemed a jumble of loosely connected ideas in search of a central core. There were too many loose ends. Upon Laffer's return from two years in Washington, I discussed my uneasiness over macroeconomics with him. He confided to me that he shared the same concerns and was searching for a new approach to macro theory. The new approach would have a global perspective and would be consistent with the theory of efficient markets. The theory would revolve around basic paradigms in which economic behavior at the individual level is consistent with economic behavior at the national or world level. We resolved to join forces in the search.

Preface

To many outsiders, Chicago in the late 1960s and early 1970s was seen as a monolithic place, dominated by Friedmanian Monetarism, which assumed that the Federal Reserve controls some definition of money within the U.S. borders and that the ups and downs of this quantity determine the ups and downs of U.S. interest rates and prices. In fact, there were two quite different monetary traditions at Chicago. The other tradition was the Monetary Approach to the Balance of Payments (MABP) in the International Economics Workshop. This tradition was sparked by separate essays written by Laffer and by Robert Mundell in the mid-1960s. Unlike the famous closed economy "oral tradition" of Friedman's Money Workshop, the MABP explicitly recognized that money markets are global, not national. In an integrated world market, the Fed is only one participant, and under fixed exchange rates the Fed could clearly control neither the money supply nor inflation.

The differing perspectives led to drastically different policy conclusions. The MABP argued that in efficient world money markets the best monetary policy was one that permitted a stable value of domestic money in terms of foreign currencies and/or commodities. In contrast, the monetarist answer to global money markets was an attempt to isolate the U.S. money market: allow exchange rates to float; do not stand behind the dollar; let it float down. A depreciating dollar might even stimulate the economy and improve the trade balance. Hence, the monetarists cheered the slamming of the U.S. gold window on August 15, 1971, and the breakdown a year and a half later of the agreement stabilizing exchange rates.

The MABP, on the other hand, held that the fall in the dollar's value would just yield more inflation in the United States relative to other countries. Unhinging money makes the value of money unstable. Indeed, Laffer and Mundell openly warned of an immediate boost to inflation caused by the dollar's devaluation and of the likelihood of higher average inflation rates and of increased volatility in the next decade. All this, they believed, would lead to slower economic growth. Their warnings proved prophetic.

So even as monetarism began to burst into the public view, its basic assertions were being challenged by the global monetary theory. The framework of the global theory had been outlined by the time the U.S. gold window was shut in 1971. It continued to provide accurate warnings of volatile money markets throughout the 1970s. In the 1970s, too, a further understanding of new phenomena like Euromarkets, domestic financial innovations, and the potential role of foreign monies helped to explain why, within global money markets, even floating exchange rates cannot prevent the money supply from being endogenous (shaped by the demands of the public) and a money supply target from being an ineffective policy. We began to see more clearly why the implications of monetarism, while appearing simple and intuitive, were largely inconsistent with the way private money markets work.

The mid-1970s also marked the initial development of a companion theory about the real side of the economy. This real sector theory is what became known as "supply-side economics." It began to show the limitations of monetarism from another perspective. Monetarism was shown to be just another version of Keynesian demand management, with varying injections of money, instead of injections of government expenditure, regulating aggregate demand.

The globally oriented research continued to provide new insights as to why monetarism would never be an effective policy guide for monetary stability. Yet, by 1981, there were monetarists firmly implanted in some of the highest economic offices of the Reagan Administration. Even the press was religiously incorporating into its analysis the monetarist assertions

Preface

that pressuring the Fed to limit the growth in money aggregates would lead to monetary stability. Each Friday afternoon, the financial markets impatiently anticipated the latest money-supply figures, as though they held the key to the future. It certainly looked as though the monetarists had the answers.

It was, of course, a misleading impression. We finally saw in the fall of 1982, for example, how a retreat from monetarist quantity targets was necessary for interest rates to decline. But nowhere was there a complete supply-side explanation of why this should be so, of why monetarism is doomed never to work, and of what should replace it. There was a need for a concise, explicit enumeration of the problems. There was a need to share the insights from my days at Chicago. There was a need to explain why price rules, and not quantity rules, are the only policies that can work. There was even the further need to explain to some of my fellow supply-siders *precisely* what *combination* of price rules might work to achieve price stability. In other words, there was a need to discuss what monetary policy lies beyond monetarism.

A book of this nature does not emerge from a vacuum. There is always a group of people who share at least some beliefs, and whose insights help to focus the story or generate new ideas. I would be terribly remiss if I did not thank these people.

At the top of the list is David Ranson. David has shared my dissatisfaction with conventional money supply and demand analyses of inflation and interest rates. (After all, if the relevant world supply of money is endogenous, so that the private sector is always making its supply equal its demand, why should there ever be inflation?) Therefore we have together probed alternative approaches to monetary theory for the past few years. The emphasis on government's role as a redeemer of money, the discussion of how prices are formed under unhinged money, and the emphasis on the need for two price rules all evolved from those discussions. My thanks are also extended to Eugene White and Alan Reynolds, who both contributed in special ways.

This book was written during my sabbatical in 1982–83. I would like to thank the Lehrman Institute in New York, whose generous Research Fellowship made the sabbatical possible. An equally important benefit of the Fellowship, however, was an opportunity to present my ideas at roundtable discussions organized at the Institute. These discussions were extremely helpful in focusing my arguments. Among the roundtable participants, I would like to thank in particular Chairman Richard Zecher, Eugene Birnbaum, Joe Cobb, Maury Harris, Graham Loving, Robert Mundell, Bluford Putnam, and Sykes Wilford for their constructive comments. While these and other people helped to save me from some potentially embarrassing mistakes, I must of course retain responsibility for any remaining errors.

The typing of the various drafts was handled by Andra Velsor, who is probably as happy as I am that the book is finally completed. I thank her for her diligence.

Finally, I would like to thank my wife Manja who graciously read more drafts than she cares to remember. Her objective opinions as a noneconomist were extremely helpful in identifying and improving vague or complex sections. Her insightful comments helped me to brush away extraneous ideas and get to the heart of the matter. More than once I vigorously opposed her comments, only to realize in a later draft that she had been absolutely right. I have also found that in editing my work all these years she has learned more economics than she ever intended, or would admit. These realizations, of course, only add to my trust in and high respect for her opinions.

Beyond Monetarism

I

The Toll of
Current Monetary Policy

THE MORNING NEWS SHOWS now tell you not only what the stock market did yesterday, but also the prevailing price of gold on the London, Zurich, and New York markets, as well as the latest quotes of the dollar against the deutsche mark, pound, and yen. Twenty years ago such detailed daily quotes were rare. But today frequent, detailed reports are a necessity. The stock market is capable of rising or falling thirty-five points in a day. Gold prices can suddenly change by thirty dollars an ounce. The dollar can swing wildly against one or more currencies. Such reports are simply a symptom of our uncertain times.

The steady decline in monetary stability over the last twenty years has triggered a continuing debate over what can and should be done. The points of the debate can be heard echoing in the chambers of Congress, the offices of the Treasury Building, and the halls of the Federal Reserve, as well as in the classrooms and seminar rooms of most universities. Yet a consensus on policy remains elusive. Newspapers report that the

President wants to "stay the course," the Fed is in the process of "modifying" its policy guidelines, and some Congressmen and academicians are calling for more radical monetary change. As the debate continues, concerned citizens must sort through a pile of conflicting ideas that mount up daily. Their confusion grows. In the homes and offices of the nation, the toll of the continuing monetary uncertainty mounts.

For example, remember how people used to manage their income when they retired? They knew they could count on a monthly check from social security, and maybe a check from their pension fund. The rest of their income was from earnings on their life savings. Their strategy for managing their savings was simple. Much of the money went in the bank. Some went into government bonds, and another chunk might be invested in bonds of a utility company their broker recommended. Their income was safe and dependable, as were their monthly expenses.

By contrast, a couple retiring today can depend on nothing but uncertainty. Their cost of living keeps climbing, but at uneven rates. In June 1979, for example, inflation was eating away at their buying power at an annual rate of 7.6 percent. Only a few months later, in February 1980, the rate had zoomed to 20.3 percent. By the summer of 1982, inflation was back to the 5 percent range. How are they to plan for the future? Could that inflation rate be expected to last? How long would it be before inflation might again bound up to near double-digit rates?

Today's retirees therefore face an extremely complicated problem of anticipating expenses. With volatile rates of inflation, they can never be sure what it will cost them to live next year. Even the periodic "low" rates of inflation provide little solace. They are still high by historic standards. In the twenty-five-year period 1947–72, for instance, wholesale price inflation in the United States averaged less than 2 percent per year. Those who have retired since 1972, however, have faced inflation averaging nearly 10 percent.

Nor can retirees find a stable hedge against the vicissitudes of inflation. Even the traditional gold haven is too volatile to depend on. The price of gold has moved like a roller coaster. In the spring of 1979 an ounce of gold sold for as little as $235. A long climb, commencing late that summer, brought the price to $850 per ounce in January 1980. The price then began to slide again, bottoming at less than $300 per ounce in June 1982. Two months later, the price of gold pierced the $400 mark. In the next month the price peaked close to $500 an ounce, only to fall again below $400. In January 1983, gold closed above $500 once more, but by March the price dropped back to nearly $400 per ounce.

Today's retirees, then, must deal with a volatile economic world. They scan the newspaper and investment service reports. They listen to financial talk shows. They search for pieces of evidence, even hints, of what to expect next.

And they are not alone. Businessmen, too, find it harder and harder to conduct their activities in this increasingly volatile world. Fluctuating inflation and interest rates wreak havoc with investment plans. Businessmen spend more and more of their time simply protecting the profit on existing deals or protecting existing assets. Fluctuating currency values complicate the picture further. Says one senior officer at an international corporation, "It used to be you could look at the [foreign exchange] currency picture once a month. Now I spend one or two hours a day on it."[1]

In this unstable world, individuals grasp for what information they can. Energies are diverted to fill the information void. Some people place their faith increasingly in highly visible "handicappers" of the future like Henry Kaufman or Joseph

Granville, whose words are closely watched in hopes that they have some secret formula for sorting out all the conflicting signals. Economic services promising to provide more accurate forecasts of interest and exchange rates proliferate. Businessmen learn how to hedge through financial futures on stocks, bonds, and foreign exchange. The variety and volume of financial futures contracts soar. In 1971 there were no financial futures contracts available. Today there are about two dozen different contracts on foreign exchange, money market instruments, and stock indices. Each day about 170,000 contracts change hands. The businessman, like the retiree, must spend more and more energy dealing with the economic volatility. Like Alice in *Through the Looking Glass,* he or she must run faster just to stay in place.

The time, effort, and resources now needed to do what used to be simple have in turn created serious doubts about recent monetary policy. People from all walks of life hunger for more monetary stability, so that they can better plan their retirements, investments, and children's educations and weddings, and even pay for their mortgages and groceries. A consensus has formed that something must be done. Inflation and interest rates must be lowered. Uncertainty must be reduced. Government policy must be redirected.

But who can we turn to for the remedies? Will Keynesian policy be resurrected to find the cure? Our experience of the last forty years has produced the growing feeling that traditional Keynesian fiscal policies do not hold out the promise of a solution. Higher tax rates are not likely to hold down inflation. Using taxes to deal with inflation is like cutting off a finger to deal with a sore nail: it does not directly solve the problem, and the side effects are even worse. If anything, the higher tax rates create incentives for people to work fewer hours and for factories and businesses to close earlier. With people and factories producing less, standards of living fall. Declining output and living standards in turn create less need for what money exists, only adding to the instability of money.

Nor would higher taxes bring down interest rates permanently. The decline in effort and output brought on by higher taxes results in shrinking government tax revenues and expanding unemployment and welfare payments. The declining revenues and expanding payments hardly help keep down either deficits or real interest rates, while the declining stability of money works to raise nominal or market interest rates. In short, the key to our current troubles does not lie in old Keynesian formulas. It is increasingly recognized that Keynesian fiscal policies cannot solve these recurrent problems of high inflation, high interest rates, and sluggish growth.

Not that traditional fiscal Keynesians have been spending a lot of time in the policy saddle anyway. The reins of economic policy were being passed from fiscal Keynesians to monetarist Keynesians even before President Reagan took office. On October 6, 1979, the Federal Reserve publicly announced it would begin basing its monetary policy on monetarism. For three years eyes were focused each Friday on the latest wiggles in the popular measures of the money supply, and how they changed the wiggles for the year as a whole. Monetarist policy operated under the belief that if those wiggles could be constrained, inflation and interest rates would be lower and less volatile.

Yet the experience with monetarism has been anything but reassuring. The shift to the monetarist "quantity rule" of slow, steady money growth was followed by even higher and more volatile interest rates and rates of inflation. The discount yield on three-month Treasury bills, for instance, which averaged 5.0, 5.3, and 7.2 percent in the three years before 1979, averaged 11.5, 14.0, and 10.6 percent in the three years after.

BEYOND MONETARISM

The experience led only to more frustration and despair over policy. Even Milton Friedman, the most famous monetarist, complains about the highly volatile monetary course the Fed has followed:

The recent "bulge" is clearly a continuation of the yoyo pattern of monetary growth that has prevailed ever since October 6, 1979. . . . The period since October 6, 1979, differs strikingly from earlier periods of comparable length in three major respects: (1) monetary growth has been far more erratic; (2) interest rates have been far more erratic; (3) the economy has been far more erratic.[2]

His fellow monetarist Allan Meltzer similarly concludes:

The Federal Reserve's experiment with monetary control is a failure. Since the experiment began in October 1979 the volatility of money growth, short-term interest rates, long-term interest rates and exchange rates has been raised beyond previous levels and more than necessary. This indicates that something is wrong.[3]

The performance of the economy has suffered accordingly. Between 1980 and 1982 the economy showed virtually no growth. By 1982 the unemployment rate had soared above 10 percent. Already there are signs that the Federal Reserve and the Treasury will abandon their flirtation with monetarist policies. The strict adherence to monetary growth targets has eased as the rosy promises have failed in reality.

Thus neither major school of economic thought has been able to provide solutions to today's economic crises. Ideas that look so promising on paper have proven to be washouts as policies. The theories in which we have been placing our faith appear bankrupt for dealing with today's problems.

Even alternatives like the "supply-side" proposals have foundered in the recent environment of high interest rates and inflation. For example, in 1981, Congress passed, and President Reagan signed, a bill promising to lower income tax rates. But year-to-year consumer price inflation was 10.4 percent in 1981 and 6.1 percent in 1982. With continued inflation, such tax relief becomes illusory. While on the one hand Congress lowers tax rates legislatively, on the other hand rates rise through inflation. Cost-of-living raises push wage earners into higher tax brackets (bracket creep); the value of inventories on the shelf rises, producing taxable, illusory profits; and businesses are forced to depreciate their investments at original cost, not what it would cost to replace them. The promises of the legislation are offset by the realities of inflation. The net tax rate "cut," if any, ends up being very small.

So whether a Keynesian or supply-sider, one can agree that the high and volatile rates of interest and inflation associated with recent monetary policy are a major contributor to the high unemployment and stagnant growth we have been experiencing. The question, of course, is how do we get rid of them? The monetarists take credit for the slower inflation experienced in 1982. But that reduction was accompanied by a very deep recession. Do the monetarists want credit for that, too? Is recession a necessary cost of lower inflation?

As the Fed has turned away from monetarist policies, we have seen a strong recovery in first the stock and bond markets, and then the economy. The accompanying rise in the price of gold, however, indicates that a new bout with higher inflation may be around the corner. Can we not break these ties of reduced inflation with stagnation and renewed inflation with recovery? Can we not find a workable, lasting solution to our monetary woes that does not conjure up austerity and pain? Clearly, without such an alternative policy we are unlikely to find a significant, stable, and lasting recovery in the growth of national income and jobs.

BEYOND MONETARISM

Policy makers and pundits appear stumped. They are confused and frustrated over how to deal with this Achilles heel of economic policy. Most would agree with the assessment of how high interest rates and inflation have been wrecking the economy. Most would also agree that the monetarist experiment has failed. Yet most are also unsure why it has failed or what needs to be substituted in its place. On Sunday mornings one can tune in the television to hear the cacophony of commentators lamenting and see interviewees busily wringing their hands in dismay.

But such pessimism is not necessary. There are alternatives, and they are not strange alternatives. Rather, they are alternatives that stem from an economic time we can all remember. There is, therefore, hope that these problems can be solved. All it takes is pointing out the proper path to the policy makers and giving them an electoral nudge.

But finding that elusive path out of the woods seems difficult today. The vines, branches, and underbrush of recent policies hide the way. Somehow we need to cut through all that bramble.

That is what this book seeks to do. It tries to work as a map and compass to current monetary policy. How did we initially get lost in monetary instability? How do we find the best way out to economic prosperity? What continues to block our path?

To clear our path, we must get at the roots of our current problems. On the one hand, the book reexamines monetarism. What promises were made by monetarism, and why have they not been delivered? Twenty years ago governments seemed capable of providing low and stable inflation and interest rates. Why can they not do so now? Can this dilemma be explained by the string of monetary experiments over the last twenty years?

From 1946 to 1971 the United States and the world were

governed by a monetary system called the Bretton Woods Agreement. Under this system, the value of the dollar was tied to gold, and other currencies were tied to the value of the dollar. Governments were recognized to have little monetary discretion. In the mid-1960s, however, the U.S. government (and other countries) began to undertake new experiments designed to permit more discretion. For example, in that period the United States began the process of cutting the dollar loose from the Bretton Woods commitment to gold. The process culminated with President Nixon slamming shut the U.S. gold window on August 15, 1971. In 1973 the value of the dollar was also cut loose from other currencies. We entered a period of the "floating dollar." In October 1979 the Federal Reserve undertook a new experiment. No longer was the Fed to target the interest rate charged by one bank lending another bank reserves (Fed funds rate). Now the Fed promised to watch closely how fast monetary aggregates were growing. Assurances were made that each of these experiments promised to usher in a "golden age" of monetary policy. Yet none seemed to work to bring down either inflation or interest rates for any extended period of time. The impact of each subsequent experiment, if anything, was only to raise further the level of financial volatility.

Why was the policy such a failure? Why could there be such a discrepancy between the promises and what was delivered? The answers arise from the deficiencies and limitations of monetarism. This book emphasizes these by raising some interesting, yet troublesome, questions about the basic logic of the monetarist assertions. For example, can the Federal Reserve really control the total *relevant* supply of dollars? Monetarist policy certainly assumes that such a quantity can be closely regulated. But how does one even define the relevant supply of dollars? Is it M1 (currency plus checking accounts), M2 (M1 plus some time accounts), or some hypothetical M36? Ask any two economists, and you are bound to get at least three different answers. What is becoming increasingly clear, however, is that it is doubtful that the Fed can control the relevant money supply.

Monetarism has ignored this problem. In a world of global, integrated money markets, monetarism has myopically concentrated on only the number of dollars within the U.S. borders. But dollars are held abroad, and foreign money finds its way into the United States. Monetarism has called on the Fed to expand and tighten its regulations. Yet increased regulation encourages domestic financial innovations such as money market mutual funds and repurchase agreements, as well as additional activity in the unregulated Eurodollar market. These new financial activities provide outlets for escape from Fed regulation. In addition, monetarism has chosen to downplay even the traditional textbook descriptions of how banks and the public can react to mitigate the impact of efforts to control the supply of money.

Even if there were full knowledge of the relevant money supply and how to control it, additional problems would remain. There are problems in estimating both how much money there actually is in the world market and, equally important, how that quantity compares with what the world would like. And even without these other problems, the evidence that monetarism works is far from compelling. It is a revelation to discover that the supporting evidence is equally consistent with the opposite scenario: that the amount of money in the economy just passively expands and contracts with the demand for it.

This reexamination concludes that focusing on manipulating or stabilizing the quantity of money is an unworkable policy. At best the quantity rule is only an indirect, imprecise way of achieving the real target—price stability. In addition to the problems of defining and measuring money, a quantity rule is not a very good system for guiding the Fed in how it should behave, or for informing the private sector whether the Fed is behaving properly.

On the other hand, the book does point a way out of the current morass brought on by the monetary experiments. Fortunately there are better, more direct ways than quantity rules for going after stable prices and interest rates. The alternative is for the Fed to follow "price rules"—that is, directly stabilize the *value* of money. The book contrasts the complexity of financial life for the Fed and the public under quantity rules with the simplicity of understanding, administering, and keeping track of price rules.

Randomly choosing price rules, however, is not a guarantee of monetary success. The actual price rules chosen are extremely important. Alternatives from a commodity standard to price controls are discussed. In the end it is argued that a single price rule, such as a spot gold standard, is not enough. Nor is the proposal recently bandied about Congress to have the Fed simply concentrate on keeping interest rates low. A policy of, say, pegging only today's value of the dollar does not give the Fed sufficient credibility. People also want to know whether the same policy will be carried out tomorrow or next year. Hence, a successful policy requires two price rules. One rule assures the public of what the Fed is doing today. The second rule assures the public of what the Fed intends to do in the foreseeable future.

Having outlined the basis of successful monetary policy, the book concludes with a specific new suggestion for a two-price-rule policy the Fed should follow. One rule would stabilize the dollar value of a basket of commodities through the financial futures market. Targeting a basket of commodities means the dollar's value is not tied to the vicissitudes of any one commodity such as gold. The use of financial futures means physical reserves of the commodities need not be purchased, transferred, or stored by the government in conducting monetary policy. The second rule would stabilize long-term interest rates. Together these two rules would stabilize both the spot and forward price of goods, giving us a monetary policy that would be an important step beyond monetarism.

2

Putting Our Problems in a Global Perspective

PART OF THE PROBLEM with current monetary policy is that policy makers forget there is a world economy. Policy makers have a tendency to believe that, in focusing on what affects prices and interest rates in this country, they need look no farther than the Golden Gate Bridge or the Statue of Liberty. Somehow the United States is an economic entity that can be picked up, examined, adjusted, and experimented with, without worrying about the impact on other countries or the feedback from other countries to the United States.

Certainly the United States is large relative to most other countries, and much of its commerce and financial activity is self-contained. But in this age of high technology and rapid communication, no country operates in a vacuum. Those who subscribe to cable television can readily appreciate this fact. On a recent night I was able to watch tennis live via satellite from Argentina, a Philadelphia television station showing a basketball game live from Boston, and a New York station broadcasting a British television series. In the course of one evening, right in my own home, I was able to share experiences with people on the next block, 50 miles away, 250 miles away, and on two faraway continents.

And more than just images are sped around the world. Commercial flights can now carry the traveler between Europe and America in less than three and one-half hours. The space shuttle revolves around the entire earth in about ninety minutes. All kinds of products from oranges to Mercedes are dispersed from where they are produced to the far corners of the earth. World trade today is roughly a $1.8 trillion business, equal to almost two-thirds of all economic activity in the United States.

Policy makers should therefore not have a map of the United States on the wall. In its place should be a picture of the earth snapped by astronauts on their way to the moon. As the policy makers contemplate their next move, they should see the picture of Earth revolving slowly in space, and realize that the United States is only one small part of that mass of land and sea. From that perspective, the importance of national borders fades, and one sees that the countries of the world are connected to each other. We are all in it together. No one part can chart its future course independently of the other parts. The world economic system is interconnected, and any policy that ignores a sizable chunk of the system has to be immediately suspect.

There exists no better example of this interconnected economic system than the international money market. Today's money market is a highly technical, highly mobile operation. Just like television, the latest movements in the money market are sped instantaneously via satellite around the world. Computers of large banks and other corporations continuously monitor interest-rate and exchange-rate quotations from markets in Europe, America, and Asia. When even slight changes occur, they are immediately flashed on computer terminals throughout the world. Behind each terminal is an individual or group of individuals ready to jump into the market to buy or sell securities or foreign exchange to take advantage of a fleeting profit opportunity. Money and securities flow quickly and easily from one country to another. In a push of a telex button, millions—or even billions—of dollars can change hands halfway around the world.

In this organized world money market, U.S. residents and the U.S. government are important participants. But a glance at that picture of the earth in space makes one realize that they still are only a few of many participants. The U.S. dollar is one of the primary monies traded, but it is still only one of several major currencies. The Federal Reserve is an important source of new money in this world, but from space it would be only one of many pins representing central banks. Again, it is only one source supplying only one of the monies.

In addition, as the world money market has evolved, intricate new ways have developed to create new money. As we look at the earth from space, we see that some money comes from the pins representing the various central banks in the world. Those pins, however, are only part of the story. The official issuers of money are today only one source of liquidity. Much now comes, instead, from private institutions.

So as we look back from space at an individual in the United States who wants more money, we realize that he or she has several alternatives. The desired money may be supplied by the Fed. But the money may also come from foreign countries or from the Euromarkets, and it may involve dollars or some other currency. The assertion, then, that the Federal Reserve is the dominant force over the quantity of money becomes rather tenuous. The Fed is but one participant in the competitive, global money market. Assuming that it can control the amount of money between the Canadian border and the Rio Grande by controlling the trickle of Fed liabilities to the market is myopic. It is a bit like trying to prevent criminals from making their getaway by throwing up a roadblock on just the main road; there are many other ways of getting out of town. As succeeding chapters will reveal in more detail, the world has developed a variety of unrestricted markets and other financial innovations to circumvent the Fed's attempts to control the quantity of dollars. So in this world of integrated, mobile money markets, the Fed's ability to carry out the Monetarists' Dream of slow and steady money growth is open to question.

Bringing Home the Idea of Global Markets

The idea of global rather than national markets may strike some at first as complicated and strange. Most people are unaccustomed to thinking about the issues of monetary policy and inflation from a global instead of a domestic perspective. But if we put the map of the United States back on the policy maker's wall for a minute, we see two things. First, there are fifty states of assorted sizes, closely intertwined in a "global" economy. Second, there are twelve central bank "pins," one for each Federal Reserve District. There are really twelve separate monies and twelve separate central banks across the United States. Each District Reserve Bank oversees the regulations concerning banking in its jurisdiction. And each District Reserve Bank issues money. A close inspection of the seals on the dollars in your wallet will probably indicate that the bills have been issued by the Federal Reserve Bank of New York, or Chicago, or Atlanta, or one of the other District Banks.

Most people take little notice of where the dollars they hold originated. The reason is that each Federal Reserve Bank has agreed to trade at face value money issued by another Bank.

So a five-dollar bill issued by the Federal Reserve Bank of St. Louis can always be exchanged for five one-dollar bills at the Federal Reserve Bank of Richmond. The convertibility of money across regions is equivalent to a fixed exchange rate among Federal Reserve Districts.

What economic phenomena are usually thought to characterize this "global" market with several "monies"? First, with the value of one regional dollar tied to the value of the dollars of other regions, prices are expected to display similar movements throughout the United States. A Boston Fed dollar is rising and falling in value at the same rate as a Dallas Fed dollar. So the amount people can buy with money where Boston Fed dollars predominate should be changing at the same rate as what people can buy where Dallas Fed dollars predominate. Indeed, few talk about Texas inflation differing significantly from inflation in Rhode Island. The most relevant level to focus on the origins of inflation is the "global" market, not the individual regions.

In this example of fixed exchange rates, it is therefore incorrect to focus on the Dallas Fed as the source of Texas inflation. The Dallas Fed may be an important supplier of dollars in Texas, but it is only one supplier. As prices rise in Texas, and individuals and firms want or need more money, Texas residents can get more dollars from the Dallas Fed, or they can get more by trading with or borrowing from people in other regions. While inflation rates are similar across states, the demands or supplies of money may change at very different rates. Hence, some areas of the country end up with more money than needed, and some areas with less. The second economic phenomenon is that, in general, we should expect to find that in this "global" market money flows from regions with excess money supplies to those with excess demands.

The third economic fact concerns the Dallas Fed's ability to implement policy. The Dallas Fed supplies dollars. Its region may be one of the largest in the country. But even so, its ability to regulate banking within the region is not sufficient to control the proportion of total U.S. money there. Banks and individuals have too many avenues for transferring money to or from any of the other regions. The Dallas Fed is therefore incapable of running a monetary policy independent of policy in the other Fed regions.

What role is left for the Dallas Fed? It cannot keep Texas inflation from exceeding inflation in the rest of the United States. Instead it focuses on maintaining convertibility. It makes the money issued by the Dallas Fed or banks in its district as useful as dollars from other districts by stabilizing the *value* of Dallas Fed dollars vis-à-vis other dollars. Maintaining convertibility maintains confidence in the relative value of Dallas Fed money today and keeps the overall level and rate of change of prices the same as in other states. The principal target of monetary policy is the value of money.

Stabilizing the exchange value of Dallas Fed dollars through convertibility smoothes out dollar values and inflation across regions. But it does not by itself eliminate inflation. Inflation is a problem of the declining absolute value of money, not the value in terms of other monies. It reflects the declining value of today's money for purchasing goods. Actually slowing inflation requires a little different policy focus: stabilizing the value of today's money in terms of goods we buy. Were one of the Federal Reserve banks, or the Fed system as a whole, to undertake that policy, dollar inflation could be reduced or even eliminated in the Dallas Fed region.

But it is not enough to have stable prices today. Most of us are concerned about what our money will buy next year or anytime in the future. A stable future value of money should also be a target of monetary policy. A policy that stabilizes the value of tomorrow's money in terms of goods eliminates expectations of future inflation. This relationship between today's price level and tomorrow's expected level is in turn reflected in the level of interest rates. A rise in next year's expected price level (more expected inflation) is associated with higher market interest rates. So a policy designed to stabilize the purchasing power of the dollar over time also helps to reduce dollar interest rates.

The analogy of the twelve Federal Reserve Districts illustrates two important points. First, focusing on money and inflation from the global perspective, rather than from the national or regional perspective, has very different policy implications. Second, the policies that are most likely to be successful in eliminating the volatility of prices are those that focus directly on stabilizing the value (versus quantity) of money. These two points are two of the central themes of this book.

The Global Market at the World Level

Now take down the U.S. map and put back the picture of the earth from space. Are prices and inflation still determined primarily at the global level? Does money flow among countries the way it flows among regions of the United States? There is remarkable evidence that the economic phenomena observed among the countries of the world are quite similar to those observed among the states.

Take, for example, prices and inflation. In the United States, where dollars trade on par across regions, prices do not differ significantly. Similarly, in years in which the world has experienced fixed rates of exchange among monies, price levels have been closely aligned across countries. Under the Bretton Woods Agreement, which operated from 1946 until about 1971, the value of the dollar was fixed to gold at $35 per ounce, and other countries maintained a fixed value of their currency in terms of the dollar. Inflation over these years was very similar across countries, as the computed wholesale price indices remained closely aligned (figure 2–1). Like Texas and Rhode Island, the United States and Germany found prices changing at similar, though perhaps not precisely the same, rates.[1]

The reason prices move together across countries and regions is the threat of arbitrage, the simultaneous purchase and sale of the same commodity in two different markets in order to profit from unequal prices. Say that you found that a can of ground coffee that sold for $4.00 in your neighborhood sold for $6.00 in the next town. It does not take a computer to realize that buying a can of coffee in your neighborhood and selling it in the next town yields a $2 profit. Putting a few gross of cans in your station wagon and driving to the next town could yield a handsome day's profit. And the venture is risk-free if the price spread continues, for every can you buy at $4 you will sell at $6. Your only costs are gas for your car and your time.

So, if the prices of oranges, shoes, or steel began to diverge across regions, some enterprising individual would suddenly find an opportunity for a safe profit. All he or she would have to do is buy the oranges or shoes or steel in the region or country where it is cheaper, rent a truck, ship, or cargo plane, and sell it where it is more expensive. Of course, this effort would not pay unless the price differential covered costs such as transportation and tariffs. But once it did, that individual and others would find the activity relatively risk-free and very profitable.

The important question, however, is whether the price differential would continue once people started moving oranges,

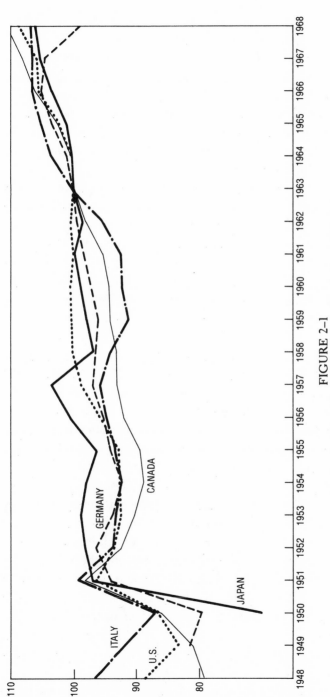

FIGURE 2-1

Wholesale Price Indices of Five Major Countries, 1948–1968

SOURCE: *International Financial Statistics*, International Monetary Fund.

shoes, or steel between markets to take advantage of it. Once the arbitrage started, prices in the two regions would quickly move back into line. The increased demand and reduced availability in the lower-price region would drive up prices. Conversely, prices would tend to fall in the other region as more oranges, shoes, or steel were brought to market. These statements are true whether we are examining orange prices between Houston, Texas, and Providence, Rhode Island, or between New York and Stuttgart.

In fact, in the modern financial world, if the prices of commodities were to differ between diverse parts of the world, it would not even be necessary to hire a car, plane, or boat to take advantage of the difference. Many commodities including grains (such as corn and wheat), fibers (such as wool and cotton), metals (such as gold, platinum, and tin), eggs, orange juice, hogs, cattle, and many others are traded on organized commodity exchanges throughout the world. Say that the dollar price of raw sugar on the Coffee, Sugar and Cocoa Exchange in New York was lower than the dollar price of an equivalent amount of raw sugar on the Sugar Terminal Exchange in London. By buying raw sugar contracts for delivery in New York and simultaneously selling the equivalent amount of contracts in London, profits could be reaped without ever physically owning the commodities.

Just as we saw in the Dallas Fed analogy, then, prices in the world are determined by monetary conditions in more than one region. Inflation in the United States is not unique to the U.S. economy. Inflation is the result of interactions of economic forces among all countries. Forces in the United States economy, such as the Federal Reserve, certainly affect dollar inflation, but only to the extent that they in turn are a part of economic forces within the world economy.

The global nature of dollar inflation in turn implies that

Putting Our Problems in a Global Perspective

some popular beliefs about the relationship between money and prices must be reexamined. The conventional wisdom is that as the Fed "eases" monetary policy, the additional money leads to higher prices. Figure 2–2 illustrates the typical evidence that changes in money cause changes in prices in the United States. It shows that price changes tend to follow money changes with a lag of two years. Does this relationship provide much insight into the interrelationship between money and prices?

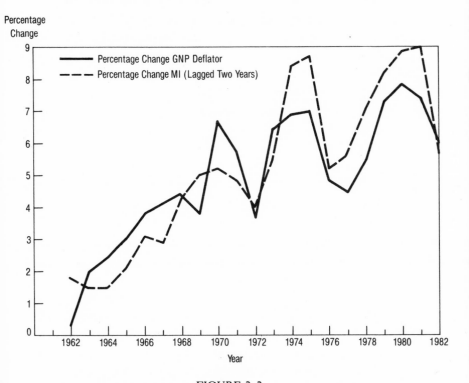

FIGURE 2–2

Money and Prices in the United States, 1962–1982

Sources: *Federal Reserve Bulletin* (Washington, D.C.: Federal Reserve Board); *Survey of Current Business* (Washington, D.C.: Department of Commerce).

BEYOND MONETARISM

Probably not. The global perspective suggests that there should be a close correlation between the rate of dollar inflation and the rate of money expansion at the global level. And so there is (see figure 2–3). In fact, in a study of the world money supply published in the prestigious *American Economic Review*, Ronald McKinnon (of Stanford University) observes, "In general, growth in the world money supply is a better predictor of American price inflation than is U.S. money growth."[2]

It is not that there should not be a relationship between money in the United States and U.S. prices. It is just that the numbers in figure 2–2 suggest the opposite of the usual monetarist interpretation of inflation. Remember the Dallas Fed analogy; when prices rose simultaneously in Texas and

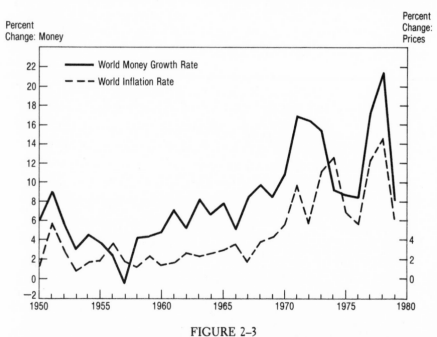

FIGURE 2–3

World Monetary Growth Rate and the World Inflation Rate, 1950–1979
Note: Reprinted with permission from Arthur B. Laffer and Marc A. Miles, *International Economics in an Integrated World* (Glenview, Ill.: Scott, Foresman & Co., 1982), 276.

throughout the entire United States, Texans scurried to find more money. The same thing is probably also happening at the national level. Perhaps anticipating higher prices, consumers and businesses allow the amount of money they hold to grow. Having more money allows them to buy before prices rise, buy at higher prices, or meet a bigger payroll. The important point is that the usual interpretation of the evidence in figure 2–2 may be wrong. Perhaps we are not seeing price changes lagging money changes by two years but rather money expanding in anticipation of price changes.

The usual interpretation implies that the Federal Reserve stands like the gatekeeper to the U.S. money market, carefully controlling through its actions how much money makes it into the economy. The implication is that the available quantity of money is *exogenously* determined by the Federal Reserve's wishes. The Federal Reserve is causing inflation. The alternative explanation, however, implies something completely different: the Fed's gates are instead a Maginot Line. While the Fed is busy monitoring its gates, the private sector is busy increasing or decreasing available money through various back doors as the need arises. In other words, the money supply is shaped by the demands of the public, not what is supplied by the Fed. The money supply in the United States is *endogenously* determined by the needs of the private sector.[3]

At the end of 1982, the portion of the money directly controlled by the Federal Reserve (the monetary base) amounted to only about $175 billion. The level of checking deposits at banks amounted to about $350 billion. The level of checking accounts is partially influenced by Federal Reserve regulations, but it is also heavily influenced by bankers' lending decisions and where the public puts its money. As described in more detail later, money market mutual funds, repurchase agreements, and Eurodollars are monetary assets under the almost complete discretion of the private sector. The level of money market funds and just *overnight* repurchase agreements and Eurodollars amounted to about $230 billion. The Fed therefore has direct control over only a small proportion of what is often considered money. There remains considerable latitude for the public to influence the ultimate amount of money in the economy.

How is the private sector able to make the money supply expand and contract? One possibility is to rely more heavily on close substitutes for traditional dollar money, such as money market funds, Eurodollars, or even foreign currencies, which are not a part of the narrowly measured money supply shown in figure 2–2. But there are still other possibilities. For example, the private sector can reduce the proportion of money held in pockets or under mattresses as currency. Less currency held makes more reserves available to banks for expanding their deposits. Or the public can free up bank reserves by shifting money from deposits with higher reserve requirements to those with lower ones.

Another possibility is to purchase or borrow money from another country. Recall that in the Dallas Fed analogy, when Texans wanted more money they could trade with or borrow from another region. Money flowed within that "global" market to where demand was greatest. The same phenomenon has been observed in the global economy. The flow of money between countries can be measured by the balance of payments. In a previous study I showed (for Germany, Japan, the Netherlands, the United Kingdom, France, and numerous other countries) how actual changes in the balance of payments (as a fraction of GNP) compare with what one would expect from changing relative net demands for money. The changes in net demand are measured by the growth of money income and money in that country and the rest of the world.[4] In most countries I found a close relationship between rising relative net demand and an increased inflow of money (improved balance of payments). As relative demand for money increases, there is a net injection of money into the country from the rest of the world. The available supply of both currency and bank reserves expands, permitting a larger quantity of even conventional measures of money.

The various ways the private sector can expand and contract the quantity of money in the United States, independently of Federal Reserve policy, is described in more detail in chapters 5, 6, and 7.

Inflation Rates and Monetary Policy in the Last Decade

Where exchange rates are fixed across countries, inflation rates should be very similar. But exchange rates have not been fixed since the early 1970s. Should inflation rates now be expected to diverge? Is the global market framework still relevant?

Both answers are yes. The global framework suggests that, where exchange rates are unhinged, inflation rates can diverge in specific ways. More precisely, a decline of, say, 10 percent in the foreign currency value of the dollar is associated with approximately 10 percent more dollar inflation than elsewhere. In other words, exchange-rate changes affect *relative* rates of inflation across countries. Countries with depreciating exchange rates experience relatively more inflation than countries with exchange rates rising in value.

The recent experience of the United States is consistent with this assertion. Despite significant ups and downs in the dollar exchange rate, wholesale prices in the United States have remained aligned to exchange-rate-adjusted foreign wholesale prices, even on a quarterly basis. For instance, in the summer of 1977, then Secretary of the Treasury Michael Blumenthal went around the world "talking down" the value of the dollar. The Carter Administration (and many economists) were under the impression then that a declining exchange rate stimulates demand and production in an economy by lowering a country's relative price level. What they found out, however, was something for which many smaller countries could already vouch: the primary effect of currency depreciation is simply a higher relative rate of inflation that offsets the decline in the currency.

Measured inflation rates in the United States took a sudden jump by October 1977. Exchange rates are immediately available market data. Changes in exchange rates are therefore immediately apparent. Changes in measured price indices, on the other hand, take time to appear. Manufacturers must first change posted prices, then data must be collected, weighted, adjusted for seasonal changes, and so on. Given the time required and the potential errors at each stage, it is therefore not surprising that the spurt in inflation appeared to lag slightly behind the fluctuation in the dollar's value. But the overall pattern is clear. As the dollar fell in value relative to other currencies, the dollar rate of inflation rose relative to inflation elsewhere. Despite the significant decline in the dollar's relative value, price levels across countries remained aligned. Conversely, as the dollar appreciated sharply in 1981–82, U.S. inflation fell relative to rates in other countries, keeping prices aligned.[5]

So under a system of nonfixed exchange rates, there are now two sources of U.S. inflation. The first, as before, is the rate of inflation that is occurring on average throughout the world. The second source is changes in the exchange rate. Were the dollar's value stable, the United States would experience the world's average inflation rate. In a global economy, the Fed has little influence over that rate. The world's average inflation, however, can be pictured as a trend line to which exchange rate depreciation/appreciation-induced inflation is added. Actual inflation can therefore deviate from the world trend.

Care must be taken, however, in interpreting the policy implications of this fact. It does imply that, under unhinged rates, the Fed can cause dollar inflation to deviate from inflation elsewhere to the extent it can influence the value of the dollar. It does *not* imply, however, that lowering the growth target of some conventional definition of money leads to less inflation. To jump from one implication to the other means ignoring the way global money markets work.

So even under unhinged rates, inflation and exchange rates must be viewed within a global framework. Two implications of this global framework are particularly important. First, the value of the dollar, like the value of other traded items, is determined in the world market. Even if the supply and demand of dollars were of primary importance in influencing the value, the conventional measures of money that have become the focus of policy are only a small fraction of the total relevant dollar money assets. The U.S. dollar market is only part of the world dollar market, and conventional measures represent only a fraction of even the U.S. dollar market. To argue correctly within this supply-demand framework that the Fed can pinpoint dollar inflation would require a Fed ability to influence precisely the much larger total relevant global market quantity of dollars.

Second, as the discussion is beginning to indicate, even an ability to control the relevant *supply* of money is at best an indirect method of influencing inflation. Any adherent to this framework would have to admit that the Fed's task is really to regulate the supply of dollars relative to dollar demand. Controlling supply alone is not enough. But even controlling dollar supply relative to dollar demand gets at the inflation problem indirectly. Inflation represents a declining purchasing value of the dollar. The direct method of controlling the rate of dollar inflation is to target the *value* of the dollar, not the *quantity* of dollars. The Fed's most direct route for stabilizing U.S. inflation is therefore a commitment to stabilize the value of money.

Current inflation, inflationary expectations, interest rates, and exchange rates have all been exacting problems over the last decade. Economists have debated how to deal with each one. Each problem involves a concept of value. A direct solution for each therefore involves adopting policies for directly stabilizing that value concept. Unfortunately, as we shall see in the next chapter, monetary policy over the last twenty years has moved 180 degrees in the other direction. Rather than maintaining a steadfast aim on the stability of values, policy makers have increasingly turned a blind eye on this goal. They have instead become increasingly fascinated, if not bewitched, by the movement of quantities.

3

The Fed Strays from the Road to Redemption

IN A GLOBAL MONEY MARKET, the Fed's primary target should be preserving the value of the dollar, but in fact recent policy has been directed quite differently. Rather than working to bolster the dollar's value, the Fed attempted, in the period of October 1979 to October 1982, to "squeeze" inflation out of the system. If only monetary policy could be sufficiently "tight," the theory went, our inflationary problem could be eliminated. High-ranking monetarists in the current administration urged the Fed to turn the screws on the money spigot tighter and tighter. Chairman Volcker reassured us that "the Federal Reserve means to do its part" by aiming for the lower end of its money-growth targets.[1] Each Friday the financial markets waited with baited breath to see if in fact the screws had been tightened another notch.

Meanwhile, back in the bond market, interest rates remained at near-record levels. Occasionally they dipped temporarily, but then they bounded right back up. Such high rates, however, seemed only to strengthen the determination of the Administration monetarists and Fed policy makers. Austerity was promoted as a necessary evil. "Turning back the inflation-ary tide isn't a simple, painless process," spoke Chairman Volcker.[2] We must tolerate a period of pain before we can enjoy the pleasure of price stability. The rapid growth of money is the cause, and inflation is the symptom. Tight money is the cure, and high interest rates are the temporary side effect.

The whole scenario had the makings of great medical drama, complete with heroes and villains. Unfortunately, it was mis-directed economics. The prescription of "tight money" may add great tension to the melodrama, but ask an economist to define what "tight" monetary policy is. How would he know if it existed? Should this not be a simple question? An econo-mist confronted with such a question would likely fumble for an answer for a few moments, before blurting out a traditional answer.

"High interest rates," he might say.

"High interest rates?" you reply. "Are you speaking of the return on capital (the *real* interest rate) or the return on money assets (the *nominal* interest rate)?"

Surprised at your persistence in pinning him down, he might answer, "The return on capital."

Fresh with your new awareness of the global nature of mar-kets, however, you can zero in a bit more. "But capital trades in a global market. Its return therefore (adjusted for differences in income taxation and other barriers) must be the same in each country. So you are implying that a 'tight' monetary policy is when the Federal Reserve alters the return on capital in international markets. But since the Fed is only one of many participants in this global market, how likely do you think such a change is to occur?"

The economist is taken aback by your response. Chances are your economist is not used to thinking about monetary policy in a global context. He has been trained to think of the good ole U.S. of A. as an island unto itself. On that island, the Fed plays the tune to which money markets dance. He therefore tries a new tack.

"Even if the Fed cannot influence the return on capital, it can affect dollar interest rates. 'Tight' policy is therefore associated with high money interest rates."

Again you can refute his assertion. Back in the beginning of the century, Irving Fisher, a renowned economist, pointed out that high money interest rates are not a sign of "tight" money. Rather they are a sign of the public's expectations about inflation.

Fisher noted that the return people expect on their money has two components. One component is the return on capital. An alternative to lending money is investing directly in capital assets. So to get people to lend you money, you must pay them at least what they could earn elsewhere.

The second component is how much inflation is expected during the period of time the money is lent. If I lend you $100 and there is inflation, the purchasing power of the $100 you give me back is less than the $100 I gave you. You are paying me back in "cheap" dollars. I want to be compensated for this loss of purchasing power, so I add this amount to the interest I charge you. With 10 percent inflation expected to occur over the year I lend you money, I charge an interest rate equal to the return on capital plus 10 percent.

Fluctuating interest rates, then, should reflect changes in the public's expectations about inflation. Expectations of higher inflation should be associated with higher interest rates, and lower expectations with lower interest rates. Some interesting evidence of this association has been provided by David Ranson.[3] Comparing the level of short-term dollar interest rates to the expected inflation revealed by consumer surveys of the U.S. public (figure 3–1), he found a close pattern of the two sets of

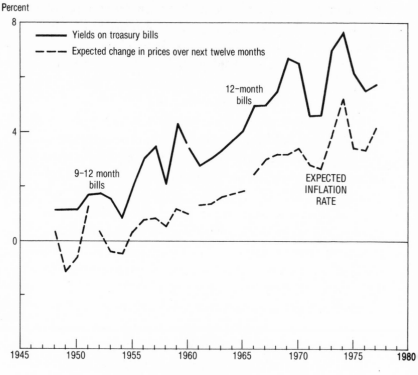

FIGURE 3–1

Actual Treasury Bill Yields Versus Consumer Inflation Expectations

NOTES: Breaks in expected inflation series reflect changes in questionnaire phraseology. Reprinted with permission from R. David Ranson, "The Real Rate of Interest," *Economic and Investment Observations*, H. C. Wainwright & Co., Economics, 3 March, 1981.

numbers rising and falling together. Your next response to the economist, then, is to remind him of this basic axiom of monetary economics.

"Why does tight money policy raise interest rates? I thought high dollar interest rates were associated with expectations of high inflation. Is high inflation associated with loose or tight money policy?"

At this point the economist is in a box. You have just exposed one of the basic, yet unresolved, conflicts in economics. Does an increase in the supply of money cause interest rates to rise or fall? The economist will try to wiggle out of this predicament by trying the other traditional response to the meaning of tight money.

"Ok," he concedes, "let's define tight money in terms of money aggregates. Tight money is a slow growth in the money supply."

"Slow growth in the money supply?" you retort. "Which money supply? Some traditional, very narrow measure like M1 or M2?[4] How absurd! That is but one component of the relevant supply of money. The market for money is like the world's oceans. Both consist of a global network of interconnected sources of liquidity. The quantity of dollars issued by the Fed, while perhaps sizable like the Atlantic Ocean, is but one source of liquidity. There are many domestic and international substitutes for these Federal Reserve liabilities which correspond to alternate sources of liquidity. Surely you are not claiming that the Fed controls all this liquidity!"

The ocean analogy is most instructive. Imagine the difficulty of controlling the level of water in the Atlantic Ocean. Even if a way could be found to drop the level of the Atlantic even slightly, water would run in from other oceans. Likewise, if the supply of money in the United States were somehow lowered, liquidity from the foreign sources would come pouring in. Money markets, like bodies of water, tend to seek their own level across markets.

This analogy can also be used to question whether the original policy objective is even a desirable outcome. Suppose the Fed could lower the level of water in the Atlantic Ocean. Would the world be better off? As the water level dropped, the Atlantic would become a less useful body of water for commercial purposes. At some point large tankers, which previously found the waters navigable, would now have to use other oceans or seas. As the water level continued to fall, more and more boats would be forced into surrounding oceans. Boston and New York, once major seaports, would no longer be centers for nautical trade. Some fishes and plants, which used to find the waters hospitable, would no longer survive the decreasing depths. The level of commerce in the Atlantic would decline.

Likewise, if the Fed were actually successful in restricting the supply of dollars, the usefulness of the dollar would decline. As dollars in the United States became harder to find, navigating commerce in dollars would become harder. Commercial activity might initially move to offshore facilities such as the Eurodollar market or other money instruments, but eventually it would likely find its way to other currencies entirely. New York's position as an international financial center would decline. The level of commerce in dollars would drop. The immediate policy goal of controlling the supply is accomplished only by destroying a priceless natural resource.

The Fed's obsession with targeting the quantity of money was therefore misdirected. At one level, as we shall continue to see, the obsession represents a search for a mythical cure which does not exist. But even worse, this policy contradicts the logic of why we have a monetary system and a central bank to begin with. *The goal of an effective monetary system should be to make money useful, not to restrict its use.* The policy prescriptions of monetarism have turned the logic of central banking on its head.

In the water example, navigation and commerce would be aided much more by attempts to keep the surface of the ocean smooth for sailing than attempts to control the quantity or level of water. Similarly, the key to making money useful is not the quantity of dollars, but rather the smoothness of its value. The usefulness of the dollar is enhanced by the certainty of its being as valuable tomorrow as it is today.

In other words, monetary policy would be enhanced if we forgot the obsession with quantity rules. Instead, interest must be rekindled in policies involving price or redemption rules.

The Fed Strays from the Road to Redemption

People need an incentive for holding more money, and what better incentive than increased certainty about the stability of purchasing power. With less emphasis on the quantity of drops passing through the Fed's spigot, and more emphasis on quality control in maintaining an even size, the attractiveness of the dollar will improve. The Fed has to move back into the redemption business.

Straying from the Road to Redemption

The policy of attempting to rein in the growth of money represents a dramatic switch from the types of Fed policies that were associated with relative price level and interest rate stability in the two decades following the Second World War. In fact, the past twenty years have represented an almost steady movement away from an initial price or redemption rule policy and towards the prescribed policy of the monetarists: quantity rules.

In 1944, representatives of the world's major countries met in Bretton Woods, New Hampshire, to iron out details of a new world monetary system. They sought to establish a system that would produce a stable financial environment to facilitate the task of rebuilding war-torn economies. This new system became known as the Bretton Woods Agreement.

The secret for creating price stability in those early postwar years was a dual set of price or redemption rules imposed by the Bretton Woods system. The dollar was the pivotal financial asset of the system. It served as the numeraire (unit of account) in which international payments cleared. Price stability therefore required that the value of the dollar remain stable and that the value of other currencies remain stable in terms of the dollar.

Hence, according to the Bretton Woods Agreement, the United States was required to redeem the dollar in terms of gold at a constant price of $35 per ounce. This policy stabilized the value of the dollar in terms of gold. It also meant that U.S. monetary policy was dictated by gold market participants.[5] If the market felt that U.S. creation of dollars was too rapid, the price of gold would rise, thereby obliging the U.S. monetary authorities to extinguish dollars by purchasing them in exchange for gold.

The other countries of the free-market world in turn had their redemption rule. They agreed to redeem their currencies at a constant dollar price. These governments' monetary policies were therefore dictated by the votes of buyers and sellers in the world's foreign exchange market.[6] If the market felt that money creation was too rapid, the country's currency would depreciate vis-à-vis the dollar. As its currency value began to fall, that government was committed by the agreement to extinguish excess domestic currency by purchasing it from the private market in exchange for dollars. Alternatively, if the market felt that money growth was too slow, the government would be obligated to intervene by issuing domestic currency to purchase dollars.

With these two price rules in place, inflation and interest rates in the United States were relatively low for almost twenty years. Between 1947 and 1964, annual dollar inflation (wholesale price index) averaged only 1.4 percent, and three-month Treasury bill yields averaged only 2.1 percent. The supply of money rose and fell with its demand at the constant value. Hence the world's quantity of money grew roughly in proportion to economic activity.

The system worked well until, in the mid-1960s, commitment to the rules began to wane. The United States, mired in Vietnam and burdened with heroic social programs, resorted more and more to monetary financing. The focus of monetary policy had begun to shift. The injection of money at a faster rate led to a burgeoning of the balance-of-payments deficit. As excess dollar balances piled up on the books of foreign central banks, the United States was obligated by the agreement to intervene in foreign exchange markets in support of the dollar. Pressure for the dollar price of gold to rise intensified as the federal government itself began to regard its lynchpin role in the world monetary system as a burden and an obstacle to its inflationary policies. The market began to anticipate that the United States could not, or would not, maintain the $35 gold price indefinitely.

Attempts were made to bolster the system by altering the initial agreement. These adjustments, however, reflected the reluctance of the United States to part with its gold reserves. Inadvertently they caused the demise of the Bretton Woods system through a steady dismemberment of its structure.

The first serious break in this agreement to stabilize relative prices came in 1965 as the United States sought to stem the potential gold outflow by removing its commitment to redeem Federal Reserve deposits in gold at $35 per ounce. Markets reacted adversely to this reduced commitment. Over the ensuing 1965–67 period, interest rates jumped to an average 4.4 percent, and inflation rose to 2.0 percent.

On March 18, 1968, the United States moved further to stop the potential gold drain by formally abolishing the 25 percent gold reserve requirement behind Federal Reserve notes and ending U.S. participation in the London gold pool. While the U.S. government retained some commitment to redeem the dollar in gold for foreign central banks, it was completely eliminating its commitment to redeem dollars in private hands at a constant price. The market's faith in the future value of the dollar was further jostled. More rapid depreciation of the dollar followed as the rate of inflation rose to 3.3 percent between 1967 and 1971. Treasury bill yields jumped to an average 5.8 percent.

The promise to redeem the dollar received another blow on August 15, 1971, as President Nixon caught wind of the intention of foreign governments to convert large amounts of dollars to gold and promptly slammed shut the U.S. gold window. The probability of even indirect dollar convertibility was now greatly diminished. Again, market prices responded with greater depreciation of the dollar relative to commodities. The decline in interest rates to 4.3 percent may have reflected reduced inflationary expectations, but actual inflation in the year and a half after this action jumped to an average 6.5 percent.

While the dollar's commodity redemption value had been eliminated, at least the dollar retained a relatively fixed value in terms of other currencies. In December 1971, countries agreed to the Smithsonian Accord, which attempted to restore fixed exchange rates, but without dollar convertibility into commodities. This limited promise of redemption was short-lived. In February 1973 the dollar was again officially devalued and redefined in terms of SDRs (Special Drawing Rights).[7] These actions ushered in the current period of "floating" exchange rates. Inflation and interest rates ratcheted up another notch. Between 1973 and 1977, inflation averaged 9.1 percent, and Treasury bill yields averaged 6.2 percent.

As if the lack of redemption under floating rates were not enough, the Carter Administration decided in mid-1977 to give the distrust of the dollar a big boost. As mentioned previously, in a misguided attempt to stimulate output and improve the U.S. trade balance, then–Treasury Secretary Blumenthal went around the world in the summer of 1977 "talking down" the dollar. The message he carried to the financial markets was simply that the United States was changing its rules about dollar redemption. The United States would now intervene in foreign exchange markets to "maintain orderly markets," or stabilize the dollar, only at much lower values. The markets responded quickly to this new policy, as the dollar plunged against major foreign currencies. Inflation and interest rates responded, too. Inflation bounded upwards at a 10.6 percent annual rate between the third quarters of 1977 and 1979. Interest rates now reached an average level of 7.4 percent.

Yet more was to come. Even as the promises to redeem the dollar's value in terms of commodities and other currencies were broken, the Federal Reserve still retained one last price rule. Fed policy in the late 1970s centered on short-term interest rates, particularly the rate on Fed funds. Fed funds are reserves that are lent by those banks that have an excess over the required amount to those banks that have fewer reserves than required. The Fed funds rate is the interest charged to lend these reserves.

Interest rates are a relative price, the value of today's dollars relative to tomorrow's dollars. Stabilize that price, and at least the market has some certainty about the value at which today's dollars will be redeemable in the future. Admittedly, stabilizing the Fed funds market rate, which applies primarily to overnight lending, involves stabilizing the relative values of the dollar over a very short time horizon. But at least there remained some reference point (though a shifting one) for the dollar's value.

The switch in Federal Reserve policy on October 6, 1979, however, eliminated even this final price rule. Volcker and company were probably sincere in their assertions that they were trying to target and stabilize the various measures of money. But the further abandonment of price rules only led to more instability. Inflation and interest rates reached new record highs in the next few months. By the beginning of 1980, inflation rates hovered around the 20 percent mark and three-month Treasury bill rates were approximately 12.5 percent. In 1981 Treasury bill yields averaged about 14 percent, spiking in mid-1981 to over 19 percent. Inflation for most of the year averaged double digits, though with the onset of the deep 1981–82 recession, the rate of inflation temporarily cooled.

So over the last twenty years, the set of signals to which the Fed has responded in setting its policy has been steadily transformed. At the beginning of this period, the Fed looked for signals emanating from market prices. Falling values of the dollar in one of a variety of financial markets meant intervention was necessary. The Fed knew it had to step into the market and redeem the dollar. With a return of market prices to the desired level, intervention could stop.

As we have seen, however, the Fed began to turn a blind eye on market prices and gave up its commitment to redemption. Attention, instead, was turned to the quantity of money and how fast it was growing. Policy no longer responded to immediate market signals. Instead, policy was triggered by numbers compiled from a variety of sources, with some difficulty and with a lag. Even worse, the new numbers no longer gave direct signals about what policy should be.

For example, does a spurt in the growth of money mean the central bank must rein in money growth to prevent inflation? The experience of the Swiss franc would indicate that the burgeoning money supply may instead reflect a growing world demand for a strong, stable money. At the beginning of 1978, as turbulence (lack of redemption) surrounded other currencies, particularly the dollar, the private market voted with its checkbooks to move to the relatively stable Swiss franc. As a result, the quantity of Swiss francs surged. Yet the Swiss franc price level continued to fall throughout most of 1978. In con-

The Fed Strays from the Road to Redemption

trast, in the United States where the Carter Administration was busy shattering faith in the dollar through "talking down" its value, dollar demand fell. While money supply growth was at about the same 8 percent rate as in 1977, the inflation rate surged from 6.9 percent in 1977 to 9.3 percent in 1978.

The quantity of money, as we shall continue to see, is therefore not a very reliable signal for a successful policy. Economists and businessmen are slowly beginning to realize this important fact. Unfortunately, the limitations of such a monetarist policy were not part of the conventional wisdom in the early 1970s as monetarism began to exert increasing influence over monetary policy.

4

The Ascendancy of Monetarism

THE FED'S U-TURN on the road to redemption did not occur in a vacuum. In fact, there were two complementary sets of forces propelling government policy in that direction. One force was the emergence of new ideas among economists about what route monetary policy should take. The second was the political and economic expediencies of the moment. These twin forces together created the initial momentum to break with prevailing monetary policies and try something new. Once in motion, these forces also successfully prevented monetary policy from turning back, leaving little option but to plunge deeper into the unknown in search of the elusive Monetarist Dream.

The Meeting of Minds

The new ideas were, of course, those associated with monetarism. Politicians are naturally reluctant to embrace new policies that do not have the imprint of "respectability." It is much easier to defend economic policy when backed by economists and students waving their studies and textbooks like Bibles in support. By the late 1960s and early 1970s, monetarism had begun to reach this point of "respectability." There was by this time a growing legion of individuals intoning a growing body of literature about how the government's policy should focus more on controlling the supply of money. A prominent leader of this legion was Milton Friedman. For over twenty years he had worked arduously to develop and spread the gospel of monetarism. His pioneering work with Anna Schwartz, *A Monetary History of the United States, 1867–1960,* had sought to detail the empirical relationship between the supply of dollars and dollar income over a century of U.S. history. Theoretical and empirical articles by Friedman and his students sought to describe the mechanism through which changes in the supply of money brought about changes in the level of economic activity and prices. By the late 1960s, the essential framework of this point of view had been described, and the basic relationships among policy targets and instruments had been documented.

What was emerging, however, was not simply a monetary version of fiscal activism. Friedman had concluded along the way that monetary policy acts with "long and variable" lags. The proper role of monetary policy was therefore not to intervene actively to obtain short-run targets. Instead, the goal of the monetary authorities should be to stabilize the growth of money over the longer haul.[1]

Friedman's mission was aided by many other monetary economists. Karl Brunner, Allan Meltzer, and other members of the Shadow Open Market Committee rose to national prominence arguing similar policies. Other economists such as James Tobin argued for a more active monetary policy within a more traditional Keynesian framework. The research staff at the Federal Reserve Bank of St. Louis became famous for its studies on the impact of monetary policy and for its advocacy of the monetarist policy of stabilizing the growth of money aggregates. Prominent economists from private banks and elsewhere in the private sector were swayed by many of these arguments and began to lend their support.

Simultaneously, there arose a political need in Washington for a new monetary policy. Economic and political realities appeared headed for a collision course. The escalating war in Vietnam and the promises of a "Great Society" required increasing annual government resources. Yet supplying those resources became increasingly difficult. The war was not politically popular, hindering the practicality of increased taxation. Raising resources by issuing long-term bonds was also limited by the fact that interest rates had exceeded the congressional limit of 4.5 percent. Instead, Washington was forced to turn to the remaining option of printing more dollars.

If the United States had maintained the strict relationship between the quantity of dollars and gold the private sector wished to hold at the official value of $35 per ounce of gold, such a dollar increase would not have been possible. So the United States began finding ways of loosening that relationship. As we saw in chapter 3, in 1965 and 1968 the U.S. government abolished the relationship between gold and Federal Reserve deposits and Federal Reserve notes.

There still remained the promise, however, to redeem in gold the dollars held by central banks of other countries. As the supply of dollars burgeoned, and more and more found their way abroad, the pressure to make good on that promise mounted. Washington was still in a bind. It was unwilling or unable to keep its promise to other central banks, but failure to keep the promise would mean a repudiation and end of the prevailing system of monetary arrangements. Washington needed a justification for such a drastic step.

The Ascendancy of Monetarism

The monetarists provided a convenient justification. They hailed the slamming of the gold window and the breakdown of the international monetary system as a victory, not a calamity. The unhinging of the dollar from gold and other currencies represented a giant step towards their avowed policy of more discretionary monetary control. Such a break was a necessary first step to a period in which a country could independently direct its monetary policy according to its own enlightened self-interests. This reasoning allowed the politicians to put up a positive front in what was clearly an embarrassing international situation.

Once the tie with past economic policies was broken, political and economic forces pushed the politicians deeper and deeper into this new territory. As chapter 3 showed, every time policy strayed a little farther from its former path, inflation and high interest rates jumped a little higher. The economy seemed to suffer even more.

This deterioration in the economy, in turn, was not lost on the voters. They, of course, clamored for a reversal of the ever-worsening inflation and interest-rate outlook. Current policies were not working, so new answers had to be found. Where might those new answers lie? Should the government retreat to a Bretton Woods system? There clearly was no stomach for that route in Washington. The desire to escape the discipline of Bretton Woods was what motivated the current experiment. Policy makers were not about to revert to that discipline. Should the government now rely more heavily on traditional Keynesian policies? Keynesianism had been seriously embarrassed by the simultaneous spurts in inflation and unemployment that occurred in the early 1970s. According to Keynesian theory, one or the other might occur, but never the two together. Keynesian theory seemed increasingly unable to explain what was happening in the world.

What option was left? The only remaining, generally accepted theory was monetarism. So monetarism was used more and more to try to explain what was going on. Increasingly, magazine articles and newspaper stories described the ups and downs of the economy in monetarist terms. More college and graduate students became exposed to the logic of monetarism, as the arguments for targeting monetary aggregates became incorporated into standard economic textbooks. The monetarists were becoming more visible, and their reasoning better known. Their arguments began to creep into everyday discussions, becoming part of the conventional wisdom.

So as each modification of the old system failed to deliver the promised bright new world, and as politicians looked for new answers, monetarism was consulted for these answers. What started out as simply an abandonment of the policy constraints of the old system became a trend toward a wholly new policy. The policy shift picked up ever-increasing momentum, as political and economic unrest spurred it on its way. By the time Ronald Reagan took office in 1981, monetarism had already become central to policy discussions.

The men Reagan brought to Washington reflected this shift in policy focus. Some of the people who had hailed the dramatic shift in monetary policy a decade earlier were now in major economic decision-making positions of the administration. For example, Friedman was a member of the panel of top economists advising President Reagan. Beryl Sprinkel, a former student and a close intellectual associate of Milton Friedman, was appointed Under Secretary of the Treasury for Monetary Policy. Jerry Jordan, the former research director at the monetarist Federal Reserve Bank of St. Louis, was named a member of the President's Council of Economic Advisors. Economists sympathetic to the monetarists' goals took other positions at the Treasury Department, in the Office of Management and Budget, on Congressional staffs, and even at the

Fed. The emphasis on the role of monetary policy within the government had changed. Together these new people tried to complete the transformation of monetary policy to targeting money aggregates.

Having reached positions of prominence and authority, these economists began to promote their game plan with missionary zeal. They had formulated policies that they felt would assure the Fed an open field for carrying the monetary football. They cheered from the sidelines as the Fed began to try their plays. They booed as the Fed tried stategies from other playbooks. They intended to win the monetary game by their game plan, and they were intent on whipping the Fed into compliance.

But precisely what vision motivated these strong supporters of monetarism? What new insights did they claim to have in their playbooks? Why did they hail the initial shift away from the Bretton Woods monetary strategy? What superior strategies did they promise? And as the decade of the eighties began and policy shifted more and more in their direction, what remaining obstacles blocked the final implementation of their game plan?

The Basics of Monetarism

The central assumptions of the monetarist philosophy can be summarized in two points:

1. The Federal Reserve dominates or controls the movements in the supply of money such as M1 or M2.

2. Movements in M1 or M2 are closely related to movements in the dollar value of U.S. income.

These are the two pistons of the monetarist engine. Properly serviced to remain in synchronized motion, these two pistons keep the economy running smoothly. If the government neglects to maintain one or both pistons, or if it periodically alters the timing, the engine will begin to knock, sputter, and work inefficiently. The focus of monetary policy should be to keep that engine running smoothly.

Adjusting the ups and downs of the money-supply piston is supposed to be accomplished through two Federal Reserve controls. One control regulates the amount of monetary base in the monetary system. The other control regulates the rate at which this monetary base can then be transformed into bank deposits. The monetary base (often also referred to as high-powered money) is the money directly created by the Fed. These Fed liabilities appear in two forms: (a) the paper currency that people hold in their wallets, pockets, and mattresses or that banks hold in their vaults, and (b) reserve deposits of commercial banks at the regional branches of the Federal Reserve Bank. These two forms of Fed liabilities are easily interchangeable.

Consider, for instance, the familiar sight of an armored truck parked in front of a commercial bank. Two guards, weapons drawn, bring money out of the bank to be loaded into the truck. Did you ever wonder where those armored trucks go at night? In the late afternoon or early morning they can be found idling outside the regional Federal Reserve Bank waiting to unload. The money that you saw the guards bring out was currency that had been deposited at the commercial bank. The bank had requested the armored service to transport the money because the bank had more currency in its vault than it needed to meet the ordinary demands of its customers. Banks typically find such excess currency accumulating in the beginning of the week, as merchants deposit their weekend receipts. The commercial bank's security procedures, and perhaps its insurance policy, requires that such excess cash not simply lie around on the bank's premises. So at the beginning of the week, the armored trucks usually carry money away. The flow of currency is typically reversed at the end of the week, as banks order currency from the Fed in anticipation of cashing pay checks.

In any case, when the money is carted away and taken to the regional Fed Bank, the account of the commercial bank at the Fed Bank is credited by the equivalent amount. What had been currency becomes deposits at the Federal Reserve. Towards the end of the week, the conversion is reversed, and Fed deposits become currency.

Whether the monetary base ends up in the commercial bank's vault or in the commercial bank's account at the Fed, it can serve as reserves behind the checking or savings deposit you have at your commercial bank. In either form the bank has a stockpile of money on which it can draw when customers ask for it. The bank, however, does not hold all its assets in this liquid form. If it did, it would not be profitable, since neither vault cash nor Fed deposits earn interest for the bank. Instead, the bank holds only a minimum of its assets in liquid reserves, investing the remaining assets in securities, loans, real estate, and other interest-earning forms.

This desire by a bank to maximize its profit by earning interest on its assets means that the bank holds less than one dollar of liquid cash assets behind each dollar of the public's deposits. Hence, you can go to your bank tomorrow and withdraw the thousand dollars in your account, but if everyone else attempted simultaneously to clear out their accounts, the bank could not meet the sudden surge in demand for liquid assets. Such a surge is what happens when there is a "run" on a bank.

In the language of economics, the tendency to hold only a few cents of every dollar of deposits in liquid reserves is called "fractional reserve banking." Notice that if only a few cents of monetary base are needed as reserves against each dollar of deposits, a dollar of monetary base can serve as reserves against several dollars of deposits. With fractional reserve banking, therefore, the receipt of a dollar in monetary base means the bank can expand its commercial deposits by more than a dollar. Commercial banks, then, are able to "multiply" the amount of money existing in the economy.

How big this "multiplier" is depends on how small a fraction is held in reserves. The fewer cents of monetary base behind each dollar of deposits, the more deposits that can be supported with a given dollar of monetary base, and hence the bigger the multiplier. So by regulating the minimum pennies that banks must hold against each dollar of deposits, the Federal Reserve is thought to exert some influence over the number of dollar deposits. More pennies required means fewer dollar deposits are likely to be created from a given quantity of monetary base. So from time to time the Federal Reserve alters the level of reserves required for various types of deposits, attempting to alter the rate at which the monetary base is transformed into deposits. This is one means of exerting control over the money supply piston.

The Fed's more active means of influencing the quantity of money, however, attempts to alter directly the size of the monetary base in circulation. There are actually two ways it can do so. One way involves the discount window. There the Federal Reserve trades Treasury bills or other securities owned by a commercial bank for monetary base. This lending of reserves with securities as collateral is referred to as "discounting" the securities, and the interest rate charged is the "discount rate." Raising this discount rate or tightening the terms on which securities can be borrowed are thought to reduce the attractiveness of the discount window.

The approach used most frequently, however, is open market operations. In this procedure the Federal Reserve buys or sells government securities on the open financial markets in exchange for monetary base. If the Fed wishes to inject monetary base into the system, it instructs a bond dealer with whom it is working to buy a given amount of government securities. The dealer in turn bids the securities away from the public, paying for them with dollars from the Fed's account. If nothing else has changed, the liabilities of the Fed, or monetary base, increase. In contrast, instructing the broker to sell government securities would cause the level of monetary base to contract. In recent years reserve requirements and discount-rate changes have occurred less frequently and have had a smaller direct impact on reserves than the level of open market operations. Open market operations are today the main day-to-day policy instrument for influencing the effective level of monetary base.

The ups and downs in the monetary base in turn are expected to influence strongly the ups and downs of the money supply. Each bank deposit is required to have a specific amount of monetary base behind it. If the supply of monetary base is reduced, the supply of bank deposits, and therefore money, also declines. An expanding level of monetary base permits the money supply to expand. So as the monetary base fluctuates, the supply of money fluctuates right along with it. The monetarist evidence of this assertion is shown in figure 4–1.

These induced movements in the dollar money supply in turn are expected to affect the level of the U.S. GNP. This is the second piston of the monetarist engine. There is assumed to be a dependable relationship between the money supply and the GNP over time (figure 4–2). Hence, if the Fed controls the level of monetary base through its open market operations, if the movements in the monetary base strongly influence movements in the money supply, and if movements in the money

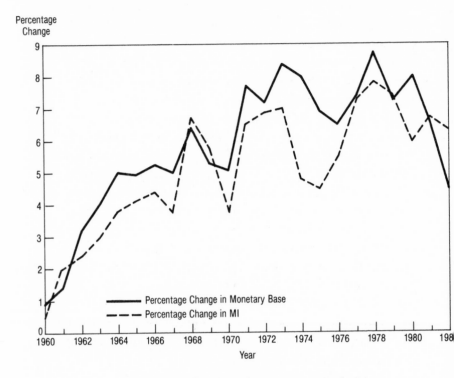

FIGURE 4–1

The Money Supply and the Monetary Base, 1960–1982
SOURCE: *Federal Reserve Bulletin* (Washington, D.C.: Federal Reserve Board).

supply are closely related to the GNP, the Fed can keep the level of economic activity puttering right along.

Notice that it is the dollar value or "nominal" level of economic activity that is expected to move with money in this way. The movement in nominal economic activity can therefore be due either to growing real economic activity or to changing prices. A sudden money expansion would likely be reflected primarily in inflation. A sudden contraction would likely yield a disruption of prices in the opposite direction.

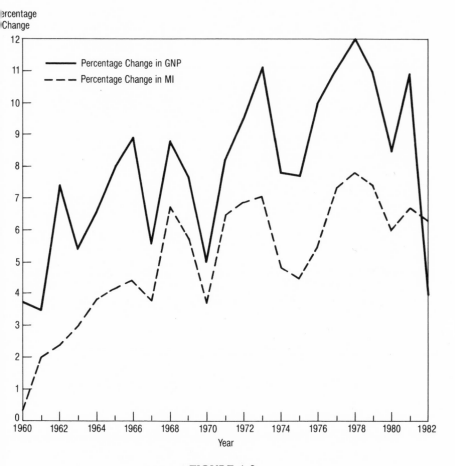

FIGURE 4-2

Money and the Nation's Income, 1960–1982
Sources: *Federal Reserve Bulletin* (Washington, D.C.: Federal Reserve Board);
Survey of Current Business (Washington, D.C.: Department of Commerce).

Sudden surges either way therefore imply trouble for the economy.

Even more disturbing is the conclusion of the monetarists that sudden surges do not produce either immediate or precise effects. According to the monetarists, the major effects take time to appear and may differ from one time to the next. Money, then, works with a "long and variable lag." To quote Friedman:

The link between the policy actions of the monetary authority and the price level, while unquestionably present, is more indirect than the link between the policy actions of the authority and any of several monetary totals. Moreover, monetary action takes a longer time to affect the price level than to affect the monetary totals, and both the time lag and the magnitude of effect vary with circumstances. As a result, we cannot predict at all accurately just what effect a particular monetary action will have on the price level and, equally important, just when it will have that effect. Attempting to control directly the price level is therefore likely to make monetary policy itself a source of economic disturbance because of false stops and starts.[2]

An expansive monetary policy undertaken at a time of economic slowdown may not have its full effect until the economy has already entered the recovery. The surge in money only adds to inflation. Alternatively, stepping on the monetary brakes in a period of inflation may have its greatest impact three, nine, twelve, or fifteen months later when the economy has already begun to slow down.

So while the monetarists claim to understand how the underlying engine of the economy works, they do not claim to be in a position to "fine tune" the total output accurately. Instead they argue that the best that can be done is to make the two pistons of that engine run smoothly together. Smooth running requires a smooth growth in the monetary aggregates. In Friedman's words:

My own prescription is still that the monetary authority go all the way in avoiding such swings by adopting publicly the policy of achieving a steady rate of growth in a specified monetary total. The precise rate of growth, like the precise monetary total, is less important than the adoption of some stated and known rate.[3]

A steady hand on the monetary throttle yields a steady rate of real growth and inflation. The monetarist wants a steady "quantity rule" of money.

The Problem of Implementation in the 1960s— Waiting for the Opportunity

While by the late 1960s the theoretical arguments for a central bank "quantity rule" had been substantially developed, there remained several impediments to putting this policy into practice. The policy required, above all, discretionary latitude on the part of the Fed over the size of the monetary aggregates. Yet, in the 1960s, even the monetarists recognized that the Federal Reserve was incapable of unilaterally altering the supply of money.

The primary barriers to monetary control were the links between the dollar and gold and between the dollar and other currencies. These price rules, tying the value of the dollar to these other assets, essentially dictated what the dollar money supply would be. Fixing the dollar price of gold, for example, constrained dollar growth to the rate at which dollar demand was growing. If the supply of dollars grew more rapidly, the relative value of the dollar would tend to fall (and the dollar price of gold would rise). The Fed, noticing the rise in the market price of gold, would be forced to step in and extinguish the excess dollars in return for gold. The Fed's role with respect to the quantity of dollars was passive. It kept the quantity of money at whatever level the public seemed to desire at the fixed dollar gold price.

Similarly, the fixed value of the dollar in terms of other currencies tied the growth in money across countries. If the Fed tried, say, to increase the supply of money by purchasing bonds on the open market, it was likely to find at least part of the resulting increase in money escaping to another country through a balance of payments deficit. The outflow of dollars would help to even out money growth rates (in proportion to income growth) across countries.

The reason money could escape is quite simple. Under fixed exchange rates the central bank is committed to fix the value of the country's currency in terms of another currency. The Bank of France, for example, fixes the franc in terms of the dollar. If people want to cash in francs for dollars, the Bank of France is obliged to do it at the promised rate. If people want francs, the Bank of France must supply francs in exchange for the stated number of dollars.

So the bottom line, as far as the money supply is concerned, is that the commitment to fix the relative values of currencies means the public can transform one denomination of money into another whenever it wants. The central bank commitment gives the public the power to decide not only the relative proportions in which different monies can exist in world markets, but also, through private market transactions, the relative amounts of money in the various countries. Any attempt by one central bank to raise (or lower) the quantity of domestic money above (or below) the level the public desires will be frustrated.

As an example, suppose that under fixed exchange rates the Fed attempted to raise the quantity of dollars through the traditional channel of purchasing bonds. Suppose the U.S. public was previously holding just the amount of dollars it wanted. Now the quantity of money is increased. With more dollars than desired, the U.S. public wants to exchange some of the extra dollars either for commodities that can be consumed now or for bonds. Say the public would now like both to buy some cheese from France and to lend money to some Frenchmen (obtain French bonds). Upon completing these transactions, the U.S. residents have more French cheese and French bonds. The Frenchmen now have more dollars.

Of course, under fixed rates, the Frenchmen would probably prefer to have French francs in their pockets. They therefore present the dollars they have received at the Bank of France. The Bank of France has promised to convert dollars into francs at a specific price, providing the public's outlet for transforming dollars into francs. So the U.S. public ends up with fewer dollars, the French public with more francs, and the Bank of France with more dollar reserves. The central bank commitment to maintain a fixed exchange rate has permitted the private sector to alter the relative amounts of francs and dollars in the world and to redistribute all or part of the initial increase in dollars to another country. The redistribution appears on the U.S. foreign accounts as a balance of payments deficit, as there is an outflow of official reserves (dollars) to the Bank of France.[4]

Thus, under the price rules, discretionary latitude over monetary policy was impossible.[5] The monetarists call for more active control over money aggregates simply could not be implemented. They had to bide their time, hoping (and lobbying) for an end to the existing international monetary ties.

Their long-awaited opportunity came in the late sixties and early seventies, as their program began to mesh with the government's perception of its needs. The monetarists provided an intellectual justification for what government officials wanted to do. The successive breakdowns in price rules would untie the hands of the Fed. At last there would be an opportunity for monetary policies tailored to U.S. needs. By eliminating the central bank commitment to exchange one money asset for another, they could shut off the international escape route for dollars. With the dollar escape route shut off, U.S. monetary policy could finally be regulated as in the monetarist scenerio.

So the slamming of the U.S. gold window in August 1971 was hailed by the monetarists. The monetary base would no longer be tied to the price or quantity of gold. To the monetarists, the politically expedient step of pulling up the gold anchor was justified by the Fed's new freedom to steer the economy over whichever course it desired.

The transition to an insulated monetary policy, however, was not yet complete. While the dollar's value could now float without the tug of gold, its ups and downs were still constrained by ties to other currencies through the Smithsonian Accord. The final breakdown of the Smithsonian Accord in February 1973 could therefore be justified as another important positive step. The breakdown severed the dollar's value from that of foreign currencies. Even more important from the monetarist perspective, the renunciation of the agreement to peg currencies meant that the flows of money between countries, which had been facilitated by central bank intervention, were now to be greatly reduced. Pulling up this second anchor was to give Fed policy even more latitude in steering its course. As Milton Friedman had written twenty years earlier:

In effect, flexible exchange rates are a means of combining interdependence among countries through trade with a maximum of internal monetary independence; they are a means of permitting each country to seek for monetary stability according to its own lights, without either imposing its mistakes on its neighbors or having their mistakes imposed on it.[6]

The Experience Without an Anchor: What Went Wrong?

So the breakdown of the international monetary system was to usher in a "golden period" of monetary policy. The hands of the Fed were free of the shackles of value-stabilizing rules. At last the Fed could concentrate on stabilizing the aggregate quantity of money, just as the monetarists wanted. The emerging monetarist theories were in turn to produce stable domestic inflation and growth. Unfortunately, things did not work out as planned. The intervening decade did not produce the stable monetary policy or stable prices that had been hoped for. In fact, as figure 2–2 reveals, both prices and money growth were considerably more unstable in the 1970s than they had been in the 1960s.

Political pressures again built to do something about this instability. Economists began anew to search for the culprits behind the escalating inflation. Part of the blame was laid at the feet of OPEC, the Organization of Petroleum Exporting Countries. Like that of other commodities in the early 1970s, the world market price of oil had risen dramatically. But because of the central role of oil in everyday life, and since oil prices seemed to be dictated by a producers' cartel, this particular commodity captured the attention of economists and politicians throughout the world. Various steps were taken to deal with the OPEC menace. In the United States a number of tacks were tried, ranging from mandating more fuel-efficient cars to imposing fees on imported oil. The important unifying aspect of these varied attempts to deal with rising prices, however, was the failure to view them as a monetary problem. Oil prices were seen as rising because Americans were guzzling gas too fast, or Arab sheiks were being unreasonable. The monetary experiments bore little direct responsibility.

Monetary policy could not escape blame, however, as the prices of other things also began to skyrocket. There were no cartels selling groceries, building homes, or knitting sweaters. There had to be other reasons why breaking from Bretton Woods was not working as promised. The monetarists blamed the ensuing ineffectiveness of their monetary policy primarily on four things. First, there was continued official U.S. intervention in the foreign exchange market. Federal Reserve policy is carried out by two desks, the foreign exchange market intervention desk and the domestic open market desk. These two policy centers can be thought of as the left and right hands of the Fed. Even if the right hand had been behaving properly, the actions of the left hand, the foreign exchange desk, were not consistent with monetarist policy.

Although the dollar was no longer fixed in value, the foreign exchange desk at the Federal Reserve Bank of New York had orders from the Treasury to intervene to maintain "orderly markets." The dollar was free to move up or down, but the intervention prevented sharp short-term movements. This intervention meant that the Fed automatically bought back dollars to prevent sudden downward shifts in the dollar's value relative to other currencies. Similarly, the Fed had orders to sell dollars in exchange for other currencies if there were a tendency for the dollar's value to rise substantially.

The intervention also meant that the Fed was still assisting the private sector in determining the currency composition of the money supply. If there were a desire in the foreign exchange market to shift from, say, dollars to deutsche marks, the dollar's value would tend to fall. In order to moderate that fall, the Fed would step in to absorb dollars in exchange for deutsche marks. The pressure of the private market to hold more deutsche marks and fewer dollars triggers an accommodating response from the Fed. This left hand was not working towards controlling the supply of dollars.

Second, the right hand of the Fed was not targeting growth in the supply of dollars either. The right-hand intervention is the open market operations desk. This desk responds with open market purchases or sales of securities within guidelines set down by the Federal Reserve's Open Market Committee. But for most of the 1970s the guidelines did not involve the movement in the aggregate quantity of money. Policy instead revolved around price targets like the Fed funds rate.

Third, the Federal Reserve's influence over the banking system continued to wane, as many commercial banks sought to leave the Fed system. The Fed already lacked the jurisdiction to regulate savings and loans or mutual savings banks. Even among commercial banks, it could directly regulate only those banks with federal charters. State-chartered banks were controlled by separate, individual state regulations. State chartered banks generally faced lower reserve requirements and could often keep part of their reserves in interest-bearing accounts or even in U.S. Treasury bills. Not surprisingly, as interest rates and Fed reserve requirements rose in the Seventies, many banks no longer felt that the benefits of Fed membership outweighed the costs. They applied for state charters. Over the 1970s the number of member banks declined by over 350 to about 5,500 banks.

Fourth, there were other, technical factors which muted the Federal Reserve's ability to control the money supply. A major complaint of the monetarists was the two-week lag in accounting for required reserves on bank deposits. With "lagged" reserve accounting, the minimum amount of reserves a bank is required to hold this week is not based on this week's deposits but on the deposits the bank had on its books two weeks ago.[7]

Some argued that the extra two weeks are needed to allow the banks to adjust efficiently. The monetarists argued that the practice hinders discretionary policy by making the monetary base essentially determined by the banks and not by the Fed. Given the deposits of two weeks ago, there is a prescribed minimum amount of total reserves the banks must hold today. If the Fed clamps down through open market operations on its target of nonborrowed reserves, it must still allow banks that are "short" on reserves to borrow through the discount window. The edge of Fed policy is blunted. The Fed must supply those additional reserves whether or not such a level of reserves is consistent with the Fed's targets.

Cascading Policies in the Seventies and Eighties

By the late 1970s, high interest rates and inflation had become part of everyday life. Families buying new homes found themselves facing the burden of high-interest mortgage payments. Planning family budgets became nearly impossible as each week's trip to the grocery store brought new inflation-induced surprises. Federal, state, and local governments struggled to deal with the burgeoning cost of payrolls, supplies, and debt servicing. Across America, people were getting fed up with the economic situation. The political pressure continued to build to do something.

The response in Washington to these monetary problems was to make the policy that had been ineffective in the 1970s effective in the 1980s. In August 1979 Paul Volcker replaced William Miller as Fed Chairman. Volcker seemed intent on tackling the problems that appeared to blunt the impact of monetary policy in the 1970s. For example, on October 6, 1979, the Board of Governors of the Federal Reserve announced a dramatic switch in policy. No longer were they to center their policy on fluctuations in the federal funds rate. Rather they now were to target monetary aggregates. In effect, the Board of Governors had been won over to the monetarist position. They had become convinced that the way inflation is brought under control is to perform open market operations, or change other Fed policies, to limit the growth in the monetary base or one of the various measures of the money supply. The Fed would no longer stabilize the rate of interest on short-term interbank loans.

. . . appropriate restraint on the supply of money and credit is an essential part of any program to achieve the needed reduction in inflationary momentum and inflationary expectations. . . . However, growth over recent months in these aggregates and in bank credit has been more rapid than is consistent with those targets, and if unrestrained, would clearly be excessive in terms of our basic economic objectives. Recent Federal Reserve actions, taking account of inevitable lags, should work to contain money and credit growth in the months immediately ahead, consistent with targeted objectives. The actions announced today are designed to provide further assurance that those objectives will be reached.[8]

The announcement signaled not only a switch in Fed policy but also a change in financial reporting. To describe Fed policy, business writers now had to couch their scenarios about the ups and downs of the financial markets in terms of apparent or anticipated changes in the supply of money. The monetarist assertions concerning the relationship between money growth rates, interest rates, and inflation took another giant step toward becoming a part of the received body of conventional wisdom.

Attempts were also made to solve the problem of declining Federal Reserve bank membership. Since this problem was perceived as diluting the influence of the Fed in directing monetary policy, the obvious solution would be simply to expand the Fed's sphere of influence over banks. In March 1980, Congress passed the Monetary Control Act of 1980. On the one hand, this legislation attempted to close off the escape route of commercial banks from Fed control. Banks could no longer avoid Fed restrictions by becoming state-chartered banks. The Monetary Control Act extended Fed control to all commercial banks, whether federally or state chartered.

But the legislation did not stop there. It extended the powers of the Federal Reserve far beyond the Fed's original jurisdiction. Not only state-chartered commercial banks were now subjected to the same regulations as Federal Reserve member banks. So, too, were savings and loan associations, mutual savings banks, and even local credit unions. In one piece of legislation the Fed extended its regulatory powers to all traditional domestic financial intermediation institutions. In addition, the International Banking Act of 1978 had put domestic branches of foreign banks on equal regulatory footing with U.S. banks. That legislation, combined with the Monetary Control Act, extended the regulatory powers of the Fed even to foreign banks operating in the U.S. From the perspective of traditional money and banking, the Fed now had been given far-reaching powers to put the control of money aggregates into practice. (The Monetary Control Act and its impact on dollar money markets is the subject of chapter 8.)

The election of Ronald Reagan turned into a further validation of these policies. As already mentioned, the new administration had strong advocates of the monetarist objectives in top policy-making positions. These individuals were naturally eager to implement their long-sought "quantity rule." They were now in a position to bring that goal within reach.

In particular, they could now make sure that the policy of the U.S. Treasury would be consistent with a quantity rule. The Treasury directs the foreign exchange desk operations of the Federal Reserve. The monetarists had recognized that the interventions of that desk were potentially offsetting any attempts by the Fed to control monetary aggregates. So in March 1981 the U.S. Treasury adopted a policy of minimal foreign exchange intervention. Beryl Sprinkel, the Treasury Under Secretary for Monetary Affairs, announced the shift from active foreign exchange market intervention in the spring of 1981. The United States would now intervene only in extreme circumstances. The shooting of President Reagan brought Fed intervention to prevent disorderly markets, but day-to-day developments did not. The assassination of President Sadat of Egypt, for example, did not induce U.S. foreign exchange intervention. In fact, the United States did not intervene again in foreign exchange markets until mid-June 1982, over a year later. The new administration was determined to allow only the minimum of leakages of dollars out of the U.S. market.

Then, in June 1982, the Federal Reserve committed itself to returning to contemporaneous reserve accounting. Stung by criticism both from within and from outside the administration for allegedly allowing sharp short-term swings in money growth rates, the Fed was trying to adjust operating techniques to zero in on money aggregates. The operational change, scheduled to become effective in February 1984, shrinks the accounting lag from two weeks to two days. The shortened accounting period supposedly will allow the Fed to control more effectively the quantity of total reserves in the banking system.

So, by mid-1982, much of the monetarist program was in

place. While a few minor technicalities remained, the final goal was within easy reach. As Milton Friedman says:

Can the Fed produce steadier monetary growth? Can it gradually lower monetary growth to end inflation? The monetarist answer is clearly yes. By changing its operating procedures and the rules and regulations it enforces on banks, the Fed could match its actions to its rhetoric. It has just taken the first step in that direction by deciding to replace lagged with contemporaneous reserve requirements. That may be a hopeful augury for the future.[9]

Yet despite all these extraordinary measures, interest rates still remained historically very high. The monetarists were very close to their final goal, but the results continued to deviate significantly from what had been promised.

Just as monetarism seemed about to reach its zenith, therefore, confidence in this approach began to wane. Monetarism had been repeatedly unable to deliver on its promises. Maybe it was not the answer after all. These doubts became reinforced in August 1982; only as the Fed appeared to move away from a strict monetarist quantity rule did interest rates fall from their historic heights. Less monetarism seemed to quell some of the uneasiness in the money markets. The uneasiness has not dissipated completely, however. Today interest rates still remain much higher than in the 1950s or 1960s, as the Federal Reserve searches for an alternative monetary policy.

5

Reexamining Monetarism I— Money: Cause or Effect?

BY THE EARLY 1980s, monetarism had worked its way into the conventional economic wisdom. One turned on the radio and heard the latest money supply figures reported. One turned on the television news and watched a debate or story about how some recent action of the Fed was affecting the money supply. One picked up a newspaper and read speculation about how some Fed-induced change in the money supply would affect inflation, interest rates, and overall economic activity. People around the world were being subtly trained to think in monetarist logic.

The monetarists, of course, felt this shift in economic reporting justified. Their basic message was simple enough for most to understand: the Federal Reserve controls or "causes" changes in M1 or M2 or some relevant monetary aggregate, and these movements in money in turn are related to or "cause" movements in the dollar value of U.S. income. The monetarists also felt that past experience justified the message. Researchers supporting the monetarist position had burned up a lot of computer circuits trying to uncover empirical support for their arguments. Volumes had been written on the subject, not to mention numerous scholarly journal articles and various investment house research reports. The point seemed proven, the issue settled.

Yet despite the acceptance of monetarism in the press, despite the ascendancy of monetarists to high policy-making positions in the United States and abroad, despite the Federal Reserve's promise to slow the growth in money aggregates, doubts remained about whether monetarists had all the answers. These doubts surfaced in actively debated policy questions. Are high interest rates simply a sign of the Fed's tight money policy? Is high inflation simply a symptom of a loose money policy? Will the Fed have the courage and ability to follow a "correct" monetary growth policy? Just below this surface lay even more troubling questions about monetary aggregates as a policy guide. For example, precisely what is money? Who really controls the relevant money supply, the Fed or the public? What other phenomena do the periodic wiggles in the reported money supply reflect? Can we really say with any certainty that changes in the money supply cause changes in the level of economic activity? How reliable, in fact, are the reported money supply numbers for guiding monetary policy?

In short, while the advocates of monetarism had presented their evidence and given a persuasive closing statement, the jury was still out. The precepts of monetarism on public trial had not yet been found reliable "beyond reasonable doubt."

Would they? The best way to anticipate the outcome is to review some of the transcript. In particular, let's review those disturbing policy questions just below the media surface. These issues are sometimes very subtle, sometimes very complex. Yet they hold the key to whether monetarism will ever be a successful policy.

So for the next few chapters we will pause to review parts of the transcript. We move from the world of black and white to the world of grey. We will see some basic issues of monetary policy that divide economists as they debate the course of future policy. This chapter raises some nagging questions about the basic monetarist scenario. Chapter 6 brings in the role of the Euromarkets. Chapter 7 examines the policy implications of the presence of foreign money. You must take the role of a jury member. You must decide if the monetarists' basic beliefs are based on fact. You must decide "beyond reasonable doubt" if in fact "the Fed controls money" and "money controls prices and income," as the monetarists assert. Look closely at the evidence as we explore it and as you make up your mind.

It would be nice if the exploration produced an unqualified answer to the question, "Is monetarism wrong?" However, as in many trials, the evidence can often be interpreted in more than one way. Those looking for a quick and final refutation of monetarism are likely to be disappointed. There is unfortunately no empirical way to rule directly in favor of the claims of monetarism versus those of its alternatives. The opposing attorney cannot decisively refute the monetarist testimony, but he or she can point out some potentially damaging holes in it. There remain those interesting and disturbing questions about basic monetarist assumptions. Chapter 2 has already raised the fact that the dollar money market is global, not national. And the transcript reveals that the apparently hard evidence in support of monetarism is equally consistent with other scenarios. These alternative explanations, it turns out, more consistently describe the way world money markets operate than does monetarism. In the end, the deficiencies of the monetarist case, along with the relevancies of the alternative view, will lead to the alternative policy approach described in chapters 9 and 10.

Question One: Does Money Cause Income?

One Type of Evidence

We begin the review by examining several important points about the relationship between money and income. The movements in M1 and M2 are supposed to be predictably related to movements in the level of dollar income. A monetarist could provide a straightforward explanation of why this relationship must exist. More money pumped into the economy means people have more money to spend. More spending boosts total demand for goods in the economy, which in turn leads to a rise in the price of goods and/or the quantity of goods produced. In either case the dollar value of income increases.

This scenario, with its direct impact of money on income, differs, of course, from the kind of story that a Keynesian would tell. In the Keynesian world, the link from money to income is very indirect. Money affects real economic activity only if it first affects interest rates. Only then can the movement in interest rates affect investment, which in turn affects total demand in the economy, which finally affects income.

So, in the Keynesian story, more money does not always mean more dollar income. Any additional supply of money might just be absorbed like a sponge into rising public money demand, in which case the chain of events never gets started. Since interest rates would not be affected, neither would income. Hence Keynesian monetary policy prescriptions traditionally center around targeting interest rates, the trigger in the chain of events, rather than monetary aggregates.

But in the view of the monetarist, money works more directly. Excess money in the pockets of people means extra desire for goods in the hand. So the monetarist's policy prescription is to control the amount of "excess" money. Since monetarists, unlike their Keynesian counterparts, believe that changes in the demand for money are stable and predictable, controlling excess money amounts essentially to regulating only the supply of money.

Studies designed to bolster the monetarist position have therefore concentrated primarily on the overall relationship between money and income. One of the more famous studies has been Milton Friedman and Anna Schwartz, *A Monetary History of the United States, 1867–1960.* [1] One type of relationship they found is an apparent, positive historical correlation between the behavior of the money supply and the stages of the business cycle. The growth rate of money rises during cyclical expansions and falls during contractions. The peak rate of money growth occurs early in the cyclical expansion and the trough early in recession. The changing behavior of money therefore comes before or "leads" the changing behavior of income.

Does this relationship prove that the quantity of money matters greatly? Some monetarists might insist that it does. Yet the evidence is far from conclusive. In this particular case, at least one problem is bothersome. The relationship described is between a physical quantity called money and a man-made concept called the business cycle. Is a comparison of such different entities meaningful?

It is beyond the scope of this book to provide an in-depth analysis of business-cycle theory. Briefly summarized, business cycles are an attempt to impose order on the world. Human beings, since earliest times, have looked for order and meaning in their world. They looked, for example, at the stars in the sky and wanted to know more about their meaning. From this quest for knowledge grew two disciplines, astronomy and astrology. The first discipline studied the nature of stars and the forces that made them move. The second searched for patterns in movement and deciphered their importance for the future behavior of humans.

Economics has also branched in two similar directions. Basic economic theory is concerned with what makes the economy work. What are the underlying forces in the economy, and what causes these forces, and thus the economy, to change? Business cycle theory, however, is more akin to astrology. Those who follow business cycles scour economic data for signs of patterns. The more regular the patterns, the happier the business-cycle analysts. Regular patterns in turn mean that economic data ("leading indicators," as they are labeled) can be read like the stars to predict the future course of human behavior.

Relating the behavior of money to the behavior of business cycles is therefore rather artificial. The behavior of a physical phenomenon (the supply of money) is compared to the behavior of data created by a committee (business-cycle turning points).[2] Not much true meaning can be gleaned from either the presence or the absence of a relationship here.

Stronger Monetarist Evidence

More convincing would be a close relationship between two more naturally observable series of numbers. Is there strong evidence that changes in the money supply are closely related to the actual growth in the economy? This relationship has also come under the scrutiny of economic investigators.

There is always the problem of selecting just a few representative studies that summarize fairly the empirical answer to this policy question. For example, researchers differ over what period of time the relationships are to hold. Some have chosen monthly data as the appropriate measurement period but have averaged the data over, say, a twenty-month period. Others have chosen quarterly data, sometimes with simple lagged data, sometimes averaged over twelve quarter periods. Still others have chosen annual data, again with differences of opinion over how to measure the year. Some prefer changes from one year's fourth quarter to the next year's fourth quarter. Others, however, compare changes between yearly averages.

There are obviously substantial differences, even among those sympathetic to monetarism, over how the desired statistical relationships can best be measured. These differences in interpretation among adherents to this school of thought can become more heated than differences between schools. With the understanding that focusing on only a few interpretations is likely to inflame passions in some, two sets of results are chosen as representative empirical evidence. One is a set of equations derived from annual data by Robert Weintraub, of the Joint Economic Committee. The other is the Andersen-Jordan equation of the St. Louis Fed model.

The Weintraub equations examine the policy questions among annual averages of money, inflation, income, and the velocity (turnover rate) of money over the period 1956–81.[3] One of Weintraub's equations estimates the relationship between percentage changes in U.S. money income and percentage changes in nominal dollar balances in the same year. He finds that nominal GNP and M1 are closely related over the period of a year. In fact, Weintraub finds that a one-percentage-point increase in M1 is associated with a one-percentage-point increase in nominal income in the same year.

Is the rise in nominal income associated with rising prices or real income? Weintraub finds little or no effect of money on real income. Money explains practically none of the annual variation in real income. Money instead affects prices. There is in particular a relationship between inflation (measured by

77

GNP deflator) and the percentage change in money two years previously. Every percentage point rise in inflation is associated with a percentage point growth in money two years before.

Weintraub also tries to show that the relationship between money and nominal income is dependable. One of the traditional arguments against the use of monetary policy is that its effects cannot be accurately anticipated. Changes in the quantity of money may produce offsetting or unpredicted changes in the velocity of money. Weintraub examines this assertion and finds no supporting evidence for it. Money and velocity appear unrelated for annual changes.

The well-known Andersen-Jordan equation of the St. Louis Federal Reserve model looks for relationships between quarterly percentage changes in the level of U.S. GNP and either changes in the U.S. money supply or changes in some measure of fiscal policy. The current version compares the effect of annualized percentage changes in M1 and the high-employment level of government expenditures.[4]

The findings of this model are similar to the findings of other monetarist models such as Weintraub's. Changes in U.S. income appear to be more closely related to changes in the money supply than they are to the changes in fiscal policy. Fiscal policy has only a small and temporary effect on nominal income. A one-percentage-point rise in the rate of high-employment government expenditures this quarter raises the rate of growth of income slightly over one-tenth of a percentage point by the end of next quarter. By the time one year has passed, however, the net effect of fiscal policy has almost completely disappeared. Monetary policy, on the other hand, has an immediate and persistent effect. A one-percentage-point rise in the rate of money growth is associated with an almost one-half percentage point rise in the growth rate of income in the same quarter. After a year monetary policy has, just as in

Weintraub's results, a percentage-point-for-percentage-point effect on nominal income.

The results, therefore, seem quite straightforward. There appears to be evidence reinforcing the one-to-one relationship between percentage changes in money and nominal income. If combined with the assumed Fed control of the money supply, the course of action is clear: stabilize money growth to stabilize income growth.

The Horse-and-Cart Problem

The Weintraub and Andersen-Jordan results are evidence of an apparently strong statistical correlation between money and GNP. But a basic rule of statistics is that correlation does not imply causation. A child grows over a period of years. In the same time, outside his bedroom window, a sapling grows into a sturdy tree. There is probably a strong correlation between the heights of the child and of the tree. It would be foolish, however, to argue that the child caused the tree to grow. In this case the two events are clearly unrelated to each other.

Similarly, just because money and income rise together does not mean that the rise in money *caused* the rise in income. Again, the two events might be unrelated. But an even more likely alternative explanation is that just the opposite causality is at work. A rise in income may have *caused* the rise in money. In other words, the observed correlations are equally consistent with the scenario that money simply adapts to the "needs of trade." We do not know whether money is the horse or the cart. We simply see money and income moving off together.

Some economists have argued that this horse-and-cart problem can be deciphered. If we only look a little harder, we might be able to tell which goes through the gate first. The first one through the gate must be the horse. In the course of this investigation several economic studies showing that the changes in money tend to occur first have received wide attention. There seems to be a lag between the time when the supply of money changes and the time when income changes. This apparent lag has been interpreted in two ways in the monetary policy debate.

First, for those monetarists who are convinced that money is the horse and income the cart, the lag has important implications for how monetary policy must be carried out. If money acts on income with a delay, but the delay is regular and precise, monetary policy might be useful for smoothing out specific ups and downs in the economy. But repeated attempts to find a regular and precise lag have been unsuccessful. The St. Louis Fed model implies that the lag is about six to twelve months. Friedman now says three to nine months.[5] Elsewhere Friedman has concluded simply that "monetary actions affect economic conditions only after a lag that is both long and variable."[6] A change in monetary policy today has an effect somewhere down the road, when quite different economic circumstances may exist. This inability to anticipate the precise effects of monetary policy has led monetarists such as Friedman to advocate a policy of steady monetary growth, rather than a more interventionist policy.[7]

Second, the lag is held up as "proof" that changes in money cause changes in income, and not the other way around. If the change in money comes first, it must be "causing" the change in income. Money must be the horse, and income the cart. In an attempt to nail down this point, various academic articles, applying sophisticated statistical techniques, have tried to show that the changes in money precede changes in income. Interestingly, the results have been mixed. In some cases changes in money appear to precede changes in income. Other articles yield the opposite conclusion.[8]

Yet even solid statistical proof that money changes first does not prove it is the cause of income changes. The fact that one event occurs before another does not mean the first caused the second event. The classic example of the phenomenon of the second event causing the first is stock market prices and corporate profits. Most observers of the stock market would agree that stock prices vary positively with corporate profits. An improved outlook for a corporation's earnings generally triggers a rise in the price of the corporation's stock. Conversely, should the outlook for future earnings suddenly become bleak, the price of the stock is likely to plunge.

The causality of corporate profits on stock prices is quite clear. Yet the observed sequence of events, using the monetarists' logic, could be interpreted to imply just the opposite. Typically stock prices rise in anticipation of higher earnings, and only later are the higher earnings actually reported. Statistical tests would always prove that stock price changes precede reported earnings changes. Yet these tests certainly do not prove that higher stock prices cause higher earnings.

The important message from the stock market example is that, statistically, there is no way to determine if the first event (a rise in the money supply or stock market prices) triggers the second event (a rise in income or corporate profits). Nor can we prove the alternative, that the first event occurs in anticipation of the second. Either explanation is consistent with observing one event systematically preceding the other. But the alternative explanations have diametrically opposite implications for policy and for the way markets adjust.[9]

In fairness, the possibility of this "reverse causation" from income to the money supply has been recognized. It pops up in many of the studies evaluating the relationship between money and income. The studies often concede that, to the extent such reverse causality exists, the correlation between money and income overstates the influence of the Fed. Yet, somehow, between evidence and conclusion, most of the correlation is ascribed to the effects of money.

What the data may be telling us, however, is just the opposite causation. When the economy begins to expand, businesses, for example, typically hire more workers. More workers mean a larger payroll, and the firm increases its money balances to cover these added expenses. Similarly, the recently hired worker probably holds more money than before. Or an employed worker may interpret the expanding economy to mean a larger end-of-year bonus check. In anticipation, the employee increases his or her money balances in order to increase purchases. In a multitude of ways, an expanding economy creates the need for an expanding supply of money. Rather than reacting to an increase in money thrust upon them by the Fed, people may be simply demanding more money from the banking system in anticipation of their needs.

Weintraub's results, for instance, are completely consistent with this alternative scenario. Money may be endogenous—in other words, responding to people's needs rather than to Federal Reserve policies. When income rises in a given year, money rises with it. Weintraub's contemporaneous relationship may support monetarism, but it simultaneously supports just the opposite theory as well.

The Seasonal Adjustment Problem—Making It Even Harder to Tell the Horse from the Cart

The St. Louis Fed model also supports the conjecture that money changes in response to income. The model does show that the ups or downs of money occur a few quarters before income has completely changed. Yet as we have seen, these correlations could be interpreted as money balances changing in anticipation of income changes. Again, the fact that income in the St. Louis equation responds after money cannot prove the importance of the quantity of money on the economy. Perhaps even more importantly, however, the observed lagged response in the equation may be more apparent than real. The source of the observed lag may be the seasonal adjustment of the data.

Economists agree that seasonal patterns have to be taken into account. The Christmas season is very busy. Retail sales, money supply, and other raw economic data tend to reach their yearly peak around this time. On the other hand, the "dog days" of August are a very slow time. People go away on vacation, and economic activity declines. Because these patterns persist from year to year, it is hard to compare raw economic numbers from December to numbers from August. Instead, the numbers must first be adjusted to account for these seasonal patterns.

There is a substantial difference of opinion, however, over which method of seasonal adjustment is most appropriate for performing statistical tests. Many economists simply rely on the economic data that have been seasonally adjusted by the government. These data are the numbers commonly reported in government press releases. Most government data are seasonally adjusted by a statistical technique called X–11. This process smooths out the seasonal troughs and peaks in the data by making the variations in one month's data a weighted average of the variations in surrounding months. In other words, the reported behavior of, say, the seasonally adjusted money supply this month depends not only on what is now happening to the money supply but also what happened several months ago.

Seasonal adjustment definitely makes the apparent behavior of the money supply smoother than it would appear if the data were not seasonally adjusted (figure 5–1). But desired smoothness is obtained at a cost. The seasonal adjustment very nicely cuts off the peaks and troughs in the raw data. Those peaks and troughs, however, contain information. Some of the information may be seasonal patterns that we want to eliminate, but some of it is not. Unfortunately the X–11 process does not discriminate well between these two types of information.[10]

So in addition to smoothing out the seasonal patterns, X–11 also rearranges the other information. Suppose, for example, a relevant, nonseasonal jump in the money supply data occurs in May. In the unadjusted data the jump contributes to an apparent peak. In the process of smoothing out that peak, however, some of the relevant information is redistributed to other months. In other words, some of the relevant jump in the data for May now may appear in the data for January, February, March, April, and even June and July. What happens if an economist looks for a relationship between, say, the growth of money and changes in a measure of income like the level of industrial production? Even if the true relationship between money and income is contemporaneous, when the information is rearranged, lead and lag relationships may appear. The seasonal adjustment process has increased the probability that an economist looking for a lagged relationship will find one.[11]

The problems of seasonal adjustment have become increasingly evident to the economics profession. There are a variety of other statistical techniques for dealing with seasonal patterns in data, many of which avoid the problems inherent in X–11. Aware of the problems, more and more economists today choose to use seasonally unadjusted data, opting instead for one of the alternative methods of seasonally adjusting the data in their regression equations.

The differences in results can be considerable. An interesting example occurred in the early 1970s. The original Ander-

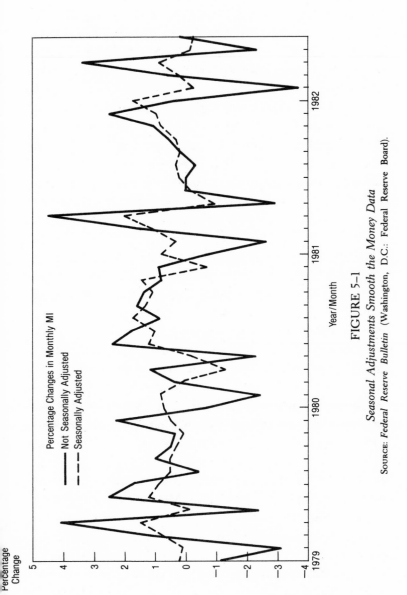

FIGURE 5–1

Seasonal Adjustments Smooth the Money Data

SOURCE: *Federal Reserve Bulletin* (Washington, D.C.: Federal Reserve Board).

sen-Jordan equation of the St. Louis Fed model had already been estimated and its conclusions widely disseminated. As in the later version, these researchers found movements in money to have a significantly positive impact on income up to three quarters later. This relationship was estimated using seasonally adjusted data.

In 1970 two researchers, Arthur B. Laffer and R. David Ranson, examined essentially the same historical relationship.[12] As did the St. Louis Fed researchers, Laffer and Ranson related changes in U.S. GNP to changes in money and government expenditure. The only major differences were that Laffer and Ranson used percentage changes instead of absolute changes in the data, and most importantly, seasonally unadjusted data.[13] Seasonal patterns were then accounted for by employing an accepted statistical procedure called "dummy variables."

In some ways the conclusions of the two studies were quite similar. As in the St. Louis Fed model, Laffer and Ranson found quarterly changes in the money supply to be more highly correlated to quarterly changes in income than were quarterly changes in government expenditure, and the net effect of fiscal policy (sum of coefficients) was approximately zero. But in one important way, the two studies were strikingly different. Contrary to the previous studies employing seasonally adjusted data, Laffer and Ranson found there was no lag between money and income. The contemporaneous correlation between money and income explained all the relationship between these two sets of numbers. Money and income were changing together.

While the estimated relationship between money and income occurred within the same quarter, the total relationship was still consistent with the monetarist studies. The coefficient on the contemporaneous money term in Laffer and Ranson's model (1.10) was very similar to the coefficient later estimated by Weintraub for annual data (1.02), or the sum of the coefficients in the revised St. Louis Fed model (1.07). A one-percent increase in nominal income is associated with a one-percent increase in money. At the time Laffer and Ranson estimated their model, that meant that a one-dollar increase in the money supply was associated with a five-dollar increase in income.

This finding that money and income change in the same quarter went against the prevailing wisdom. The results were naturally received with skepticism. Some people tried to deride these findings as the "Laffer-Ranson Money Machine." Just pump more money into the economy, and income responds five-fold immediately. These skeptics, however, failed to see the potential implications of these findings because of their own viewpoint. Laffer and Ranson were not showing that an injection of money produces prosperity. All they had done was estimate the historical relationship between money and income. What they had discovered, however, was that removing the X–11 seasonal adjustment removes most of the apparent lagged response of money to income.[14]

A subsequent updating of the model did uncover some lag between the time that money changes and the time that income does.[15] The average lag, however, was only about ten weeks, less than one quarter. The empirical relationship remained essentially contemporaneous, certainly far more contemporaneous than other models of the day.

The possibility that money and income are contemporaneous reinforced in the minds of some the likelihood of "reverse causality." While even a lag between changes in variables does not rule out causation running in both directions, the absence of a lag makes the concept of income determining the level of money more attractive to many people. Maybe all Laffer and Ranson have captured is the money supply rising by one dollar when nominal GNP rises by five. If so, the probability that the Federal Reserve can influence the country's income by influencing money is not very great.

Question Two: Is It Likely that the Fed Will Ever Control the Money Supply?

How solid is the other link in the monetarist chain? Is the Fed really the force behind the movement in M1? The monetarist scenario certainly confers such omnipotent powers on the Fed. The technicians at the Fed are seen as resembling the gatekeepers who regulate the flow of water from a dam. The gatekeepers are skilled at delivering water downstream to meet the needs for consumption, irrigation, recreation, and maybe even hydroelectric power. The Fed's technicians similarly are viewed as closely monitoring the flow of money, making sure that the right amount is making it from the central bank to the market to meet the needs of the private sector. Too much and the city will be flooded. Too little and the city shrivels from a drought.

The Fed technicians, however, are not believed to be mere human workers. Rather, they are assumed to have almost superhuman powers and skills. For example, it is not enough that just a given amount of money makes it to the market. No, all along the money waterway, with the aid of sophisticated instruments, they are constantly monitoring the speed and size of the flow headed for market.

These Fed technicians are naturally assumed to know precisely what the market downstream needs, and they are supposed to deliver only that amount. But the focus of their concern is more than just the total number of dollars making it to the market. They are also supposed to watch carefully the time at which the dollars arrive. Money is not supposed to show up at the market in one large swell, even if the market should want it that way. Monetarism insists that money should trickle in bit by bit. So the sophisticated monitoring equipment lining the waterway to the market is supposed to ensure that money flows in a dependable, steady stream.

Meanwhile, back at the gatehouse, the gatekeepers are busy monitoring the dollars leaving the dam. The wider the dam gate is opened, the more money that flows at one time to market. In days when the liquidity value downstream is rapidly falling (inflationary periods), the gatekeepers are concerned that the gate not be opened too wide. They try to squeeze the opening in the gate to reduce the liquidity making it to the market. The squeezing, they believe, will make the fall in value slow down. Simultaneously, the technicians are put on full alert to monitor more closely the activity along the waterway to market. Their instruments maintain a watchful eye over how fast the money is moving, providing an early warning should the liquidity begin to lap the tops of the banks. And perhaps most importantly, as the sun sets slowly in the West, the gatekeepers issue press releases, hailing what a fine job they are doing. The people in the city below can sleep soundly at night, they are told, knowing these gatekeepers are defending them from a flood of money.

This monetarist scenario is very straightforward and appealling, and it certainly instills confidence that stable money is only a few Fed directives away. Yet even since the October 1979 decision to monitor the total quantity of money, the apparent actions of the Fed have received a lot of criticism. For the most part, the Fed has been berated for not constraining the various Ms sufficiently. There have been periods in which the popular

M1 has grown beyond the Fed's announced targets. In other periods, M1 has flowed nicely within the waterway, but M2 was busy lapping over the top of its banks. Such apparent inconsistent or incompetent behavior has become the target for monetarist criticism. The Fed is not doing its job. It is not following its own directives. It is technically lax in following its directives. Its directives are misdirected.

The monetarist criticism, however, is probably unfair. The source of the apparent breakdown in policy is simply that the Fed's control is not as omnipotent as the scenario would suggest. The Fed is only one of many fallible participants in the money market. The other participants also have considerable clout. There are many ways beyond the Fed's sphere of influence for the private market to circumvent the Fed's money growth policies. Not only does money find its way out of the waterway the Fed has set, but there are other dam gates and other waterways as well. The Fed has trouble controlling its own supply route, and there are competing supply routes over which it has little, if any, control. Money markets are changing rapidly these days, and it is unlikely that a staid institution like the Fed can keep pace with, much less control, the evolving markets.

Question Three: Will the Real Money Supply Please Stand Up?

The Fed therefore faces many difficult problems in living up to the legend the monetarists have created for it. About the most basic is the problem of the money supply. The Fed is supposed to control the money supply. But what is *the* money supply?

The literature of monetary theory abounds with articles trying to define precisely what should be included in a relevant definition of the supply of money. The debate is far from resolved. Ask any two economists, and you are bound to get at least three different answers. But particularly in the last decade, as inflation and regulation have spurred financial innovations, economists have increasingly come to realize that what is used for money in the U.S. extends far beyond the traditional concepts such as M1 or even the new M2.

Today M1 includes currency in circulation, demand (checking account) deposits, and other checkable deposits such as NOW accounts and credit union share draft balances. Traditionally these currency and checkable accounts have been forms in which people and institutions held money for their everyday use. These components are all liabilities of institutions that at least appear to be under the control of the Federal Reserve. Hence the attractiveness of M1 as a policy guide. This is a number which the Fed might be able to influence directly.

There are today, however, numerous domestic financial alternatives to the money assets included in M1. For example, there are time deposits, certificates of deposit, money market shares, repurchase agreements, commercial paper, credit cards, and so on. There are also international alternatives such as Eurodollars. These alternatives clearly represent a spectrum of monetary assets that fall less and less under the control of the Federal Reserve regulations. They therefore represent a spectrum of assets whose availabilities are increasingly likely to respond to the demands of the private sector. They provide direct methods for the public to get around the dollar liquidity policy of the Fed.

Even the Fed realizes the limited value of their traditional money measures. In fact, the increasing importance of alternative monies was part of the motivation behind reformulating the definitions of money in February 1980. At that time, M2 was greatly expanded to add to M1 not only small time deposits but also such assets as overnight repurchase agreements, overnight Eurodollar deposits in the Caribbean, and money market mutual fund shares. This bowing to reality was thought to enhance the effectiveness of Fed policy guidelines. But the new numbers also represented an admission that the Fed's power is limited. While the inclusion of these additional assets made M2 closer to a relevant market definition of money, the newly included assets are simultaneously clearly outside the Fed's control.

Is even M2 the relevant definition of money? Probably not. If overnight Eurodollars at Caribbean branches (included in M2) are relevant, why not overnight Eurodollars in other banks? And why not longer-term Eurodollars? Longer-term Eurodollars at even Caribbean branches do not appear until the broad measure L (liquid assets). Overnight Eurodollars at other than Caribbean branches do not appear in any definition of money. Longer term repurchase agreements do not appear until M3.[16] Money market funds that belong to institutions also do not surface until M3. In addition, with the current incentives to increase returns and reduce costs in financial markets, new financial innovations continue to appear. Witness, for example, the development of "sweep" accounts.

These financial innovations will have to be included in any relevant money supply. Such innovations occur, of course, because the financial markets see a need for the new money instruments. Yet even the monetarists would have to agree that the Fed does not control this broader range of assets. It is quite likely that the innovation occurred in the first place to avoid a Fed regulation or barrier. For instance, money market mutual funds began to flourish as banks were constrained from paying competitive interest on smaller deposits. As the next chapter describes in more detail, the growth of the Eurodollar market has also reflected efforts to avoid domestic interest-rate ceilings, as well as rising reserve requirements and other Fed imposed restrictions.

Given these alternative assets, were the Fed, say, to reduce the supply of monetary base in an attempt to reduce M1, the private sector could respond with greater use of money market funds, repurchase agreements, and credit cards. The Fed's policy might even successfully reduce M1. But since the relevant definition of money instruments includes more than what is measured by M1, the decline provides a false signal. The decline in M1 is offset by the rise in the alternative instruments. While the Fed, through its limited powers, might alter the relative proportions that the public holds in regulated versus unregulated money, it is unable to directly control the total relevant quantity of money.

For example, repurchase agreements, or repos, provide a way for banks to handle a shortage of required reserves without having to go begging at the Fed. The repo is a transaction between two private market participants, the bank and one of its customers. Suppose that one day the treasurer of Bank A notices that, given the deposits on the bank's books, Bank A does not have enough liquid assets in the form the Fed requires. The bank is not insolvent; it is just that only reserves held as cash in the vault or deposits at the Fed can be legally counted as official reserves against deposits. So the treasurer must do something. He could, for example, go begging, Treasury bills in hand, at the Fed's discount window. Or the bank could try to bid away reserves from other banks in the Fed funds market. But a third alternative is for the treasurer of the bank to call the treasurer of Acme Corporation, one of the bank's customers. Maybe Acme Corporation has some funds deposited in the bank that it is not planning to use for one, two or even a few days. If so, Bank A and Acme can enter into a repurchase agreement.

Under the agreement, Acme lends the money in its account back to the bank. In return, Bank A gives Acme title to an equal amount of Treasury bills in the bank's portfolio. The bank then promises to "repurchase" the T-bills at a specific date. Acme is happy. Instead of a deposit, it now has a repo that pays interest over the days the cash is unneeded. Acme has simply traded one type of money asset for another. To Acme the repo is as liquid as money, for the company gets the cash back precisely when it thought the money would be needed. The bank is also happy. By borrowing back the money, the deposits on its books subject to required reserves are reduced. Hence, its required reserves are reduced. The economy is also benefitted. By changing the form of the money assets from deposits to repos, the banking system is able to keep up the level of money without having to depend on the Fed to pump more monetary base into the system. A dollar of monetary base, so to speak, "goes farther." Repos, then, make the relevant money more elastic. The relevant supply of money can be more responsive to the needs of the market and more independent of the Fed.[17]

What to include in the relevant money supply is an empirical question that may never be resolved to everyone's satisfaction. However, it can be argued that the empirical justification for L (which the Fed clearly does not control) is at least as strong as that for M1. If M1 is replaced by L in Weintraub's set of equations, precisely the same qualitative results are produced. This year's percentage change in nominal GNP, for example, is significantly related to this year's change in L. Statistically there is a percentage-point-for-percentage-point change in the two numbers. In fact, the movements in L even explain marginally more of the variation in GNP than do the movements in M1.[18]

Certainly as the restrictions on interest payments banks can pay are phased out between now and 1986 (see chapter 8), the problem for the Fed will only increase. Writing in the Federal Reserve Bank of New York's *Quarterly Review,* Betsey Buttrill White speculates on what the phasing out of Regulation Q restrictions will mean:

In short, the spectrum of financial assets will be much fuller than at present. Traditional distinctions between transactions balances and investment balances, between near money provided by banks and market instruments, will become even more blurred than at present, *and in the case of M-1 an "appropriate" definition will be difficult, if not impossible to determine.* (emphasis added)

She continues about the difficulty of measuring money:

Since it may not be possible to measure a transaction-related aggregate in any reasonably accurate way, greater reliance on a broader monetary aggregate may be necessary. But, when all deposits pay a market related rate of interest, *not even a broader aggregate will be a viable intermediate target in the sense that the Federal Reserve could control it over some period of time.* (emphasis added)[19]

The Bank for International Settlements in Basel, Switzerland (the central banks' central bank) agrees with her analysis. Its 1982 annual report says about the phase-out of interest rate ceilings in the United States:

Holdings of transaction balances may continue to decline in relation to GNP. While this process is going on the demand for money will be difficult to estimate. And even when the transition is completed the monetary aggregates may be less useful as indicators or intermediate targets than they have been in the past.[20]

BEYOND MONETARISM

This realization that the money supply figures are becoming meaningless was echoed by Frank E. Morris, president of the Federal Reserve Bank of Boston. Writing in the *Wall Street Journal*, Mr. Morris comments:

Economists in recent years have been writing prolifically about a new phenomenon—sudden, unanticipated shifts in the public's "demand for money," shifts which have not been explained by the traditional determinants of the rate of growth of the nominal GNP and changes in interest rates. This much greater instability in money demand coincided with the increased pace of financial innovation. . . . The pace of innovation has led us to the point where any definition of the money supply must be arbitrary and unsatisfactory. . . . I have therefore concluded, most reluctantly, that we can no longer measure the money supply with any kind of precision. . . . We have exhibited in recent years a strong nostalgic urge to retain a statistical concept of transactions balances, even though we understand intellectually that innovation and the computerization of the financial system have made it impossible to draw a clear line between money and other liquid assets.[21]

One may wonder, given that even the Fed and perhaps the monetarists recognize the extent and potential impact of alternative monies in the U.S. economy, why so much time and effort is still spent tracking, analyzing, explaining, and projecting the paths of M1 and M2. The monetarists' rationale for still zeroing in on M1 is probably similar to the rationale of the man in the old story who one night lost his watch in a field. The man's friend found him frantically searching in the street.

FRIEND: What's the matter?
MAN: I've lost my watch!
FRIEND: I'll help you look. Where did you lose it?
MAN: Over in the field.
FRIEND: Over in the field! Then why are you looking so hard in the street?
MAN: It's the only place I have a light.

Question Four: Who's Really Behind the Ups and Downs of M1?

For the moment let's forget the problem of what is money. Let's close our eyes to reality and assume the monetarists are correct in tracking a number like M1. How well would the monetarist scenario work then? Would the Fed now be able to regulate the "money supply" adequately to bring down inflation?

Problems still remain, problems which have been recognized for many years. Pick up any standard money and banking textbook and turn to the chapter on the money supply. Invariably the chapter will describe how the money supply like M1 is the final result of decisions by the Fed, the public, and the commercial banks. The Fed, as we saw, has a number of ways to influence M1. It could directly alter the level of the monetary base, alter minimum reserve requirements behind bank deposits, or change the terms at which it lends to the banking community. More monetary base or more lending helps expand the potential money supply. Higher required reserves lowers it.

The public affects the level of money by choosing how much of its money to hold in currency versus deposits, and by deciding what proportion of deposits will be transaction versus time deposits. Holding currency deprives the banking system of potential reserves, reducing the amount of money which can be created through financial intermediation. Holding more time deposits rather than transaction deposits makes the potential money supply larger, because banks are not required to hold as large reserves against time deposits.

Banks can influence the supply of money by deciding whether to hold reserves over and above those required by the

BEYOND MONETARISM

Fed. If banks wish to hold "excess reserves," the monetary base that banks hold will be spread over fewer deposits. The money supply is smaller than in the absence of excess reserves.

This textbook discussion will summarize these various influences of the Fed, the public, and banks in the product of two components, the monetary base and something called the "money multiplier." This product literally illustrates how much M1 could result from a given monetary base. The larger the multiplier, the bigger the potential M1. The smaller the multiplier, the less money there is likely to be in the economy.

This multiplier largely reflects the influence of the public and the commercial banks. The only potential Fed influence included is the adjustment of required reserves. The important policy question, then, is which of the two components exerts more influence over the level of money? Is it the money multiplier, which reflects largely non-Fed decisions? Or is it the monetary base, whose behavior is mostly controlled by the Fed?

The monetarists, of course, assume that the Fed's behavior "dominates" movements in the money supply. To them, the movements of the monetary base signal the movements in money. But that relationship has been far from perfect. In fact, it has been demonstrated that, historically, the swings in the money multiplier have had a significant effect on the movements in money.

For example, back in the 1960s, Phillip Cagan, a former Friedman student, wrote a widely known volume that was supposed to show which influences had been most important in determining the money supply over about the last century.[22] Cagan was probably interested in demonstrating how important the Fed had been. His results, however, did not support that conclusion. The monetary base and the Federal Reserve's actions were by no means the dominant force determining the course of money. In fact, the public's ability to vary the amount of currency relative to bank deposits they held (the currency ratio) accounted for about one-half of the cyclical variation in money over that period. The movements of high-powered money, or monetary base, explained only about one-quarter of the ups and downs of money, about the same effect as the banks' adjustments of their excess reserves (the reserve ratio). Cagan noted that the "important role of the currency ratio reflects two facts: the comparatively large amplitude of its fluctuations, and the regularity of its cyclical pattern."[23] In other words, the public's ratio of currency to deposits held regularly follows, inversely, the ups and downs of the economy.

It was only after Cagan began applying a statistical technique to adjust for related, offsetting contributions among the three determinants that the movements in the base or the Fed's actions began to account for more than half of the variation. Even then, the Fed's actions dominated only in a few parts of the entire period analyzed. Cagan comments this way about these results:

Although the corrected figures may overemphasize, if anything, the contribution of high-powered money, they may still seem surprising, because they do not attribute all variations in the money series in the later period to high-powered money, and because they attribute an important role to the currency ratio in both periods. . . . [I]n discussions of cyclical movements, high-powered money and the reserve ratio have generally received all the attention, while the currency ratio has been little noticed. One reason for the differential treatment is that sources of variation in high-powered money and the reserve ratio involve activities of the government and banks—both easy to discuss (and exaggerate)—whereas sources of variation in the currency ratio involve actions of innumerable holders of money and are, except in panics, obscure. While many students of the money supply have been aware of variations in the currency ratio, the present results highlight their importance, not only in panics but also for all cycles in the money series.[24]

A subsequent study, by Arthur Laffer and this author, of the post–World War II period reinforced Cagan's findings.[25] We found that over months, quarters, and semi-annual periods the public's abilities to influence the ratio of currency to deposits and the composition of deposits were far more important than changes in the monetary base for explaining the movements in M1. Not until annual changes were considered did the influence of the monetary base begin to become important. But in most of the years which were examined, the United States was under the Bretton Woods fixed exchange rate system, which permitted monetary base to flow easily into and out of the country. With integrated global money markets, it is quite possible that even these annual changes in the monetary base reflect changes caused by the public's demands as much as by Federal Reserve policy. We concluded that short-term changes in the money supply do not materially reflect Federal Reserve policy.

Given the ability of the public to stretch out money when more is needed, the technicians at the Fed are likely to be frustrated in their attempts to keep even M1 growth within targets. The Fed operates under the belief that a dollar more of monetary base in the system means a few extra dollars of money. Less base, less money. That may be true sometimes, but other times it will not. The Fed, for example, could try to put the squeeze on the money markets. It could follow the policy of pulling in monetary base to get M1 growth down to target. If the public and banks sat idly by, this policy might work. But the public and banks have incentives not to sit idly by. They want to hold more money. So the public economizes on the existing monetary base by holding less currency. More of base money finds its way into bank vaults, where it can be "multiplied" through financial intermediation. In addition, the public can expand the broader, more relevant money supply by making greater use of financial market innovations like money market funds, which do not require base money. Banks, too, turn to their alternatives for making the remaining monetary base "go farther." Banks hold fewer excess reserves, make more use of repurchase agreements, and direct more of their financial intermediation to offshore or "Eurodollar" branches. Together these actions blunt the Fed's intentions concerning the total supply of money. The money market, then, is just like water: it tends to seek its own level. Try to push the supply of money below the level of demand, and the market quickly reacts. Ways are found of getting around the force holding down the supply of money. New routes appear that permit total money assets to rise to the level the private sector wants.

Question Five: How Reliable Are Reported Money Figures for Planning Policy?

The responsiveness of money to its demand makes successful control of total money aggregates extremely unlikely. But we could even overlook this problem. We could assume that the Fed somehow can manipulate money the way it wants. Even with this highly questionable assumption, is the monetarist scenario likely to succeed? Could a quantity rule be smoothly implemented?

Implementation requires information, which raises some additional problems. Part of the information required concerns money demand. Monetary economists have noted considerable shifts in money demand across countries over the last decade. A profession that is still debating "The Case of the Missing

Money" cannot be relied on for consistently accurate forecasts of money demand. After all the information is in, economists are often able to explain what happened. But before events occur, their success is quite limited. In September 1982, for example, the Congressional Budget Office reported that it had used three prominent statistical money demand equations to estimate the level of money demand in the first two quarters of 1982. These estimates used preliminary actual figures (not even forecasts) for all variables but the money supply. Yet each equation underestimated the demand for money by $8 to $10 billion![26] The CBO concluded that an unanticipated shift in money demand had occurred. We can conclude that forecasting money demand is not an exact science.

Money supply is another piece of information required for implementation of a quantity rule. Even if we knew what money was, even if we could estimate the demand for it, even if the Fed could control it, we would still have great difficulty measuring the actual supply of money. If policy makers are to determine a course of action, they need to know not only where they want to be, but also where they are. They need an estimate of how fast money is growing. Yet the existing money supply data are not sufficiently reliable for this purpose.

How can there be such a problem? The newspapers are full of talk about M1 and M2 and how these figures have gone up or down. Why not use those numbers?

Many people probably do use these reported figures as a guide to Fed policy. But increasingly, over the last few years, they have found the reliability of the numbers wanting. One problem is the accuracy in collecting any numbers. The Fed itself does not have the number of bank deposits. These numbers must be collected from the various banks. In the process, the numbers pass through many hands, creating the possibility for error at each stage. The possibility for substantial measurement error is great. The financial markets had a taste of what such error can be like in the fall of 1979. It seems that the person at Manufacturers Hanover in New York responsible for transmitting this weekly data to the Fed was on vacation. The substitute inadvertently placed some figures in the wrong column. The result was that the weekly money supply figures were misquoted by $3.5 billion!

This experience produced turmoil in the financial markets and created a lot of red faces. Fed Chairman Volcker was hauled before Congress to explain how such a mistake could occur. A vice president at the Federal Reserve Bank of New York, which processes the weekly figure, was fired. A lot of hand waving occurred, but it could not hide the fact that the Fed does not have a consistently accurate measure of the money supply.

The problems of measurements are exacerbated by the need to correct the data for seasonal patterns and trading day variations. These adjustments are estimates, just like the raw numbers. The opportunities for misleading errors compound.

So policy decisions are based on the movement of the money supply as the Fed records it. But with all the potential errors, policy may respond to an unrealistic set of numbers. For example, as time goes on, the Fed continually updates the money supply statistics. New, more accurate information appears about the actual level of currency and deposits, and what the seasonal adjustment should really be. The Fed from time to time issues revised money supply figures that one hopes more accurately reflect how much money there was in the economy. Yet policy decisions are often based on the first set of preliminary numbers issued. Are the preliminary numbers and the revised numbers similar? Even if changes in the money supply figures reflect Fed policy, can one get relevant and reliable information from the reported figures?

Arthur Laffer and this author examined these questions for monthly money statistics over the twenty-year period 1954–73.[27] Our conclusion was that the figures are not very useful either as information or as a policy guide. The data collection procedures employed by the Fed produce two troubling sets of problems.

First, there is very little relationship between the pattern of period-to-period changes in the initially released data and the pattern in the data after final revisions have occurred (figure 5–2). Historical relationships between the money supply and the economy, for example, are estimated from the much smoother final revised data. Policy decisions are then made based on these historical relationships. Yet it is quite clear that the initially released data are almost a totally different data series from the repeatedly revised numbers. The final data are a much smoother series. There are smaller differences in month-to-month percentage changes, and large monthly percentage changes that appear in the preliminary numbers have been eliminated. The variance of the preliminary series is more than three times that of the final series. The preliminary series is clearly more volatile. The correlation between the percentage changes in the two series is only about one-third. Hence, recently released data are likely to be an unreliable guide to the policies the Fed should follow.

Second, even the final numbers are distorted. The seasonal adjustment procedures are unsuccessful in completely eliminating seasonal patterns and introduce new forms of distortion. Time series analysis of the data shows that even the final seasonally adjusted money supply series is not free of observable seasonal patterns. Simultaneously, as we have seen, the seasonal adjustment procedure transfers relevant information to irrelevant time periods, producing new distortions in the numbers.

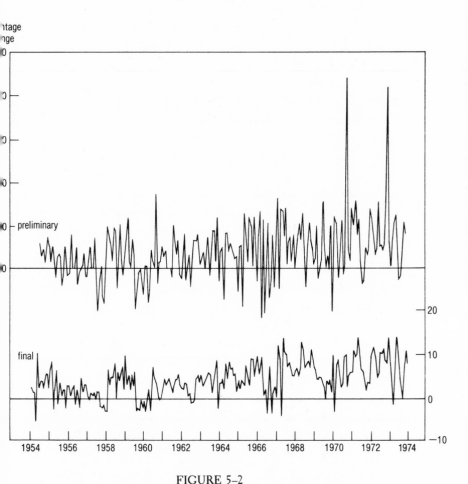

FIGURE 5–2

Preliminary Versus Final Data on Money Supply Growth Rate

NOTE: Reprinted with permission from Arthur B. Laffer and Marc A. Miles, "Constraints on the Usefulness of Just-Released Money Supply Figures," *Economic Study*, H. C. Wainwright & Co., Economics, 13 December, 1977.

These conclusions imply that the current money supply figures are probably useless at best and may be misleading indicators of monetary pressures on the economy.

These problems have not gone unnoticed by the Fed. In the spring of 1982, the Fed acknowledged that its method of seasonally adjusting weekly figures had been very inexact. While seasonally unadjusted weekly figures would continue to be furnished, seasonally adjusted numbers would appear only as an average of the four previous weeks. In other words, it is as though the Fed is to provide a "monthly" number every week. There is no reason to believe, however, that these "monthly" numbers will not have the same revision problems as monthly data in the past.

A monetarist might retort that the objections to monthly data can be overcome by using data measured over a longer period of time. If monthly numbers are unreliable, then watch quarterly or annual numbers. Every month one can compute a monthly, quarterly, or annual moving average of the money supply figures. These data will change very little as revisions emerge.

In one sense this argument is correct. Averaging figures over longer and longer periods certainly makes the historical number series much smoother and reduces the impact of revising the data for any particular date. In another sense, however, the argument is misleading. The purpose of a policy indicator such as the money supply is to tell the policy maker what to do next. The desire of the Fed to have weekly figures reflects its need for up-to-date information about the money markets for formulating today's policy. While averaging data over longer periods makes them less volatile, it also makes them less up-to-date. If for some reason the money supply suddenly jumps or falls, averaging the current numbers with those in the past blunts the current recorded change. Only part of the relevant information about what is happening today makes its way to the policy maker. The policy maker does not have all the information needed to respond properly to today's money market. The value of the money supply as a policy indicator has been reduced further.

The Monetarist Dilemma

Together these questions that have been raised and arguments that have been made emphasize a basic dilemma for those who favor a quantity-rule policy. This dilemma, however, is not a recent discovery. Alan Reynolds points out that Friedman's predecessor at the University of Chicago, Henry Simons, recognized these inadequacies of a monetary rule. As Reynolds relates,

"The obvious weakness of fixed quantity," responded Simons, "as a sole rule of monetary policy, lies in the danger of sharp changes on the velocity side." Moreover, "the abundance of what we may call 'near moneys,' " Simons wisely added, creates a "difficulty of defining money in such manner as to give practical significance to the conception of quantity."[28]

In today's regulated banking climate, these words ring true. The regulations may or may not have been instituted to make control of the money supply seem manageable. Interest-rate ceilings on deposits may have been mandated to hold down banks' costs. Required reserves may have aimed to reduce the incidence of bank failures. Whatever the reasons, these regulations have created incentives for financial innovation. The innovations in turn have created new forms of the near monies Simons mentioned. The presence of the near monies makes Federal Reserve control of the total relevant money supply an impossibility.

BEYOND MONETARISM

If the problems of monetary control are exacerbated by bank regulation, would the task be easier without the regulations? At one extreme, all regulations could be thrown out the window by abolishing the Federal Reserve. Certainly few would argue such a scenario would give the government control of the money supply. The private market would simply find new ways to create money. An interesting recent example illustrates this point. A strike among bank employees in the Republic of Ireland closed down the monetary system for six and a half months in 1970. The private sector, caught without its customary system of making payments, developed a new system. Corporations set up their own system for clearing debts, relying in part on North American and merchant banks that remained open. For the individual private citizen, retail shops and local pubs served as cash banks. These small businesses relied on their knowledge of the local customer in deciding whether to accept a check that might not clear for some time. Without a working central bank, then, the private sector developed its own institutions to permit the supply of money to rise and fall with demand.[29]

A more moderate case might be that a central bank exists, but its only source of influence is injecting and extracting monetary base through open market operations. Without the assorted other regulations that exist today, financial innovations such as money market mutual funds or repurchase agreements might never appear in such a world. Would the Fed now be able to control money aggregates? Again, probably not. While fewer near monies would likely appear, some are bound to remain. Even more important, however, the Fed still could not dictate the amount of conventional money. The public still retains the choice of how much of the monetary base ends up at banks as reserves. Banks would have even more latitude over how many reserves they held. The Fed would still be lender of last resort through the discount window.

In none of these cases does Federal Reserve control approach anything close to absolute. This lack of control in turn has important implications for the policy conclusions of the monetarists. The monetarists, for example, are fond of pointing out that even with innovations like money market funds the ratio of M1 to nominal income (M1/Y) is a stable function over time. The ratio is not a constant, but it can be anticipated ahead of time. Given that it can be anticipated, so the logic goes, any change in M1 is associated with a proportional change in income. A moderate, steady rise in M1 yields a moderate, steady rise in Y.

Whether the ratio of money to income is sufficiently stable to be forecasted accurately and dependably is a subject of controversy. But suppose it is. Does it necessarily follow that the Fed should target M1 money growth? The three scenarios illustrate why not. The rises and falls in M1 quite likely do not reflect primarily Fed policy. Instead they reflect the public's responses to their rising and falling needs for money.

Yet monetary policy continues to proceed as though the Fed at least potentially has control over the relevant Ms. In the last decade, the monetarists have thrown off the alleged shackles of fixed exchange rates. Unhinging money was to provide effective control of the monetary base. But simultaneously the unhinging resulted in soaring inflation and high interest rates. These shocks to the financial markets spurred financial innovation, creating new money assets which assured that M1 and M2 would become irrelevant.

So the monetarists are in a real bind. What they want to control (the relevant money supply) they cannot. What they might control (the monetary base) is not terribly relevant. On top of this problem, they recognize that with the two-week lagged reserve accounting that has existed in recent years, the Fed must open the discount window when the market asks.

Even the monetary base changes in response to the needs of the market.

In addition to the problems of relevancy and control, there is the problem of measuring the numbers. We simply do not have good estimates of this thing we are supposed to be closely watching. Yet the shouting matches among partisans, over whether money growth has been one-half percent too high or too low, continue throughout the country. These debates, however, are more form than substance. They are a symptom of how the monetarists are using the debates over money supply figures much as a drunk would use a lamppost—more for support than for illumination. The monetarists are trying to hide the fact that they are in a no-win situation.

6

Reexamining Monetarism II—Whoops! We Forgot About the Euromarket!

TO LISTEN TO A MONETARIST, the Federal Reserve is like a mighty dike protecting the U.S. money market. Dollars are the liquidity that allow the economy to grow and prosper. Too much liquidity and the economy drowns in inflation. Too little, and businesses wither on the vine. The wisdom and strength of the Federal Reserve stands between us and financial calamity!

The agents of the Federal Reserve, the Board of Governors and the Open Market Committee, are the keepers of the sluice gates. They closely monitor what dollars exist in order to keep the economic environment properly irrigated, and carefully allow in only those few additional dollars that can be readily absorbed into an expanding trade. So the Federal Reserve system, through its power to regulate domestic banking, shores us up from the oceans of liquidity lapping our shore, and helps to keep domestic liquidity at "reasonable" levels.

While this analogy for the Fed may be intellectually satisfying to some, it clashes head-on with reality. Those dikes are full of holes. The external oceans of liquidity, responding to changing domestic needs, ebb and flow almost at will across the U.S. economy, and the Federal Reserve Board and Open Market Committee have little power to prevent it. Rather than mighty gatekeepers, they are more like the little Dutch boy trying desperately to plug the holes in the dike. It seems, however, that every time the boy sticks his chubby little finger in one hole, a new leak appears.

These holes exist because the market for dollars, like the markets for other currencies, is global. In global markets the opportunities for getting around domestic regulatory barriers increase greatly. Banks, like other businesses, want to get as much profit as possible from each transaction. Regulations imposed on them by the Federal Reserve reduce the profitability of each transaction. New ways of doing business, not subject to the regulations, must be found. Profit becomes the mother of circumvention.

One such avenue of circumvention is the Eurodollar market. Rumor has it that the Euromarket started as a Russian ploy. The Russians pay for Western goods in major western currencies such as the dollar. The Russians therefore maintain sizable dollar bank deposits. During the height of the cold war, however, they became concerned that such dollar deposits in the United States could be easily expropriated by the U.S. government. (Remember what happened to Iranian assets in 1980?) They therefore transferred their dollar deposits to London, beyond the jurisdiction of U.S. monetary authorities.

Whether or not the story of the Russians' part in starting the Eurodollar market is true, it illustrates the most significant aspect of the Eurodollar market: it is beyond the jurisdiction of the Federal Reserve or any other monetary authority. As such, it permits financial intermediation to occur without the burden of costly rules, regulations, and other taxes. Banks can lend to whom they wish at the best rates they can get. Banks can borrow from whom they want at competitive rates. There are no reserve requirements, no debt-equity requirements, no regulators looking over the banks' shoulders. Hence, from the banks' perspective, Eurobanking is more efficient and profitable. It takes only a small rise in the relative cost of domestic banking to produce a sizable expansion in Eurodollar activity.

What Is a Eurodollar?

Many readers of this book have probably never come in contact with Euromoney. What does it look like? Is it a piece of paper you can stick in your wallet? No. But Eurodollars are bank deposits denominated in dollars, just like the accounts you now hold at your local bank. Holding a Eurodollar account is a lot like a Chicagoan having a bank account in New York. The bookkeeping may not be done in your hometown, but a few dollars of that account buy as many jars of peanut butter as the same number of dollars from a local bank. Don't ask your local branch manager, however, to open a Eurodollar checking account for you. He probably won't be able to do it. Eurodollar deposits are part of the wholesale banking market. That means the accounts are large (at least $100,000) and involve time accounts of varying maturities. So Eurodollar lending and borrowing primarily involves large corporations and institutions, and even the flow of money between the banks themselves.

Unless it is small, however, your local bank is probably engaged in some Eurobanking activity. Eurobanking is one type of financial intermediation of modern banks. The other types are just more familiar. For example, the checking accounts, savings accounts, certificates of deposit (CDs), and so on are part of what can be labeled traditional domestic financial intermediation. In these cases U.S. banks borrow dollars from domestic depositors and lend to others in the country who want to borrow. A similar type of banking activity is conducted by the foreign department of the bank. Again funds are borrowed from one group and lent to another. The distinguishing characteristic of foreign department lending and borrowing, however, is that deposits and loans are often denominated in different currencies. The bank may borrow dollars, for example, but make the corresponding loan in pounds sterling.

A third type of activity is foreign branch banking. A U.S. bank may have a London branch that is booking sterling deposits and making sterling loans. This branch is behaving just like other British financial intermediaries. And just like accounts of British institutions, these sterling accounts are subject to the banking regulations of Britain.

Each of these activities is a legitimate form of financial intermediation, but none is Eurobanking. Each may involve Eurodollars, but none is beyond the regulations and control of all the world's monetary authorities. Eurobanking that takes place in the London branch, for instance, differs from traditional foreign branch banking by involving currencies other than sterling. Otherwise, it would be classified as a type of British domestic banking and fall under the Bank of England's purview. Only if the accounts are denominated in dollars, deutsche marks, Swiss francs, or other foreign currencies will the Eurocurrency transactions be viewed as foreign banking activities by the British officials and not be subject to British banking regulation.

U.S. banks are not the only ones to take advantage of this absence of regulation. Banks of other countries, including Britain, engage in Eurodollar and other Eurocurrency business in London. The British banks avoid regulation, for example, by forming separate units to handle their dollar operations in London. Their sterling activities, however, are still regulated. Eurosterling activities of the British, American, or any other banks therefore must be conducted in another Eurocurrency center such as Paris or Luxembourg in order to avoid regulation.

Because Eurodollar banking is unregulated, it is highly mobile. In a stroke of a pen, or more accurately a push of a telex button, Eurodollars can be transferred swiftly and efficiently from one country to another. The Eurodollar market is therefore going to choose a hospitable country in which to grow and will be very sensitive to any changes in the regulatory climate. Eurodollar activity has flourished in economies with traditional "hands-off" policies with respect to foreign currency deposits, such as Britain, Luxembourg, the Bahamas, the Cayman Islands, and Hong Kong. Countries with histories of close banking regulation, such as the United States or Germany, have not reaped the benefits of becoming Eurobanking centers.

The next time you are in the Cayman Islands, however, do not waste time looking for avenues lined with large marble bank buildings. The Eurodollar market is a wholesale market. It deals with smaller numbers of large deposits. People do not come to Eurobanks to deposit or withdraw $1000, let alone $100. Funds, instead, are transferred, as deposits mature or loans are made, through telex systems. In fact, most of the Eurodollar activity of the Cayman Islands actually is processed in New York. The Cayman Islands address is often only a postal box or small office, the legal minimum needed to justify ascribing accounts to a location where little bank regulation occurs. The deposit of the individual or corporation is physically a certificate of deposit, which simply says it is payable in the Cayman Islands rather than in New York. However, upon maturity, the owner of the certificate probably receives a check drawn on the New York home office.

The Eurodollar market therefore represents a legitimate loophole for avoiding the regulation of the Fed. Banks appear to be taking increasing advantage of this loophole. At the end of 1971, the net size (excluding interbank deposits) of the Eurodollar market was only about $20.9 billion (figure 6–1). By 1975 this figure had more than tripled to $63.8 billion. By the end of 1982, it had surged to at least $290.8 billion.[1] The average annual growth during the period 1975–82 was over 21 percent. At the end of 1982, these Eurodollars amounted to 59 percent of M1, 15 percent of M2, and even 12 percent of M3.[2]

Are Eurodollars Money?

The fact that Eurodollars are beyond the control of the Federal Reserve and have grown so rapidly does not necessarily mean that the Fed will be frustrated in its attempt to influence domestic money markets. For that to occur, Eurodollars must actually be part of the relevant dollar "money supply." Do Eurodollars serve the same purpose as more conventional money?

The issue remains unresolved in the minds of some, but meaningful answers to this question can be generated by relying on the adage "If it looks like a duck, waddles like a duck, and quacks like a duck, there is a good chance it is a duck." The question becomes, do Eurodollar deposits allow depositors to do the same things they could do with domestic deposits?

There are at least two different ways of trying to answer this

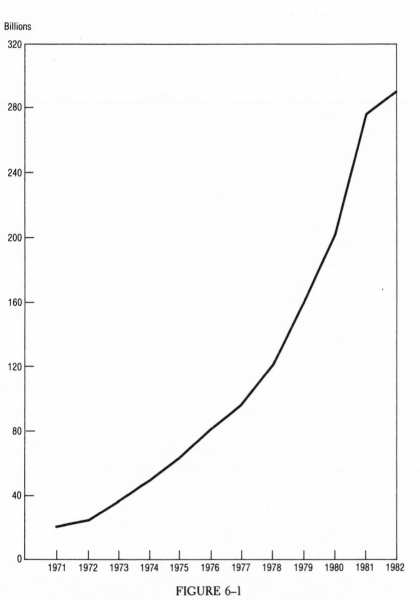

Billions

FIGURE 6–1

Net Eurodollar Deposits, 1971–1982 (Billions of U.S. Dollars)

SOURCES: *Federal Reserve Bulletin* (Washington, D.C.: Federal Reserve Board); *Bank for International Settlements Annual Report* (Basle, Switzerland); *Bank of Canada Annual Report* (Ottawa, Canada).

question. One is to examine the similarities between Eurodollars and better-known monies. Of course, to do this we must first decide what constitutes well-known money, and, as chapter 5 pointed out, economists have difficulty agreeing on this basic question. The economics profession remains unable to resolve whether even time deposits, savings-and-loan deposits, money market funds, and CDs should be included in the traditional definition of money.

Eurodollars are a type of time deposit. They represent a bank borrowing from one group and lending to another group, just as deposits at domestic commercial banks and savings and loan associations do. They are therefore close substitutes for other sorts of money, such as time deposits at commercial banks or savings and loans, or CDs. This fact would seem to argue that all or part of Eurodollars should be included in the broader definitions of money (M2 or M3), which include time deposits.

But on the other hand, about 30 percent of Eurodollar deposits are of very short maturity (less than thirty days), and many of these are overnight deposits. Unlike domestic banks, Eurodollar banks are not prohibited from offering very short-term time deposits. So even if Eurodollar deposits do not appear to satisfy a transactions demand for money (you cannot write a check on a Eurodollar account), there are substantial Eurodollar deposits that clearly resemble demand deposits, except that the short-term Eurodollar deposits pay interest like NOW accounts or money market funds. Hence at least part of the Eurodollar market provides an alternative even to domestic M1.

With rapid developments of alternatives to conventional M1, such as money market funds, NOW accounts, repurchase agreements, and so on, it has become increasingly obvious even to the Federal Reserve that M1 no longer (if it ever did) accurately reflects the conditions in the nation's money markets. As pointed out in the last chapter, in February 1980 the Federal Reserve began reporting a reformulated M1, which includes some of the domestic near monies, a reformulated M2, which includes some overnight Eurodollar deposits at Caribbean branches of U.S. banks, and L, which includes U.S. resident holdings of longer-term Eurodollars at Caribbean branches. Eurodollars, then, are becoming increasingly recognized as an alternative source of monetary liquidity in even conventional measures.

A second way to test the importance of Eurodollars as a source of money is to estimate whether they are empirically relevant as a measure of what the public uses as money. For example, the monetarists would argue that over time the public tends to hold a fairly constant fraction of income in the form of money. A rise in the level of income is associated with a rise in money holdings. A drop in income often corresponds to a decline in the quantity of money held.

If the quantity of money remains roughly proportional to the level of income, then the velocity of money remains roughly constant.[3] The relevant concept of money might therefore be defined as the one that yields the most stable velocity of money. This definition may include Eurodollars.

If it does, then the Eurodollar-inclusive definition should produce a more stable measure of velocity than one which excludes it. As, say, income rises, the combined demand for Eurodollars and more conventional dollars rises. However, since it is the combined demand that rises, it is impossible to say whether the increased demand is reflected primarily in more Eurodollars or more conventional dollars. If we measure money as only the more conventional forms, we may be misled. The observed supply of money may rise more or less than would be proportionate to income, depending on whether it is conventional money or Eurodollars which primarily respond to rising demand. Observed velocity under the conventional definition is less stable.

While the empirical importance of Eurodollars continues to be debated, Bruce Brittain and Henri Bernard have given an important clue. They found that adding Eurodollars and other Eurocurrency deposits held by Americans to more conventional money measures makes U.S. money demand more stable.[4] Whether M1 or the broader M2 is used, including Eurodollars reduces the volatility of measured velocity. The Eurodollar-inclusive definition appears closer to the relevant definition of money.

The Regulation "Wedge": The Incentive to Use the Eurodollar Market

The incentive for using the Eurodollar market comes from regulation. Regulation is equivalent to a tax on the activity it governs. Like a tax, regulation drives a wedge between the gross price charged and the net return received by the labor and capital which generate the activity. In the case of banking, the activity is financial intermediation—that is, lining up those who wish to lend with those who wish to borrow. As figure 6–2 shows, the gross price of financial intermediation is the market interest charged on loans. The net return consists largely of the return to debt capital paid through interest on CDs. The difference between the gross and net prices consists of two cost components. First, the bank must collect fees for performing the service of financial intermediation. This is the return to bank labor and equity capital. Second, taxes or regulation imposed on the banking system must be paid. This is the regulation "wedge."

Whoops! We Forgot About the Euromarket!

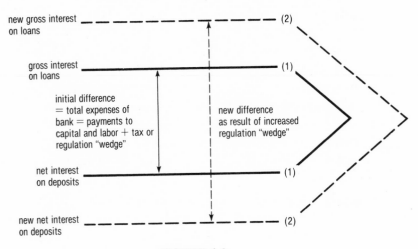

FIGURE 6–2
The Regulation "Wedge"

Figure 6–2 illustrates the immediate impact of increasing the "wedge" (dotted line). On one side of the market, the additional regulations make loans more expensive. On the other side of the market, they lower the return paid to debt capital through CDs. In between they may also lower the return to bank labor and equity capital. Bank loans become a less attractive source of funds to potential borrowers. CDs become a less attractive debt instrument to potential depositors. Domestic banking becomes less attractive to banking institutions. All these effects serve to discourage financial intermediation and to make the dollar a less flexible currency to hold.

This regulation "wedge" or "tax" may take several forms. A prominent form is minimum reserve requirements. Suppose a bank is required to hold a larger fraction of its liabilities as non-interest-bearing reserves. The cost of loans and the value of deposits are affected. For a loan of a given size, more deposits have to be attracted. For example, with a 2 percent reserve requirement against CDs, a $1 million loan would have to be matched with a CD of roughly $1,020,000. If the reserve requirement were raised to 4 percent, the same $1 million loan would require a CD about $20,000 larger. The bank's cost of providing the loan, and the gross interest rate charged, rise.

Similarly, a given deposit creates fewer loans. In the example above, the $1,020,000 CD initially could be matched with a $1 million loan. But when minimum reserve requirements were raised to 4 percent, that same CD could be matched by the bank with a loan of only about $980,000. The deposit is less valuable to the bank, and the compensation the bank is willing to pay the depositor falls.

If the difference between gross and net returns increased by the full amount of the increased cost, while gross and net returns to borrowers and lenders would be affected, the return to the labor and capital providing banking services would not. However, unless the level of loan demand is inelastically set regardless of cost, or the supply of deposits is the same regardless of interest paid, the difference between the two interest rates will not expand by the full added cost. The failure to cover the total added cost means the return to bank labor, equity capital and debt capital fall.

The larger the proportion of reserves required, the larger the tax, the higher the interest rates paid by borrowers, and the lower the interest rate paid out on CDs. Higher loan rates cut back borrowing demand. Lower CD rates curtail the supply of funds for loans. Smaller compensation attracts fewer resources to the banking industry. Less financial intermediation occurs.

Other "regulation taxes" include reporting requirements and restrictions on interest payments. A requirement to fill out detailed forms on liabilities and assets entails hiring additional accountants, clerks, and lawyers. The cost of engaging in financial intermediation rises. Prohibitions or restrictions on interest payments lead banks to compete through indirect and less efficient payments. Branches proliferate beyond optimal numbers. Banks "hide" interest payments in other services such as reduced-fee checking accounts. Certainly few would argue that the department-store atmosphere at thrift institutions offering depositors and their "friends" premiums is the most efficient method of compensating customers. Picnic coolers add little to the efficiency of financial intermediation.

A less direct form of taxation is restrictions on activities in which an institution may engage. They diminish its ability to adjust quickly and efficiently to changing economic conditions. Restrictions on savings and loan associations are a good example. In addition to reserve requirements, these institutions face limits on the interest rates they may pay on some of their liabilities, while their assets are largely restricted to fixed-interest, long-term loans (mortgages).

In a static world banks would just have to "grin and bear" the increased regulation. But financial markets are very dynamic, adapting quickly to changing incentives or disincentives. Whether the increased regulation wedge takes the form of minimum reserve requirements, restrictions on interest payments, or reporting requirements, the larger wedge has an important effect on the institutions regulated. Financial institutions look for ways to adjust to avoid as much of the cost of regulation as possible. Those that succeed are likely to be observed expanding relative to those institutions that cannot easily adjust. The latter find it increasingly difficult to adapt quickly and efficiently to changing economic conditions.

The behavior of the Eurodollar market is a good example of institutions that adapt to avoid regulation. Given the greater cost of borrowing under increased regulatory wedges, as well as the reduced return to lenders and bankers, banking institutions have an automatic incentive to move more of their activities out from under the shadow of the regulators and into the sunshine of the unregulated market. The tremendous growth of the Euromarket in the 1970s is also a legacy of the regulation of that period.

How the Eurodollar Market Is Used to Offset Fed Policy

The existence of this additional source of money called Eurodollars provides an important avenue for offsetting the Federal Reserve's targets concerning the quantity of money. The Eurodollar market can provide a cushion for the private market against the Fed's policy. As, say, the Federal Reserve attempts to tighten monetary policy, Eurodollar activity can expand. Domestic borrowers discover that at prevailing interest rates they cannot find as much financing as they desire, so they turn to the Eurodollar market to borrow more for their projects. With higher loan demand, Eurobanks offer slightly higher interest rates to attract more deposits to finance the loans. Eurodeposits expand.

But as both lenders and borrowers are attracted to the Euromarket, is not the expanding Eurodollar financial intermediation simply offset by a corresponding decline in domestic dollar deposits? Not quite. The secret is the form in which Eurobanks hold reserves. Domestic banks are permitted to hold reserves in only one type of asset—monetary base (currency in the vault or deposits at the Fed). Eurobanks have no such requirement. So when a Eurobank has dollars deposited into its accounts, it transfers any monetary base assets back to the home office in the United States. In return the Eurobank receives a deposit on the home branch to use as its reserves. The Eurobank has its necessary reserves in a useful form. The home offices have the monetary base they need for creating new deposits. Total reserves available in the U.S. banking system are the same as if the Euromarket did not exist, and domestic deposit expansion can proceed normally.

So even if the Fed were able to reduce the quantity of deposits created in the United States, the expanding quantities of Eurodollar deposits help to keep the total quantity of dollar deposits unchanged. Alternatively, suppose the Federal Reserve increases the monetary base in an attempt to increase the dollar money supply. The better terms on which loans and deposits can be made in the United States expand the quantity of domestically created monetary assets, reducing the need for Euromarket activity. Corporations simply reduce the quantity of their Eurodollar borrowings. Eurodollar deposits decline by a corresponding amount. Thus the Eurodollar market acts as a conduit for arbitraging differences in the form reserves are held in the regulated and unregulated markets. In this capacity it serves as a buffer for counteracting and easing the effects of domestic monetary policy.

One offsetting nature of the Eurodollar market is portrayed vividly by figure 6–3. The figure compares the growth rate of Eurodollars and the growth rate of the U.S. monetary base. The two sources of money move in opposite directions. When the growth in the monetary base slows (contractionary policy), the Eurodollar market expands more quickly. And when the monetary base grows rapidly (expansionary policy), the growth of the Eurodollar market slows. It is as if the Fed were attempting to control the quantity of air in a long balloon. As it squeezes the domestic end of the balloon, the Eurodollar end simply expands. As it relieves the constraints on the domestic end, the Eurodollar end contracts.

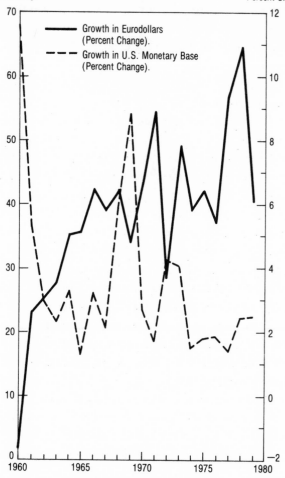

Eurodollars[b]
Percent Change

Monetary Base
Percent Change

Growth in Eurodollars
(Percent Change).

Growth in U.S. Monetary Base
(Percent Change).

FIGURE 6–3

Eurodollars and the U.S. Monetary Base, 1960–1979 [a]

NOTES: Reprinted with permission from Arthur B. Laffer and Marc A. Miles, *International Economics in an Integrated World* (Glenview, Ill.: Scott, Foreman & Co., 1982), 270.
[a] End of year data.
[b] External liabilities of banks in eight reporting European countries, in U.S. dollars.

Whoops! We Forgot About the Euromarket!

So, just as the Fed is powerless to control the total air in the balloon, it is powerless to control the total relevant quantity of dollars in the money market. Eurodollars provide the private sector one more means of circumventing Federal Reserve restrictions. By flexing its powers sufficiently, the Fed may be able to influence the proportion of dollars in the domestic market. Controlling the total relevant quantity of dollars, however, is clearly beyond the Fed's ability.

The Euromarkets are also useful for circumventing other (nonquantity) types of Federal Reserve restrictions. One important restriction that private markets sought to avoid in the 1970s was regulation Q. Regulation Q is a Fed restriction limiting interest that can be paid on time deposits. Regulation Q is the reason all the commercial banks in your neighborhood pay 5-1/4 percent and all the savings and loan associations pay 5-1/2 percent on simple passbook accounts. Prior to May 1973, however, Regulation Q also controlled the maximum interest rate payable on large CDs. No such restriction, of course, existed in the Eurocurrency market. So as interest rates on U.S. deposits reached their maximum, but world rates continued to rise, U.S. bank deposits became relatively less attractive investments. Investors, particularly large ones, had an incentive to place their money in alternative investments.

This inability to compete as interest rates continued to rise presented a potentially dangerous situation for U.S. banks. If, say, an Arab sheik withdrew a $1 million account in order to take advantage of higher interest elsewhere, the bank would suffer a severe loss of income. With a fractional reserve banking system, a $1 million withdrawal in the form of monetary base would require a multimillion dollar contraction in the loan portfolio.

Luckily for the banks, they had the Eurodollar option. While they were prohibited from paying higher rates of interest in New York, they could pay a competitive rate on dollars in their London or Bahamian branch. So the banks simply transferred (for the cost of a telex) more of their large accounts to the foreign branches. In this way the monetary base never had to leave the books of the New York branch. The Euro-branch deposit could simply be created with a simultaneous deposit in New York as its reserves. A realization by the Federal Reserve that the Regulation Q ceiling was simply driving business to the Euromarkets was largely responsible for the removal of interest-rate ceilings on CDs over $100,000 in May 1973.

Another interesting, and more recent, example of how the Euromarkets are used to circumvent Federal Reserve policy is the reaction of banks to President Carter's November 1, 1978 attempt to restrict the growth of dollars. Part of that proposal was a directive by the Federal Reserve doubling the reserve requirements on large CDs from 2 to 4 percent. The change was intended to slow the rate of growth of the U.S. money supply. The major effect of the change, however, was simply to switch part of the CD market from the U.S. to the Eurodollar market. Creating dollar CDs now became relatively more expensive for home offices in the United States and relatively cheaper for Euromarket branches. The change therefore probably had only a minor effect on the total supply of dollars, as Eurodollar CDs replaced domestic CDs, and any monetary base that found its way to the Eurodollar market was transferred back to home offices to serve as reserves against other outstanding deposits.

The relative amount of large denomination CDs issued in the Eurodollar market rose steadily in the months following the November 1978 reserve requirement increase. The dollar liabilities of foreign branches of U.S. banks as a percentage of large U.S. domestic market CDs grew from 12.8 percent in November 1978 to 23.0 percent in August 1979, when Paul

Whoops! We Forgot About the Euromarket! Volcker was named Fed Chairman. The influence of the Fed was clearly being dampened as more banking activity moved beyond the Fed's control.

Why the Federal Reserve Will Never Control the Eurodollar Market

If the Euromarkets permit the private sector to avoid government restrictions, why does the government not simply try to restrict Euromarket activity? The obvious answer is that since Euromarkets are beyond the control of any government, no government can regulate them by itself. All that any one government can do is to restrict the activity of its country's banks in the Euromarkets, worsening the competitive position of those banks but doing little to stop the circumvention of government policies.

Not that governments have not tried. A classic example is the Bundesbank's attempt to control the Euromark activity in 1968. Concerned about the quantity of external deutsche mark accounts held by German banks, the Bundesbank decided to stop that activity by requiring all German banks to keep 100 percent reserves against these accounts. This policy was partially successful in the sense that all Euromark activity dried up in Frankfurt. However, the Euromark market had simply picked up and moved to Luxembourg, where no such regulations existed. Today Luxembourg is the center of Euromark banking.

The United States has also tried to regulate Eurodollar activity. In October 1969 the Federal Reserve instituted Regulation M, which assessed reserve requirements on deposits of the

Eurobranches held at the home office (liabilities to foreign branches). When Eurobranches lent funds to the home office, these deposits were now taxed. Initially the reserve requirements were set at 10 percent, and in January 1971 they were raised to 20 percent. The idea behind these restrictions was to reduce the attractiveness, and therefore the incentive, for U.S. banks to transfer part of their activities to the Euromarket. There was now an additional cost to banking diverted through the Euromarket in the form of the noninterest-bearing reserves the home office had to hold.

Regulation M probably did retard the Euromarket activity of domestic banks. But the primary effect of the restrictions on U.S. banks was to affect the competition between U.S. and foreign banks. The Federal Reserve did not have the jurisdiction to impose these restrictions on foreign-based banks. The foreign banks were therefore not subject to such a reserve requirement on their Eurodollar activities. Hence Regulation M made Eurodollar activity relatively more expensive for U.S. banks. The foreign banks then used the change in competitive advantage to gain a foothold in the domestic U.S. market. The realization of the negative effect on the business of U.S. banks probably played a large part in the decision to lower Regulation M reserve requirements. Marginal reserves were lowered to 8 percent in June 1973, later to 4 percent, and then to zero in August 1978.

Regulation M was thus zero in November 1978, when U.S. banks used the Euromarkets to circumvent President Carter's desire for slower dollar growth. Perhaps with the frustration of November 1978 in mind, a restriction similar to Regulation M reappeared in October 1979. The new restriction added an 8 percent reserve requirement against any additional deposits to foreign branches above a prescribed level. As in November 1978, the Fed was again trying to reduce the dollar money supply by raising reserve requirements against domestic CDs. An additional reserve requirement of 8 percent was being applied against CDs of domestic banks above a certain base level. This time, however, the Fed was trying to plug the Euromarket loophole by simultaneously raising marginal reserve requirements on net liabilities of parent banks to foreign branches. This additional tax was the Fed's attempt to "head the banks off at the pass." But as before, the banks found ways to circumvent these restrictions on managed liabilities.

To the extent that the deposits of U.S. banks exceeded the base levels, the Federal Reserve's new restrictions did impose new taxes on U.S. banks and made U.S. banks less competitive in world money markets. Deposits of U.S. banks would contract. But in the highly mobile world money market, the actions of the Fed did not necessarily reduce total dollar deposits significantly. Within the month, descriptions of how banks were now circumventing Fed policy began to surface.[5]

When reserve requirements on CDs were raised in November 1978, U.S. banks had responded by raising funds through the Eurobranches instead of the domestic market. The money raised in the Eurodollar market could then be lent to the parent bank and in turn lent to the U.S. private market. The rise in reserve requirements on domestic CDs in October created similar incentives. However, the simultaneously imposed reserve requirements on liabilities to foreign branches reduced the profitability of this avenue of circumvention. It was time for a new avenue to be found.

The new loophole appeared because not only do banks have a choice of whether to raise funds through the parent bank or Eurobranches, but they can choose as well which branch will make the loans. There is no requirement that money raised in the Euromarket be lent again to the U.S. private market through the parent bank. The loan to the U.S. private market could just as easily be booked through the Eurobranch. U.S. banks now found the reserve requirements on liabilities to foreign branches taxing the first lending route, but not the second. Hence as the marginal reserve requirements on net liabilities to foreign branches rose, banks simply conducted more of their lending, as well as borrowing, outside the United States. A greater proportion of funds borrowed through Eurodollar deposits were lent directly to U.S. companies (or their foreign subsidiaries) by the foreign branch. Since no U.S. deposit was necessary, the Fed's new restrictions were ineffective at stemming the growth of dollar deposits and loans.

This reaction of the U.S. banks to the imposition of the new regulation wedge can be documented. Figure 6–4 illustrates the fluctuations in the percentage of total foreign branch lending offered directly to the U.S. private market versus the percentage offered through the parent bank. For example, true to form, the proportion of direct lending began falling in August 1978, when a previous 4 percent reserve requirement on liabilities to foreign branches (Regulation M) was eliminated. With the imposition of marginal reserve requirements in October 1979, this proportion began to rise again.

The following March the Federal Reserve raised the marginal reserve requirement and widened the range of liabilities to foreign branches to which the marginal reserve requirement applied. Once again, foreign branches responded in predictable fashion as the proportion of direct lending rose sharply. Following the elimination of the marginal reserve requirements in July 1980, the proportion of direct lending again decreased.

Frustrated, but refusing to admit defeat, the Federal Reserve did not stop there in its cat-and-mouse game with the foreign branches. Today, not only do CDs and liabilities to foreign branches have reserve requirements but the same requirements also apply to the direct *loans* of foreign branches

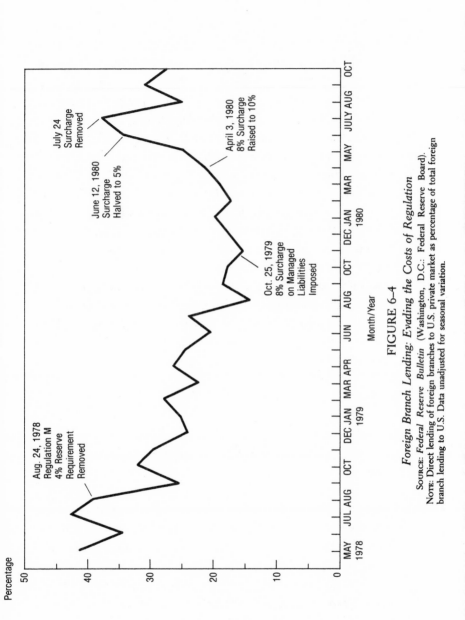

FIGURE 6-4

Foreign Branch Lending: Evading the Costs of Regulation

SOURCE: *Federal Reserve Bulletin* (Washington, D.C.: Federal Reserve Board).
NOTE: Direct lending of foreign branches to U.S. private market as percentage of total foreign branch lending to U.S. Data unadjusted for seasonal variation.

to U.S. residents. If Chase-Manhattan's Cayman branch lends dollars to GM in Detroit, Chase-Manhattan in New York has to hold noninterest-earning reserves against the loan. To the extent that the new restriction is effective, it only hurts the competitive position of foreign branches of U.S. banks relative to foreign branches of foreign banks. Quite likely, however, there are sufficient ways to circumvent the new restrictions to make them ineffective as well. For example, the Cayman branch could lend to a foreign subsidiary of GM, which in turn could lend to the Detroit office. Or GM could borrow from the Cayman branch without receiving a direct loan, say by floating debt on the Euro–commercial paper market.

The U.S. monetary authorities are thus incapable of unilaterally eliminating or even controlling the Eurodollar market through restrictions. The Eurodollar market operates outside the jurisdiction of the U.S. monetary authorities. All the Fed can do by flexing its powers is reduce or eliminate the U.S. banks' share of the Eurodollar market, not eliminate the market.

The Continuing Urge to Control

From time to time, as awareness of the effect of the Eurodollar market on monetary policy is particularly heightened, some member of Congress or foreign official will call for international cooperation in controlling Euromarkets. A frequently cited plan for such control is to have all governments subject the foreign branches of their domestic banks to the same (or even worse) regulations as the domestic offices. If all governments simultaneously undertook such a policy, the influence of the Euromarkets might be tempered. But such international cooperation is highly unlikely. All governments simply do not have the same incentives. Some governments look covetously on the Euromarkets in their own or other countries, and on the jobs and income they generate. Those governments are unlikely to take restrictive steps that would destroy these markets.

Some monetary officials eager for Euromarket controls respond by arguing that the cooperation of all countries is not even needed. All that is required is for the governments of *major* banking countries to impose Eurodollar restrictions. "Don't worry about Pakistani banks," they would argue. "Those banks have such a small share of the Euromarket business as to be inconsequential." But in such a highly mobile money market, if all other countries imposed severe Eurodollar restrictions and Pakistan did not, today's inconsequential banks would become tomorrow's Euromarket center.

Of course, the United States could try to reduce the attractiveness of the Euromarkets with a carrot instead of a stick. The Fed, for example, could reduce the added cost of financial intermediation in the domestic market. One way would be to eliminate or drastically reduce domestic reserve requirements, thereby reducing the domestic wedge. This step, however, would amount to the Fed yielding much of its pretense that it controls the supply of money. A second way to cut the wedge is to pay interest on the required reserves of domestic banks. Such an action, however, would mean that the money the Fed now turns over to the U.S. Treasury (interest from government bonds in excess of expenses) would go to banks instead. A Congress concerned with eventually balancing the federal budget is not likely to go along with such a plan, and it is excluded at present under the Monetary Control Act. So the Fed concentrates on using the stick in its attempt to harness the Eurodollar market.

If You Can't Beat Them, Join Them: The Fed Goes Half-Way

Perhaps learning from experience, or bowing to reality, the Federal Reserve has recently been moving away from further controls on Eurobanking. In fact, in 1981 the Federal Reserve authorized the formation of International Banking Facilities (IBFs), in which, for the first time, trading in nondollar accounts could take place in the United States. The move had all the signs of an "if you can't beat them, join them" push. The Federal Reserve, and other federal and state government agencies, began to promote the potential additional jobs created or tax revenues collected from these facilities.

In the typical compromise style of government agencies, however, the Federal Reserve failed to lift all the restrictions necessary to make the IBFs truly competitive in world markets. For example, still failing to grasp completely the full integration of world money markets, the Fed has clung to the concept that it can keep the IBFs from interfering with domestic monetary policy. So within these IBFs, banks are forbidden to borrow from or lend to U.S. residents. Furthermore, the Fed has ruled that IBF deposits are still subject to FDIC insurance premiums, raising the relative cost of Eurobanking in the United States. In highly mobile money markets, which respond quickly and efficiently to small changes in relative costs, such continued restrictions will only keep the U.S. Euromarket from developing to its full potential.

The permission to form the IBFs, however, is indicative that even the Fed must recognize its limitations. Despite what the Fed or the monetarists want to believe, in today's global money market no country can effectively control the relevant quantity of money.

7

Reexamining Monetarism III—Dollars Are Not the Only Game in Town

SO FAR the discussion has centered exclusively on dollars. Monetarism, like any other theory, relies on a few crucial assumptions. One of these is that dollars are the only game in town. The only kind of money Americans even think about using is dollars.

To recognize a legitimate role for foreign monies in America would strike at the heart of the Monetarist Dream. Only by limiting the discussion to domestic money can the monetarist argument remain plausible. Only with Americans holding just dollars in their wallets and bank accounts could the Federal Reserve possibly exercise control over the quantity of money Americans possess. So the monetarists try to keep the discussion in terms of M1 or M2. Having successfully limited the scope of the discussion, they are then in a position to confine any further discussion to questions like "Can the Fed control

M1?" or "Are the supply of dollars and dollar income closely related?" These are the only debates that they have at least some chance of winning.

Perhaps because the dollar has been one of the most stable currencies in the twentieth century, many Americans find it quite reasonable to restrict monetary policy discussions to the number of dollars. Until the last few years, there simply has not been the incentive for Americans to consider diversifying into other monies. Through much of the twentieth century the dollar has been tied to gold and other currencies. The link to gold stabilized the purchasing power of the dollar relative to commodities. The link to other currencies stabilized the value of the dollar in terms of other monies. Holding a dollar was like holding a corresponding amount of francs, deutsche marks, or pounds sterling. There was little, if anything, to be gained financially from holding one versus the other. Since dollars were more convenient for making deals within the United States and were also a convenient medium for international transactions, U.S. residents dealt almost exclusively in dollars.

The experience of residents in other countries, particularly those with unstable currencies, however, has been quite different. Certainly the residents of Germany in the 1920s, when prices were rising as much as 7 percent per day, came to realize the benefits of holding and dealing in foreign money rather than the unstable mark. People in other European or South American countries with a history of hyperinflation are also familiar with this phenomenon. Even today without hyperinflation, Europeans who travel or trade frequently among their neighboring countries find it useful to keep money balances in several currencies. In addition to their demand for European currencies, they may also have found the dollar and yen useful in their international transactions. Stories abound about how Italians, who have faced severe monetary instability in the last decade, trek through the Alps with suitcases full of money in order to avoid border guards. Currency controls try to force Italians to keep their money in lira, but Italians want to convert their money into something more stable like Swiss francs. Israelis are another good example. An Israeli today thinks of prices as much in terms of the relatively more stable dollar as in shekels.

So the fact that money diversification is not part of our American tradition does not mean it is not relevant to today's American economy. The recent monetary experience of exceptionally high and volatile inflation and interest rates is also foreign to the American tradition. One has to go back to the period prior to the 1850s to find annual commercial paper yields averaging over 15 percent. But changing times bring changing traditions. Economists are increasingly uncovering evidence that incentives for such diversification now exist and that such diversification occurs.

The potential for this change has been there a long time. We have already discussed how the United States is only one of many places in the world where dollars are bought or sold, borrowed or lent. The dollar money market is global. But that is not all. In that global market dollars are only one of several monies that people and institutions use for trading or making investments. Americans, then, are not confined to the dollar market. They have a choice. There are abundant opportunities for dealing in other monies. They could, for example, conduct their international business in Swiss francs or deutsche marks, money assets over which the Federal Reserve has little, if any, direct influence. Their options are limited (as Adam Smith might put it) only by the diversity of the market.

To assume that Americans just ignore these alternative opportunities, especially if they are more profitable, does not make much sense. Such an assumption certainly runs counter to the conventional wisdom about how Americans handle other assets in their portfolios, such as stocks and bonds. When it comes to money, investors want to maximize returns and minimize risk, just as they do with stocks and bonds.

The domestic portfolio diversification process becomes more complex. It is no longer just a question of how many dollars Americans want. They may also want varying amounts of Swiss francs, deutsche marks, and pounds sterling. The international portfolio choice also becomes important. Whether foreigners are increasing or decreasing the quantity of dollars they hold becomes crucial for anticipating dollar prices. The basic analysis of money demand, prices, interest rates, and exchange rates has to be seriously reexamined. It must be expanded, reshaped, and made consistent with global money diversification.

What Does the Presence of Foreign Money Mean for Monetary Policy?

Assume that dollars are not the only game in town. Americans have the option of holding and using foreign money. Foreigners have the option of holding and using dollars as well as their national monies. Dollars flow back and forth among countries as money portfolios adjust to shifting relative expected values and risks of monies, or as economic activity picks up or falls in individual countries. The accompanying injections or spillovers of dollars must be affecting current U.S. monetary policy. The influx or outflow of foreign money must be throwing a monkey wrench in the monetarist plans. How extensive is the damage?

These private market flows of money strike at the very heart of the Monetarist Dream. Part of that dream was the hope of floating exchange rates. As long as the Fed did not intervene in foreign exchange markets to influence the dollar's value, monetary policy in the United States could be isolated from monetary policy elsewhere. This hope was the basis for the Reagan Administration's decision, shortly after taking office, not to permit the Fed to intervene in exchange markets on behalf of the dollar. The Reagan team, led by Under Secretary of the Treasury Beryl Sprinkel, was firm in its resolve. Neither the assassination of Sadat, the leftist victory in France, nor the Israeli invasion of Lebanon brought the Fed into the foreign exchange market. Only the intense pleas of U.S. allies at the Versailles Summit in June 1982 brought even a reconsideration of this position. The Reagan administration was intent on providing an environment in which the Fed could flex its muscles.

The presence of the potential private market flows of money that we have just described, however, shows why this Monetarist Dream is but an illusion. Little could be accomplished in the way of monetary control by shifting from fixed to flexible rates. The monetarists already knew that fixed exchange rates were inconsistent with their dream. Under fixed rates the balance of payments provided an easy escape route for excess money, or a convenient avenue for extra money if the Fed did not supply enough. The reason that the pumped-in money escapes in this case is the promise by central banks to fix exchange rates. Say that the Fed increases the number of dollars, and some of these escape to France. Monetarists believe French men and women have use only for francs, not for dollars. But they also know that under fixed rates the Bank of France stands ready to convert dollars into francs (or vice versa) at the promised rate. Hence, those dollars the French get are turned by the Bank of France into the francs the French want.

With floating rates, however, the central banks are not supposed to be so accommodating. As long as monetary authorities refrain from intervening in foreign exchange markets, the net flows between countries are supposed to stop. The balance of payments is supposed to be zero. If dollars leak to France, the French do not have a friendly central bank ready to transform foreign money into francs. What are the French to do? They have dollars but are assumed to want only francs. Obviously they are forced to trade for francs in private exchange markets. They have to buy francs from the only people who hold dollars, Americans. In this way, the dollars eventually find their way back to the United States through foreign exchange markets. As long as central banks refrain from intervening, the impact of their monetary policies is confined ultimately to their domestic countries.

So the U.S. Treasury ordered the operators at the foreign exchange desk of the New York Fed to sit on their hands, hoping that the influence of the domestic open market operations desk would be enhanced. The added influence, however, was but wishful thinking. It was true that since the U.S. Federal Reserve was no longer intervening, they were no longer transforming dollars into other currencies for foreigners. And it was true that if dollars leaked to France, the French might not find a central bank to give them francs in exchange. But that does not mean that those dollars were now automatically finding their way back to the United States.

Remember that the French can hold diversified money portfolios. They may be holding francs, dollars, and other currencies. So when the dollars leak to France, some of them may just stay there in private portfolios. Net flows of dollars to France and other countries are generated, not through central bank intervention, but through private market transactions. Simply slamming shut the central bank's foreign exchange window does not stop these flows. Even without the help of any central bank, newly introduced dollars can become dispersed through-

out world markets. The dollar has become truly international-
ized. The Fed's influence has been further blunted.

The extent of the new problem for the Fed does not stop
there. Even if by some quirk the Fed could control the quantity
of dollars within the United States, such domestic control of
dollars is no longer sufficient to produce the monetarists'
desired independent monetary policy. With the private sector
holding diversified money portfolios, domestic dollars are only
part of the relevant "money supply." The remaining portion,
foreign currency–denominated money, flows in and out un-
checked by the domestic monetary authorities. Flows of the
foreign money prevent the monetary authorities from "tuning"
the relevant money supply or the economy.

An Analogy Revisited

An analogy first used in chapter 2 helps to illustrate this point.
The twelve Federal Reserve districts in the United States are
very much like twelve separate regions with twelve separate
monies. Each Federal Reserve District has a central bank capable of issuing paper money with its own special seal. Furthermore, the Federal Reserve Banks historically have had a degree
of control over the commercial banks in their districts, setting
both reserve requirements and the terms on which banks can
borrow money reserves. The private sectors in these twelve
regions, however, view the different monies as substitutes for
each other.[1] They therefore are likely to hold money portfolios
that are diversified across monies of the different regions.
Someone in Kalamazoo may hold money from the Cleveland,
Chicago, and New York regions. This diversification makes

targeting monetary aggregates within any one region an ineffective policy.

Consider, for example, the plight of the bright young economist at the Federal Reserve Bank of Atlanta, who is ordered by his superiors to estimate the relevant monetary parameters within their district in anticipation of running a separate, regional monetary policy. It seems the Atlanta Fed, imbued with a new sense of the monetarist spirit, has decided to try to run a monetary policy more consistent with regional rather than national goals. So the young economist has been ordered to estimate money demand, money velocity, and inflation involving only dollars directly under the control of the Atlanta Fed.

The young economist soon discovers how impossible his task is. For instance, in considering the demand for money, he quickly realizes that there are three potential money demands. First, there is the demand for "Atlanta Fed" dollars. But dollar bills bearing the Atlanta Fed seal are likely to circulate throughout the United States. In addition, deposits at southeastern banks may be held by anyone in any part of the country. They could easily belong to Georgians who now reside in Washington, or New Yorkers who spend their winters in Florida. Clearly, the demand for these dollars spans more than just the Atlanta district.

Second, there is the demand for dollars in the Atlanta region. This demand can be met by "Atlanta Fed" dollars. It can also be met by dollars originating in any of the other eleven districts.

Third, there is the demand for "Atlanta Fed" dollars in the Atlanta district. This third definition is the money demand in which his superiors would traditionally be interested. But this definition is only a narrow subset of the other two. Hence it would be expected to have the least stable relationship to other economic variables.

Dollars Are Not the Only Game in Town

For example, as income rises in the Atlanta district, the demand for money should also rise. But because dollars from other Fed districts serve the same purposes as "Atlanta Fed" dollars, there is no way to guess which regional dollars will be used to satisfy the increased demand. The regional demand for all the various dollars as a group is more closely related to regional income than is the specific demand for "Atlanta Fed" dollars.

The fact that people in the southeastern part of the United States hold dollars from throughout the country also makes the velocity of "Atlanta Fed" dollars very volatile. Velocity, as we have seen, is the ratio of income to money held ($V = Py/M$). It is roughly equal to the number of times money has to change hands in the economy in order to "finance" the current level of market activity. If people in the Southeast used only "Atlanta Fed" dollars, the quantity of those dollars held would be a stable proportion of the level of economic activity. Velocity would be stable, rising only as, say, higher interest rates led people to economize on money in general.

But with people holding all kinds of dollars, when income rises the amount of "Atlanta Fed" dollars held can rise proportionately, rise more than proportionately, or even fall. Velocity can move in any direction. Any measured velocity of "Atlanta Fed" dollars in the southeastern United States is likely to appear unstable.

This analogy sheds light on current monetary policy. The Fed is resolved to limit the growth in monetary aggregates. But which monetary aggregates? For the policy to be effective, even monetarist theory agrees that the relevant monetary aggregate must be controlled relative to its demand. Which aggregate is relevant? Again there are three possibilities. The first is the total quantity of dollars. But dollars are held by more than just Americans. Individuals and firms in Canada, South America,

Europe, Asia, and elsewhere hold dollars, too. The Fed is hardly in a position to alter the quantity of dollars these people in other countries hold. Dollar deposits are accepted from and dollar loans made to people throughout the world by the Euro-dollar market. The Fed's inability to regulate or deter this source of dollar financial intermediation has already been de-scribed. But the total world supply of dollars may well be the relevant monetary aggregate from a monetarist perspective. Controlling that aggregate may well be the key, from their perspective, to controlling dollar inflation. If it is, the Fed is in trouble.

The most the Fed can hope to do is control the quantity of money held by Americans. But still, which money is that? Just as the bright young economist at the Atlanta Fed found more than just "Atlanta Fed" dollars lying about in wallets and bank accounts, his counterpart at the Federal Reserve Board in Washington is likely to find that Americans use more than just dollars. Americans along the borders likely hold currency of or deposits in Mexico or Canada. People engaged in international trade and frequent international travelers retain money of the country in which they do business. Multinational corporations maintain balances in several monies. Corporations may decide to borrow or invest through the Eurocurrency market, perhaps in currencies other than the dollar. Those wishing to protect themselves against an expected decline in the dollar's purchas-ing power may switch their assets to more stable currencies such as the Swiss franc.

So if the Fed is to control the quantity of money in the United States, it somehow has to control the quantity of for-eign money as well as of dollars held. Few would argue that the Fed is up to this task. Clearly, in our current atmosphere of free capital mobility, foreign money can flow in or out at will. The only possible hope of restricting these flows would be a drastic step such as capital controls. Even capital controls, however, are not likely to succeed in accomplishing this goal in a world of highly integrated money markets.[2] Furthermore, introducing such distortions into the economy greatly reduces economic efficiency. Even if the controls could be successful, the Fed would be achieving a modest gain in something that is of concern only to it (monetary control) at great expense to the overall economy. It hardly seems worth the effort.

You may have noticed, therefore, that the Fed does not talk about controlling either of those at least potentially relevant money supplies. Instead, all the discussion is restricted to targeting only the quantity of dollars held by Americans. Notice, however, that this quantity is the least relevant of the three potential money supplies. It is only a subset of the other two. The dollars Americans hold are only a fraction of the total world supply of dollars and are only part of the total money Americans hold.

Some Empirical Implications of Diversification

What does it mean that money portfolios are diversified? Does it mean each of us must be holding foreign bank accounts? Does it mean that the average shopper on Main Street in Des Moines walks around with deutsche marks and guilders in her purse? The answer to both questions is no. It does not mean that every person in the economy becomes enamored with foreign money.

Diversification is not an argument about the *average* amount of foreign money held. It is an argument about the *margin.* One rule of economics is that "decisions are made on the margin." It is always those last few or "marginal" units that determine market prices. Alternatively, when the cost of the last few units changes, people change how many units they use.

So money diversification is just an extension of the basic idea that people respond to incentives. In contrast, monetarism denies this fundamental rule. Individuals and firms in a particular country are assumed to demand only the money of that country, regardless of the cost or risk. In other words, regardless of how reckless U.S. monetary policy becomes, it is assumed that Americans will cling unflinchingly to dollars.

With rational money management, however, when the incentives for holding foreign versus domestic money change, people should respond. The quantity of foreign money used should rise as the incentives to hold it increase. This is precisely how the owners of bonds and equities are already assumed to diversify their portfolios, in order to reduce overall risk. One obvious source of risk is uncertainty of exchange rate depreciation, which can potentially inflict capital losses on assets denominated in a given currency. Faced with exchange rate uncertainty, bond and equity owners diversify the currency denominations of their assets, thereby reducing the risk of capital loss. The money diversification argument simply extends this common sense behavior to the decisions about how to hold money.

Perhaps only a few people actually hold foreign money today. That fact would not make money diversification irrelevant as long as money holders continue to respond to incentives. For diversification to have significance, it is enough that, as the expected outlook for the dollar becomes increasingly dismal relative to that for other monies, more individuals or firms begin dealing (or expand their dealings) in foreign money.

Dollars Are Not the Only Game in Town

Some Evidence of Money Diversification

Over the last decade, we have certainly witnessed a change in marginal incentives for holding dollars versus other monies. For example, two economists, Haim Levy and Marshall Sarnat, have calculated how the average rates of return and risks of foreign currencies differed during the Bretton Woods fixed-rate period and the more recent period of floating rates.[3] They conclude that during the fixed-rate period, the changes in the exchange rate were not sufficiently large to create an incentive for money portfolio diversification. But with the breakdown of the Bretton Woods system, the average rates of return and fluctuations in these returns rose dramatically, providing a strong incentive for money diversification.

In other words, the transition from a fixed-rate system to a floating one changed the rules of the game. With fixed rates, central banks promised to make one currency the same as another. In economic language they made all currencies "perfect substitutes" on the supply or central bank side of the market. If you had dollars, the Bundesbank would always provide deutsche marks at the promised conversion rate. If you had deutsche marks, you could always trade them in for francs at the promised rate. So by holding a dollar or a deutsche mark, you simultaneously held an equivalent amount of all other convertible currencies.

Since the various monies were linked in value by the central banks' promises to exchange one for another, there was little, if any, difference between the expected returns or risks of return from holding individual currencies. But when the central banks stopped guaranteeing the values of their monies during the floating-rate period, the costs and risks of holding specific monies diverged. The private market now had the incentive to deal with the new uncertainties by diversifying or substituting among monies.

It is one thing to recognize the possibility of the international diversification among monies; it is quite another to demonstrate that diversification actually occurs. Does the private sector actually respond to these incentives?

One way to find out is to examine the relative amounts of domestic and foreign money held within a country, and measure how these relative amounts change as incentives change. Three incentives are usually thought to affect how portfolios are diversified: relative expected returns or costs from holding different assets, the relative risks of the assets, and the degree to which the returns among currencies are correlated. The higher the expected return or the lower the expected cost from holding one denomination of money (holding other factors the same), the more of that money demanded. The lower the relative risk of a money, the more of it will be held. The amount of a money held is also expected to increase the more the behavior of its return or cost differs from that of other currencies. For example, under fixed rates, when the costs of currencies moved essentially together, there was little incentive to hold foreign money. When the cost of domestic money increased, the cost of foreign money moved in lock step. There was no way to spread the risk over several currencies.

Research on the United States, Canada, and Germany has demonstrated that not only did the advent of floating rates create an incentive for money diversification, but the private sector responded to these incentives.[4] Not only the absolute amounts, but also the relative amounts, of foreign money held responded differently in these three countries once the exchange rate had become unhinged as compared with when the exchange rate was rigid.[5] The research involved measuring, for each of these three countries, the degree to which relative holdings of foreign and domestic money responded to changing expected relative costs. Monetary theory asserts that the opportunity cost of holding money is the interest rate associated with it. Interest rates show how much lenders demand to be compensated for expected depreciation of their money during the period it is lent out. So dollar interest rates reflect lenders' feelings about dollars, and deutsche mark interest rates feelings about deutsche marks. Changing relative interest rates reflect changing relative expected costs of monies.

The traditional argument is that the relative amount of foreign money demanded will always be unresponsive to changes in expected costs. People and firms demand only domestic money regardless of its relative cost. In contrast, the portfolio diversification argument states that small changes in relative cost produce little or no change in relative amounts, but large cost changes produce significant diversification. So in fixed-rate periods, when relative costs are fairly constant, no incentive for diversification exists. Relative money holdings will be unresponsive to the fluctuations in relative interest rates. But when exchange rates become unhinged, relative costs begin to fluctuate. An incentive to diversify arises. A significant degree of responsiveness of relative money holdings should appear.

Interestingly, in all three countries during fixed-rate periods the measured degree of responsiveness of relative money holdings to changing relative expected costs was statistically insignificant. But during floating-rate periods, just the opposite behavior occurred. The relative holdings of foreign money became very responsive to expected costs in all three countries. The consistency of the evidence represents a rejection of the traditional argument.

Evidence of the money substitution phenomenon in response to changes in relative risk exists as well. For instance, one might expect the currency chosen for a Eurocurrency market loan or deposit, or for an international trade transaction, to depend on the risk of contracting in the different currencies. Suppose a hypothetical German company and its customers in South America initially decide to value their transactions in dollars. The dollar in its role as an international reserve currency is readily accepted in most countries, and it is the most convenient form in which the German company can denominate these international transactions. However, if the risk or uncertainty of holding dollars increases, the company and its customers may decide to switch their transactions to more stable currencies. Even if the expected depreciation or appreciation of the dollar does not change, an increase in uncertainty makes the dollar less attractive. Greater uncertainty or variance of return increases chances that either seller or purchaser will experience a capital loss.

Similarly, when dollar risk increases, both borrowers and lenders in the Eurocurrency markets now find contracting in dollars more risky. Hence, both groups should now be expected to desire more of their agreements to be denominated in other, relatively more stable currencies. In other words, the risk of a currency becomes an important issue affecting *both* the asset and liability sides of the ledger sheet.

Bluford Putnam and D. Sykes Wilford have presented evidence of precisely this type of effect on the currency denomination of Eurocurrency assets and liabilities.[6] They found that increased risk (standard deviation) in the dollar-mark exchange rate is positively and significantly correlated to the proportion of nondollar Eurobanking. As dollar risk rises, so does the percentage of nondollar-assets and liabilities in Euromarket banks' portfolios. In fact, the exchange risk explained about 42 percent of the variation of this ratio on the banks' asset side, and about 29 percent of the variation on the liability side.

A similar measure of risk was found to be important in determining the relative holdings of foreign money in U.S. portfolios. In research with Marion Stewart, I found that the ratio of dollars to foreign money held in the United States depends on the relative risk of the dollar in addition to the relative expected cost.[7] American money portfolios do respond to incentives.

As portfolios have responded, foreign money has made its way into the U.S. economy. The quantity of measurable[8] foreign money held by U.S. residents has grown tremendously in the last two decades, from about $0.3 billion in 1961 to over $3.5 billion in 1981. This measured money, however, is only the tip of the foreign-money iceberg.

The inflow of foreign money in turn may in part explain the instability of U.S. money velocity in the 1970s. An interesting insight to this point has been provided by Bruce Brittain.[9] Brittain found that not only was money velocity in the United States unexpectedly bouncing around, but so was velocity in European countries such as Germany, Switzerland, the United Kingdom, and Italy. Furthermore, the movements in velocity were not random. The deviations from what one would have expected appear systematically related across countries. A high velocity in the United States tends to be statistically associated with high velocity in the United Kingdom and Italy but with low velocity in Germany and Switzerland. Brittain showed that if these interdependencies are included in the attempt to explain the behavior of U.S. velocity, many of the apparent surprises disappear. With the additional information, one now expects velocity to be high in periods in which it is actually unusually high, and low in periods in which it is, in fact, unusually low.

What had Brittain shown? Again, that money portfolios are diversifiable. The positive relationship between velocity in the United States and the United Kingdom or Italy means that when people are moving out of dollars, they also tend to be diversifying out of pounds sterling and lira. The negative relationship with the deutsche mark and Swiss franc means that money holders are shifting into these two monies when they are moving out of the others.

Some Evidence from Mexico

Another interesting example of how money portfolios respond to changing incentives comes from the devaluation of the Mexican peso in August 1976. The Mexican peso has traditionally been closely tied to the dollar. From 1954 until 1976, the dollar value of the peso was maintained at a constant value by the Mexican central bank. Mexicans (and many Americans in the Southwest) came to view the dollar and peso as interchangeable. In the past, the use of dollars in Mexico stemmed from the proximity of Mexico to the United States. Mexicans, for example, often cross the border at towns like Laredo, Texas, to purchase appliances, clothing, and other items. Similarly, Americans often cross and buy items in Mexican border towns. Prices in such places were often denominated simultaneously in both currencies prior to the devaluation.

Dollar usage also came from the substantial tourist trade between the countries. Those who have traveled to Mexico City or Acapulco are probably familiar with prices denominated in both dollars and pesos. Furthermore, the Mexican banking system, unlike that in the United States, had been free to accept deposits in foreign currencies such as the dollar. The availability of dollar accounts made dealing in dollars in Mexico less difficult. Given prices simultaneously denominated in both currencies and the access to both dollar and peso bank accounts, merchants from Laredo to Acapulco held some desirable ratio of both monies in order to be prepared to complete a transaction in either one.

Prior to the devaluation of the peso, with the dollar having been freely convertible into pesos at a stable price, the incentives for Mexicans to hold substantial quantities of dollars were not great—mainly the saving of bank fees for converting dollars to pesos and back again. However, as the likelihood grew that the Mexican government might be forced to devalue the peso, the incentives to hold a larger share of money in dollars grew. The future of the peso became more uncertain. The expected gain from holding dollars increased.

The incentives to hold dollars grew even more following the devaluation. The Mexican government showed that, after twenty-two years of stable money, it no longer was committed to policies required to keep the dollar value of the peso stable. The value of the peso in foreign exchange markets plunged below even the new devalued level the government had initially set. Where the peso might eventually come to rest became the subject of intense speculation.

In this atmosphere of uncertainty, patterns of transactions changed. In the U.S. border towns, merchants now denominated their wares in the more stable dollar. Mexico, too, experienced increased "dollarization" of its economy. The tourist industry, for example, moved from a dual price system to prices denominated almost exclusively in dollars.

As Mexican merchants moved to dollar prices in order to protect the value of what they sold, the proportion of their money held in dollars rose. Mexicans with wealth also wanted to protect their assets, and stories of Mexicans crowding airplanes to Texas with suitcases of money became very common. Their proportion of dollars held rose too. The monetary uncertainty brought about by the devaluation changed the way Mexicans held money.

Evidence in this shift towards holding dollars is provided by Leroy O. Laney.[10] Laney looked at the quantity of dollars held by Mexicans in U.S. and Mexican banks, versus the quantity of pesos held. The data are measured at the end of quarters. He finds that the proportion of dollars held rose dramatically around the 1976 devaluation. In the beginning of 1976, Mexicans on average held less than one U.S. cent for every peso held. By mid-1977, after the devaluation and related uncertainty, Mexicans were holding almost 1.3 U.S. cents per peso. The average ratio of dollars to pesos rose by over 40 percent. By the end of 1977, however, when the uncertainty had largely subsided, the relative dollar holdings had returned to their previous levels. So the relative amount of foreign money held responded swiftly and significantly to changing incentives.[11]

Where Does This Leave Us?

Diversified money portfolios are one final way for money to make its way from country to country. They are one more hole in the dike that the Fed is busy trying to stick its fingers in. With the other sources of refuge from Fed policy, there are a lot of potential holes. There are international holes, Eurodollar holes, foreign currency holes, and domestic alternative asset holes.

The Fed has only so many fingers, and the fingers on each

hand can stretch only so far. So the Fed's fingers may be outnumbered, or the holes may be too far apart for the Fed to be able to stop each one up. The distinct possibility arises that the Fed cannot hold out long, that water from the oceans of domestic and world liquidity will be pouring in. Water seeks its own level, and the Fed may be unable to keep it from rising higher. Instead, the Fed may be swept away with the tide.

8

The Monetary Control
Act of 1980—
The Fed's Last Gasp?

ON OCTOBER 6, 1979, Fed Chairman Paul Volcker announced a new Fed policy. No longer was the monetary authority going to target short-term interest rates. Instead the Fed now was to adopt the monetarist goal of maintaining a slow and steady growth in monetary aggregates. This was to be the Great Monetarist Experiment. At last the Fed would be unleashed to flex its muscles. The monetarists and others sat back to wait for the beneficial results of this radical policy switch. Unfortunately they were in for a cruel surprise. Rather than falling, inflation and interest rates both shot up. In October 1979 the U.S. consumer price inflation and interest rates (T-bills) were 12.5 percent and 11.7 percent respectively. These were very high by historical standards. But they ended up looking good compared with the rates of 18.6 percent and 15.2 percent, which occurred in March 1980. The aggregates policy was not working as planned.

The last three chapters have detailed why this outcome simply reflects the failure of monetarism. But somehow, failing government agencies or policies are seldom viewed as having outlived their usefulness. Instead, inability to carry out policy is usually interpreted as a sign that the agency needs more powers. The Fed just needs some more assistance in controlling monetary aggregates. Obviously, if the current regulatory dikes are leaking, the answer must be bigger and stronger dikes. So the Fed convinced its friends in Congress to come to its rescue and to reinforce it against future floods, and Congress obliged.

The helping hand from Congress in this case was the Monetary Control Act of 1980. It represented an elaborate set of plugs for the old dikes plus a whole new set of dikes, all in one piece of legislation. It was supposed to pluck the Fed from the troubled waters of 1980 and to give it increased protection from world liquidity. The Monetary Control Act greatly extended the scope of regulatory powers of the Federal Reserve in order to make it a more dominant factor in U.S. money markets.

The effort, however, proved largely futile. More regulations do not always mean significantly more effectiveness for the Fed. The new regulations reduced the attractiveness of intermediating in dollars and therefore probably resulted in less of the world's financial intermediation occurring in dollars. The Fed may have had a better grip on what it can control, but it found that more and more of its potential domain had again slipped through its fingers. An action intended to extend the Fed's limits only served to underscore the Fed's limitations. Far from the ultimate weapon in controlling monetary aggregates, the Monetary Control Act proved another costly market barrier around which the market sector once again found circumventions. This episode illustrates once more why the Monetarist Dream cannot succeed.

BEYOND MONETARISM

The Stage Is Set for the Fed's Power Play[1]

How was it that, despite monetarists in high policy-making positions, despite the Fed's publicized quantity targets, the Fed's big experiment with money aggregates failed? Some blamed the Fed. These critics complained that, while adopting the stable quantity rule in rhetoric, the Fed had not adopted the rule in practice. (Don't watch the lips of the Fed Board, watch its feet!) The Fed was either going too fast or repeatedly stepping on first the brake and then the accelerator. Velocity appeared unstable. The money fluctuations in turn were associated with the fluctuations in market prices.

In the six months following the Fed's historical announcement, the pressure kept growing. The United States had never before had inflation of 20 percent in nonwartime. And the prime rate now bulged at over 20 percent. Had the Fed gone mad? Or had they simply lost control?

The Fed's initial response was predictably to try to patch up its operating techniques. The staff economists finally convinced the Fed Board members that perhaps the old money supply numbers were no longer meaningful. With the rapid acceptance of checkable NOW accounts and money market fund shares, the traditional target of currency plus checking accounts hardly seemed relevant anymore. So on February 7, 1980, the Fed Board redefined what they thought was money. NOW accounts were included in the new narrow-target M1, and money market shares, along with some overnight Eurodollars and repurchase agreements, were lumped together with more traditional small time deposits in the reformulated M2.

The Fed now thought it had a better handle on policy. The Fed knew all its powers would not bring about a more stable

at the Fed). In contrast, state banks were allowed to hold reserves in the form of demand deposits at correspondent banks. In return for these deposits, the correspondent banks paid implicit interest through services provided. Federal Reserve members also receive services in exchange for having deposits at the Fed. But it has been estimated that the average, implicit rate of return on these correspondent balances exceeded the equivalent return on Federal Reserve deposits by over 300 basis points.[2] Furthermore, in about half the states nonmember banks could hold at least part of their required reserves in interest-earning assets such as U.S. Treasury bills. In six states nonmember banks could meet *all* reserve requirements with interest-earning assets.[3] In other words, the state-chartered banks in these six states had no cash reserve requirements at all.

Other important differences existed as well. While all but one state (Illinois) had reserve requirements on demand deposits, a couple of other states (Massachusetts and Rhode Island) did not require reserves on time and savings deposits. Also, what was counted as reserves was much more liberal at the state level. Member banks can count only balances that have been collected (cleared the Federal Reserve collection process). In many states, however, nonmember banks were permitted to count or effectively counted "checks in process of collection" (CIPC) as part of their reserve balances at correspondent banks. The more liberal definition helped nonmember banks to hold a substantially smaller ratio of cash to total deposits, thereby lowering reserve costs.

Not surprisingly, as interest rates and Fed reserve requirements rose, many banks no longer felt that the benefits of Fed membership outweighed the costs. As mentioned in chapter 4, they then applied for state charters and withdrew from the Fed system. As banks withdrew, the Federal Reserve found itself exerting regulatory powers over a shrinking proportion of the banking industry.

The steady erosion of regulatory power alarmed officials in the Federal Reserve and in the government. The fraction of commercial bank assets regulated by the Fed declined from almost 75 percent during the mid-sixties to only about 67 percent in 1979. By the mid-seventies, the Fed-controlled fraction of all assets at depository institutions had declined to less than 50 percent. Meanwhile, the fraction of commercial banks belonging to the Fed fell below 40 percent. There were almost 250 fewer member banks at the end of 1979 than there were only two years previously.

Newspapers and magazines began writing about this flight from Fed membership. Congress held hearings on how to reverse the tide or blunt its impact. While there may have been differences over possible solutions, all parties could agree on one point: the influence of the Fed was clearly dwindling.

The Fed Strikes Back

The Fed used this crisis atmosphere of March 1980 to try flexing its muscles again. The first step was the announced credit controls, made possible under the Credit Control Act of 1969. Traditionally the Fed had jurisdiction over the borrowing and lending policies of member banks. But now, suddenly, here was the Federal Reserve telling money market funds, credit card companies, and even retailers like Sears Roebuck what to do.

The Fed imposed reserve requirements on money market shares above a base level. The reserve requirements, of course, were designed to raise costs to money market funds, reduce the interest rates they could offer the public, make them less attractive, and thereby reduce their presence in money markets. The regulations on credit cards were designed to reduce that source of funds. Credit card companies and retailers were now also subject to reserve requirements on their lending above a certain base level. Again, the controls raised the cost of this economic activity. Credit card companies and retailers tightened their credit terms and greatly reduced the number of new customers accepted.[4]

These credit controls, however, were only the beginning. The Fed still had to do something about those Eurodollars and fleeing banks. The Fed had a plan. In the excitement of the times, many failed to notice, or at least to comprehend fully, the scope of a second and long-planned move by the Fed. Passed on March 31, 1980, the Depository Institutions Deregulation and Monetary Control Act was disguised as essentially a deregulation bill. A close examination of the legislation's title, however, reveals what a paradox of conflicting goals it contained.

The Act had many important, far-reaching regulatory aspects, but initially few people were aware of its existence. It sailed quickly and quietly through Congress with almost no resistance. It received only scant news coverage. Those publications that did mention it gave the legislation little more than cursory treatment.

What attention it did receive tended to emphasize the deregulatory aspects of the Act. Deregulation was a hot item at the time. During that year, the airline and trucking industries were deregulated, and railroad deregulation was initiated. Many policy makers wanted to add banking to the list. Also, deregulation made the bill more attractive from a consumer lobby standpoint, since it meant banks could pay higher interest rates. The consumer angle made this regulation bill more salable.

The new law did promise a modicum of bank deregulation. The Act phased out over six years the Regulation Q limits on interest and dividend rates. The immediate effects, however, were small. In the first year it eliminated the 1/4 percent interest rate differential between money market certificates at commercial banks and those at thrift institutions. It also permitted thrift institutions to service demand deposit accounts, make commercial loans, and issue credit cards. But the Regulation Q ceilings were lifted only slowly. The precise schedule was determined by the Depository Institutions Deregulation Committee. Ceilings on deposits with a maturity over 3 1/2 years were lifted on May 1, 1982 and on those with a maturity of at least 2 1/2 years on April 1, 1983. Deposits with a maturity of 1 1/2 years were not scheduled to be deregulated until April 1, 1984, and six-month certificates on April 1, 1985.[5] The last savings instrument to be freed will be, of course, the familiar passbook account. The ceiling on this instrument will probably not disappear until the twelfth hour in 1986. The low interest rate makes these accounts very profitable for banks, and they are lobbying heavily to keep that ceiling. There is little countervailing pressure, since the very small saver has few alternatives. As usual, the "little guy" with the fewest options gets help last.

Eliminating market-distorting controls such as Regulation Q is indeed a noble cause. The drawn-out process of deregulation, however, minimizes the immediate gains from the phaseout. So while deregulation comes first in the name of the Act, it is not of foremost import. The short-run significance of these provisions was dwarfed by another purpose.

The primary and immediate effect of the law was summed up by the word "control" in the title. The legislation granted the Fed sweeping new regulatory powers over additional financial institutions. They became effective September 1, 1980, and the Fed began exercising them at the beginning of November 1980. These broad powers were aimed particularly at the remaining two phenomena that were undermining the existing authority of the Fed. The Act was a last attempt to keep member banks from fleeing and to plug up those Eurodollar loopholes. But, as the Fed had learned on previous occasions, markets adjust, particularly mobile ones like the global money market. While the provisions of control might appear on paper to extend Fed powers significantly, markets continue to find ways to get around regulations, or at least to minimize their impact. Another attempt to regulate was likely only to result in more money market activity moving away from the United States.

What the Monetary Control Act Did

How broad are these new powers? Broad enough to cast a shadow across all depository institutions in the United States and their foreign branches. The Fed and Congress chose what appeared to be an easy way out of their predicament. If banks think the grass is greener on the other side of the Fed's regulation, why not just kill that grass? That is what the Monetary Control Act did. It effectively eliminated the difference between members of the Fed and nonmembers. Beginning in November 1980, the Fed's ability to set minimum reserve requirements on deposits was extended beyond member banks to all U.S. banks.

In other words, the Fed now dictates regulations to all federally chartered banks, state-chartered banks, mutual savings banks, savings and loan associations, and even your company's credit union. All these depository institutions are subject to the same reserve requirements. They also now have access to the same benefits including the discount window, check clearing, and other services. The only remaining difference between members and nonmembers is that only members can hold stock in the Federal Reserve Banks. Loopholes such as state charters and noncommercial bank status have been closed.

The proportion of the assets of depository institutions controlled by the Fed now suddenly approximates 100 percent. The Fed thinks it has solved the problem of domestic banks wiggling out from under its thumb. It also thinks it has caged in the Eurodollar market more effectively. Recall that the Fed's last move against the foreign branches of U.S. banks had been to impose reserve requirements on money lent to the home office by foreign branches. The foreign branches had been issuing CDs, thereby avoiding the Fed's higher domestic reserve requirements, and in turn lending the funds to the home office for lending in the U.S. market. Recall, too, that the response of the foreign branches to this new tax had been simply to lend more of the funds directly into the U.S. market.

Now the Fed tried one more time to control this elusive market. The Monetary Control Act empowered the Fed to require reserves not only on funds borrowed by the parent banks, but also on the direct loans of foreign branches of U.S. banks to U.S. residents. The Fed was intent on restricting the amount of Eurodollar money getting into the United States. So it is now empowered to manage not only the liabilities of U.S. banks but also the *assets* of foreign branches. One more attempt to plug one more regulatory loophole.

In addition to these two major changes, the Monetary Control Act made other regulatory changes. For example, the Fed lumped the various types of bank deposits into new categories and imposed new uniform reserve requirements. Previously, reserve requirements were divided by type as well as by location of the deposit. Member bank reserve requirements on demand deposits could vary from 7 percent for a small rural bank to 16 3/4 percent for a large bank in New York or Chicago.

Demand deposits, however, were now renamed transactions accounts. They now had a flat reserve requirement of 12 percent (for amounts in excess of $25 million) and were lumped together with all other checkable deposits, such as NOW accounts, many of which previously had been labeled savings accounts. The Fed was free to change the initial 12 percent reserve requirement to any value between 8 and 14 percent. Furthermore, if five Board members find that "extraordinary circumstances exist," this range can even be expanded for renewable 180-day periods.

Time, or nontransactions, deposits are divided into "personal" and "nonpersonal" categories. Passbook accounts and other nontransferable personal time deposits no longer have a reserve requirement. Required reserves on nonpersonal deposits vary with the length of time to maturity. Those maturing in less than four years are subject to an initial requirement of 3 percent. The net liabilities of U.S. banks to their foreign branches and the direct loans of foreign branches to U.S. residents both fall into this nonpersonal time deposit category, subject to the same 3 percent reserves. The Fed's discretionary range for the requirement is 0 to 9 percent, but again five members of the Board can alter this range.

The Monetary Control Act also increases reporting requirements. All depository institutions with deposits of more than $15 billion must now submit weekly statistical reports to the Fed. Nonmember institutions with deposits between $2 billion and $5 billion are required to submit quarterly reports. Institutions with deposits of less than $2 billion are currently exempted.

So the new Federal Reserve powers fell across all depository institutions. They constrained the institutions to within earshot of the Fed's piper. As the piper played a tune, all depository institutions had to dance the same jig. The time when banks could chose a more appealing tune and dance by fleeing to the safety of state regulations was over.

Making the Powers a Little Broader— The International Banking Act

The shadow of the Fed's new powers fell even beyond domestic banks to another group of relatively regulation-free banks operating in the United States. These were the agencies, branches, and subsidiaries of foreign banks. The Fed's regulatory control was extended over these banks by the International Banking Act, which did for them what the Monetary Control Act did for nonmember banks.

The International Banking Act was a companion piece of legislation to the Monetary Control Act. While it had been enacted in 1978, many of its provisions took effect only in 1980. Essentially the legislation sought to put foreign banks operating in the United States on the same footing with respect to restrictions on banking as their U.S. competitors. What is good enough for Citibank should be good enough for Barclays.

For instance, the Act subjected foreign banks to the same prohibition as domestic banks against accepting deposits in more than one state. It also subjected the foreign banks to the same required reserves and limitations on the payment of interest as U.S. banks. The Fed did not want foreign banks in the United States competing on better terms, or domestic banks might just sell out to foreigners.

In addition, those foreign branches engaged in retail deposit-taking were required to have and to pay for federal deposit insurance. The foreign banks were therefore required to hold, at member banks, deposits or investment securities equal to 5 percent of their liabilities. The Act also made their operating agencies and branches in the United States subject to nonbanking prohibitions of the Bank Holding Company Act.

In sum, the International Banking Act tightened the Fed's regulation of agencies, branches, and subsidiaries of foreign banks operating in the United States. It paved the way for the Monetary Control Act to bring foreign branches and agencies directly under Fed control.

Whose Welfare Is at Stake, Anyway?

One quickly realizes that the primary goal of the Monetary Control Act, and the related legislation, was to stop the erosion of Federal Reserve control. Control over the banking industry and the money supply is certainly viewed as a worthwhile goal by the Fed, which currently is busy claiming monetary control as its mandate. But what about the viewpoint of the average person? What about the country as a whole? The world? Are we better off for what Congress has done? Even if the Fed could now achieve its objective, should we be happy?

These questions reveal the dilemma of those who argue for slower money growth to reduce inflation. With global money markets, the Fed is likely to need severe restrictions if it is to increase significantly its control over the dollar money supply. But those same restrictions reduce the attractiveness of transacting in dollars, leading to an international flight from the dollar and further dollar inflation. A policy aimed at maximizing the power of the Fed Board members to control money aggregates quite likely does not maximize the benefits to the rest of us.

The problem is that the Fed's control depends on the Fed's ability to regulate. But, as we saw in chapter 6, regulation is equivalent to a tax on the activity it governs. As figure 6–2 showed, higher regulation drives a "wedge" between the gross price and the net return of an activity, reducing incentives for all participants. As a familiar economic adage tells us, "the more you tax an activity, the less of it you get; the more you subsidize an activity, the more of it you get." The activity here is financial intermediation, and the country ends up receiving fewer of the benefits associated with efficiently lining up borrowers and lenders.

A good example of this impact of regulation taxes is the decline of savings and loan associations in the late seventies and early eighties. Much has been written in the last few years on the plight of the savings and loans. Many of these financial institutions, on the brink of collapse, have been rescued through discretionary or forced mergers with banks on more solid financial footing. Some have even failed, requiring FSLIC bailouts. In contrast, reported problems among commercial banks have been few and far between. Why have financial problems plagued the S&L's in particular?

Like commercial banks, savings and loans are subject to reserve requirements and limitations on the interest rates they may pay their depositors (Regulation Q). But unlike commercial banks, their assets have also been restricted, largely to fixed-interest, long-term mortgages. As a result, the decade of the 1970s was not kind to savings and loans. In the early seventies, as deposit interest rates rose above the fixed ceiling, disintermediation occurred. Depositors simply moved into higher yield securities outside the banks. The government tried to ease the problem caused by this interest-rate ceiling distortion. The minimum size of Treasury bills was raised from $1000 to $10,000. But the situation was not eased by this new distortion. Large savers still purchased T-bills directly, and new, unregulated institutions such as money market funds developed to satisfy the needs of smaller savers.

Development of money market certificates in the late 1970s helped to stem the drift of large savers to other markets. But this movement towards deregulating bank liabilities left the S&L's financing largely long-term, fixed-interest mortgages with short-term, variable-rate deposits. New problems arose as the cost of borrowing exceeded the return on the portfolio of mortgages.

At each step the S&L's found their ability to adjust to new situations hindered by various regulations. They struggled to survive in their highly regulated, but rapidly changing, environment. Many S&L's found themselves in the position of the gasoline station on a highly competitive corner. The station had a large sign that proclaimed, "We lose 2 cents on every gallon! How do we do it? Our large volume!" Like that gasoline station, many S&L's found their marketing strategies forcing them out of business.

The Impact of the Monetary Control Act on Dollar Banking

The description of regulation as a tax is useful for analyzing the impact of this new legislation. The impact is likely to be felt in two places. First, the legislation could alter the composition of U.S. financial intermediation. Is the legislation likely to favor large banks over small? Domestic banks over foreign? Short-term borrowing over long-term? Second, it may change the form or place of dollar financial intermediation. Will more occur in the United States or abroad? And of what remains in the United States, will more occur inside or outside the banking system?

Regarding domestic banking, the new rules seem to favor large banks over small, domestic banks over foreign and short-term instruments over longer-term ones. The old reserve requirements on demand deposits, for instance, ranged from 16 1/4 percent for large member banks to as low as 7 1/2 percent for small member banks. Nonmember banks (which tend to be smaller than average) had reserve requirements in some states that were the same as the Fed's, but ranged down to zero percent in Illinois. The introduction of a flat 12 percent requirement therefore reduces the tax for large banks and raises it for smaller banks.[6] In addition, the nonmember banks now have to keep their reserves in a noninterest-bearing form, can no longer count checks in process of collection, and have additional statistical report burdens. The relative position of the large member banks is improved.[7]

Now that branches and agencies of foreign banks in the United States are subject to the International Banking and Monetary Control Acts, they also will find their costs of intermediation rising and their flexibility diminished. The competitive edge of these U.S. offices is dulled, and their share of the U.S. banking market is likely to contract.

The average yield on CDs is also likely to shorten because of reduced reserve requirements on short-term deposits. Prior to the new law, requirements on CDs varied by maturity length: for 30 to 179 days, the requirement was 6 percent; for

180 days to 4 years, it was 2 1/2 percent; for 4 years or more, it was 1 percent. The new 3 percent requirement on all nonpersonal time deposits significantly lowers a bank's cost of short-term borrowing and significantly raises the cost of borrowing for more than four years at a time.

Even more important, however, is the likely impact of the new laws on the proportion of dollar financial intermediation actually occurring through the U.S. banking system. From a first glance at the impact of the new laws, it might appear that they are likely to increase the proportion of domestic banking activity. For example, one might think domestic banking is likely to increase relative to Eurobanking. After all, reserve requirements on liabilities to foreign branches have been raised for foreign as well as for U.S. banks. Both domestic and foreign banks now find it more expensive to choose the route of raising funds in the Euromarket and channeling the funds to the United States in order to finance loans through U.S. banks. Should not more CDs therefore just be issued directly in the U.S. market? In addition, the reserve requirements against loans of foreign branches of U.S. banks to residents in the United States probably also make it more expensive to raise funds and make loans directly from the Eurodollar markets. Should not such activity therefore decline, and the proportion of U.S. banking increase?

Not quite. The new laws certainly were aimed at plugging Euromarket loopholes by raising the cost of that loophole activity. But there are other types of loopholes of which the dollar market can take quick advantage. Markets are quite efficient at finding new loopholes in order to avoid the tax or at least minimize its impact. For instance, now that domestic banking is more regulated, the borrowing and lending that remains in the United States may now proceed through other channels. While borrowing and lending through the banking system are subject to the increased regulation, borrowing and lending through, say, the commercial paper market are not.

Interestingly, previous attempts by the Fed to slow money growth by raising reserve taxes on banks apparently resulted in increased use of the commercial paper market. As mentioned in chapter 6, the Fed had raised marginal reserve requirements on CDs between December 1978 and June 1980. In that eighteen-month period, outstanding nonfinancial paper rose $22 billion, while large bank business loans rose $25 billion. In other words, 47 percent of the combined $47 billion growth was due to commercial paper. Yet in December 1978 commercial paper represented just 13 percent of the initial combined stock ($130 billion in bank loans, $19 billion in paper). And in the eighteen months preceding December 1978, when marginal requirements were much lower, commercial paper expanded by only $6 billion, only 20 percent of the combined total growth.[8] The larger wedge in commercial banking provided the incentive for business borrowers to rely more heavily on nonbank financial intermediation.

There were also new loopholes to be found in the Euromarket. One possible evasion might be to lend to foreign subsidiaries of U.S. corporations, instead of directly to the U.S. parent. Loans to foreign subsidiaries are not subject to reserve requirements, and the corporate subsidiary could always in turn lend to the parent. Or the same phenomenon could occur in the Euromarket as in the U.S. market. The Eurobranch could lend to U.S. corporations by buying their Eurocommercial paper instead of making direct loans. Again, no reserve requirement is involved. A likely by-product of the new restrictions is therefore a relative expansion of commercial paper markets in the United States and abroad.

And there was one more problem with this attempt to close the Euromarket loophole. While the Euromarket branches of

U.S. banks were subject to the reserve requirements on direct loans to their outlets in the United States, branches of foreign banks in the same market were not. The Fed had tried to reduce the drain on its power by taxing U.S. banks out of some Euromarket business. But foreign banks were waiting in the wings. To the extent that foreign banks have the ability to undertake sizable additional Euromarket activity for very small increases in reward, the Fed's plan fails. Foreign bank activity simply replaces U.S. bank activity in the Eurodollar market. The fully flexed muscle of the Fed can probably manage only to hurt the competitive position of U.S. banks by taxing them out of the market. There remains, however, a leaking hole in the new dike.

Can the Fed Now Keep Its Head Above Water?

As we have seen, the Monetary Control Act was designed to pluck the Fed out of its predicament and to build sufficiently strong barriers to prevent the flood waters of world liquidity from bursting in again. At first glance it appeared that the Monetary Control Act might accomplish its mission. The Federal Reserve regulatory power had been extended to all U.S. depository institutions, including foreign banks in the United States. The relative cost of Eurodollar activity appeared to have been raised. If so, that could drive a larger share of dollar financial activity into the regulated U.S. market. On the surface the Fed seemed to have just what it needed to whip the Ms into better shape.

But such regulatory powers are achieved only at a price. The extended powers have raised the tax on foreign banks operating in the United States. The reporting requirements on nonmember depository institutions have been increased. The tax on utilizing the Euromarket has been raised, and any bank wishing to participate in the U.S. money market must subject itself to the Fed's restrictions.

In short, the new legislation has raised the tax on financial intermediation. In particular it raises the cost of borrowing and lending in dollars relative to other currencies. The added tax raises the cost of borrowing and reduces the returns from lending, making the dollar less attractive. Both borrowers and lenders have an incentive to shift to other currencies, further eroding the position of the dollar as an international currency. If anything, that adds to dollar inflation.

The Fed has approached the problems from a narrow viewpoint. It has set its sights on winning skirmishes in the battle for control of domestic money aggregates. In the process, however, it has, if anything, put itself in a worse position in the war on inflation. Any increase in domestic Fed authority comes at the expense of declining world dollar demand.

The Fed's plan for getting itself out of its regulatory jam had been to apply new regulatory taxes to head off responses to old regulatory taxes. The Fed wished to stem the flight from membership in the Federal Reserve System, but the flight was in response to the rising relative costs of membership. In the previous year and a half the Fed had been busy driving a wedge between member banks' borrowing and lending costs by raising marginal reserve requirements. These actions were aimed at gaining control over the domestic money supply and slowing its rate of growth, but instead they were driving domestic banks from the Fed system and the wholesale money market beyond Fed control to the Eurocurrency centers. The Fed's effort to block the escape from regulatory taxes only caused taxes on domestic banking to rise further. So the Fed's plan only

The Monetary Control Act of 1980

speeded up the process of moving the money market beyond the Fed's authority.

Those who felt the Monetary Control Act was the Fed's salvation were being myopic. Given the existence of highly integrated global money markets, such an extension of taxing authority is likely to produce results quite different from those intended. Faced with greater barriers to efficient financial intermediation, domestic and foreign banks can be expected to alter business procedures to minimize the impact of the Fed's new restrictions. Less of the world intermediation will be in dollars. More of the remaining dollar intermediation will occur in the unregulated foreign markets. More of the foreign dollar banking will occur through foreign banks. Remaining domestic financial intermediation will occur less and less through the regulated banking system. Commercial paper, money market funds, and perhaps further financial market innovations will become increasingly dominant forces in the U.S. market.

Does this sound as though the Fed is now more in control? Does this sound as though the Fed can target relevant money aggregates even generally, much less with pinpoint accuracy? Does this sound as though quantity rules are likely to be successful? No, quite the opposite. It sounds as though the Fed will again be in peril if it maintains a quantity rule policy. The Fed has been attempting to achieve a goal beyond its reach. No wonder it has failed!

The Fed, however, prompted by Treasury officials, keeps trying to tinker with the system. It keeps hoping that one day it will find the magic loophole that, once closed, will provide it with the elusive control it seeks. It tried one more time in June 1982 by adopting contemporaneous reserve accounting, effective February 1984. Instead of having two weeks in which to add up deposits and post reserves, banks and S&L's would now have only two days. As we saw in chapter 4, this change was high on the monetarists' agenda for regaining control over total bank reserves and the money supply.

The contemporaneous reserve accounting is hardly the magic loophole. Even the supporters of stronger Fed control were less than confident of the prospects of serious change. Treasury Secretary Regan commented, "To the extent that contemporaneous reserve requirements move us in the direction of less volatile money growth, this is certainly welcome news." Fed Chairman Volcker was even more to the point: "I still have a major concern that it promises more than it produces."[9] Perhaps even these officials are beginning to grip the realities.

This latest tinkering is not without its costs. The staff of the Federal Reserve Board estimates that compliance will initially cost banks and S&L's $103 million to adopt new computer and reporting procedures and $29 million in each subsequent year.[10] The regulatory wedge just keeps getting bigger and bigger.

In the long run, perhaps it is useful for the monetarists to achieve a change that they perceive to be so important. Perhaps we should even test monetarist policy by yielding to all the monetarists' demands. If the monetarists are allowed to run the nation's monetary system the way they think is best, we can see how well M1 and M2 stay within the proposed targets. We can see how high inflation and interest rates remain. Even more important, we can see how *volatile* inflation and interest rates are. The chances are that nothing would speed the adoption of an alternative policy faster than the fulfillment of the Monetarist Dream.

9

Beyond Monetarism: Focusing on Price Instead of Quantity

FROM OCTOBER 1979 into 1982, the Fed remained fixed on money aggregates as a primary indicator of future policy. The Fed was apparently accepting the monetarist argument that a quantity rule is a star by which to steer the ship of state. Yet, as we have seen, the quantity of money is not a stable marker from which policy makers can get their bearings. Far from a star fixed in the heavens, the money supply is more like a kite rising and dipping in the wind currents. But gazing into the night sky, the monetarists have somehow mistaken the kite for a star. With eyes fixed steadily on that kite, the Fed has no reliable guide to a straight course of action. The money supply numbers are at best an indirect policy indicator and more often contain little relevant information. Difficult policy decisions result, as the Fed often finds itself caught between the demands of the marketplace and the demands of the monetarists and their political allies.

Trying to follow that monetarist kite, then, leaves the Fed on an unstable course. Sextants fixed on the bobbing kite, the economy sails about in circles, never seeming to reach that golden port the policy had promised. While the economy continues to be tossed about in the sea of liquidity, the monetarist crew keeps frantically looking for the port. It must be just ahead. But hopes are continually dashed as in the place of the port we find more rocky shoals that threaten the existence of the economy.

It is time, then, to admit that monetarism has been a failure and will never work. It is time to admit that monetarism has only added to the economic volatility and that some other policy is urgently needed. It is time to admit that the new policy should focus directly on restoring stability to prices, not controlling elusive, mercurial quantities.

These conclusions seem obvious. We know that life has been more tumultuous with unhinged money. Anyone who has tried to obtain a mortgage, manage assets, plan production or inventories, or just anticipate weekly food bills knows how economic life has become so much more difficult and unsettled since the early seventies. This period has coincided with the final breakdown of the previous system of price rules. The key to understanding the current monetary uncertainty must lie there.

But why should a system of price rules be superior? Is the focus of policy so different? What essential role does the central bank play that is missing with a quantity rule? Why do financial markets seem so much more jittery today than ten or fifteen years ago? Do current policies keep them more in the dark?

Understanding the difference in how policy and money markets operate under hinged and unhinged money opens our eyes to how current policies must change. This chapter will show why economic life under a complex, confusing set of rules about the shape, size, and direction of money has become so cumbersome. The discussion emphasizes the hopelessness and irrelevancy of a quantity rule and the urgency of returning to a stable value of money. It sets the stage for the final discussion —precisely which set of price rules will bring back stable money.

From Stargazing to Heeding Market Signals: Focusing on What Really Matters

The amazing thing about the monetary kite is that the Fed and the monetarists are probably the only people who really care about it. When you wake up in the morning, is the money supply one of the first things you think about? When you buy groceries or buy a house, do you worry about whether this week's or this month's money supply has risen? When you decide whether to put a few more dollars into your savings, do you anguish over whether the money supply has fallen?[1] In each case the answer is undoubtedly no.

What you probably do worry about, however, is what is happening to the value of your money. Are the dollars in your wallet today shrinking in value? Does your weekly food budget buy as many jars of peanut butter as it used to? Are dollars you put in savings today going to be worth much in a few years, even with the interest payments? Are antiques a better value?

The changes that have occurred in monetary policy are reminiscent of the story of the emperor's new clothes. The emperor's elaborate new clothes, remember, were supposed to be visible only to the "wise." Lest anyone be thought unwise, all pretended to marvel at the detail and beauty of the imaginary garments.

So it is today. Academicians and officials tell us that an elaborate new policy centered around the supply of money is the key to the future. Keep that money growth rate low and stable, and inflation and high interest rates will be a thing of the past. All eyes turn to the money supply. Newspapers and magazines give front page treatment as it wiggles up and down. Wall Street begins to bet more intensely on the outcome of the weekly estimates. Congress begins to hold hearings on why the money supply is not behaving better. Everyone begins to speculate about what each dip or burst may mean for prices today or tomorrow. After all, these academicians and policy researchers are wise, learned, and respectable people. They have powerful computers at their disposal, which can quickly produce sophisticated analyses showing why money growth is so important. Money must be the key.

No one stops to ask, "Do I really care what the money supply is?" Occasional rumblings are heard in the business community about how the money supply figures are not really informative, but these rumblings are quickly drowned out by the daily chorus of available quotes about how "tight" money will choke off inflation, or how the Fed needs to ease up to prevent depression. What we need in the current situation is that little boy in the crowd who, unimpressed by all the pretense, observed, "The Emperor is wearing no clothes!"

How do we put clothes back on Fed policy? By refocusing the Fed's efforts directly on what is bothering the public. Even under the most optimistic scenario, the money supply is of only indirect interest. The narrow Ms are only an arbitrary fraction of relevant money that is difficult to measure or control. Even if we could control it and knew its value at every instant, the supply of dollars by itself is still not the critical factor. Successfully manipulating the quantity of money requires continually adjusting it to the demand for dollars. Yet attempts to estimate demand again face unresolved measurement problems.

A policy rule for the quantity of money, then, involves manipulating with great uncertainty something with little direct value to the public. How much better it would be instead to redirect policy towards stabilizing the things people really care about, the money values of the goods people buy now and in the future. The Fed should permanently abandon the role of "keeper of the quantities" and resume the role of "redeemer of the values." That is the crucial first step on the road to renewed monetary stability.

Life in the World with the Fed as a Redeemer

To emphasize why the return to price rules is so crucial, let us contrast the world where the Fed stands behind the value of money with the world where the value of money is completely unhinged. We start with the simpler world, where the Fed has agreed to stabilize some relevant market prices. The question of precisely which prices is left for the next chapter; they could be the dollar prices of corn, gold, deutsche marks, or bricks for delivery today or two years from now. Whichever prices are chosen, however, the Fed's task is straightforward. A target value is chosen for each price, and the Fed's sole goal is to keep that value stable.

This "redemption" or "price" rule works because the Fed is defining the basic monetary unit of account in terms of something observable. The Fed calls the basic unit of its liabilities the dollar. It then tells the market that these dollar liability units will always be redeemable at a certain price in terms of that observable item. The basic dollar unit now has a specific value. Even better, so too do all the forms of money that are convertible into the basic unit. Bank accounts, Euromarket accounts, money market mutual funds, and so on may not be controlled directly by the Fed. But as long as the issuers of these monies define and redeem these accounts in dollars, the Fed is stabilizing the *value* of these monies too. Immediately we see that the Fed need no longer worry about the quantity of monies it cannot control. Instead the Fed need only concern itself with the value of the money it issues directly, stand ready to defend it, and as a result help bring stability even to the monies beyond its direct grasp.

As an illustration, assume the Fed chooses (perhaps among other things) to stabilize the dollar price of silver in spot commodity markets. A target spot silver price would be selected (say, one ounce = $12). If the price begins to deviate from the targeted value, the Fed must act. Say the spot dollar value falls (the dollar price of silver rises above $12). The Fed must prop the price back up by showing the market it stands ready to redeem. The Fed must buy back dollars at the targeted redemption price. In the opposite case, where the spot dollar value rises (silver falls below $12), the Fed must also stand by its promise. The rising value is met by the Fed selling dollars at the targeted price. The aim of the policy is simple. No matter which way the dollar tends to move, the Fed stands ready to anchor that price through redemption. This commitment clearly defines the new dollar standard for the market.

One of the nice qualities of such a policy is that it eliminates most of the current guesswork. Today we find businesses and commentators trying to read tea leaves. Will the money supply be up or down? How will the Fed respond to such a change? What is the probable impact of the Fed's reaction? The Fed's choices are also full of uncertainties. How big is the money supply? Is that too much money? How much, if any, intervention is necessary? The potential problems and errors multiply.

In contrast, the price rule requires little if any guesswork. Information is directly transmitted through the marketplace (through silver price quotations) to both the Fed and the private sector. Both the Fed and the private sector know what must be done. The Fed knows precisely when to redeem and how much. Any tendency for the target value to move requires the Fed to step into the market. The Fed also knows that it must remain in the market as long as the tendency for movement remains. No elaborate information-gathering or ad hoc policy planning is required.

The private sector also knows what to expect. This side of the market is interested in the Fed continuing to "play by the rules." A continuing commitment by the Fed means prices remain stable. Is the Fed standing behind this commitment? The private market has only to check the targeted value. If, say, spot silver prices are targeted, is the dollar price of silver stable? If the price does move from the target value, does it start moving back? If the answers are yes, the Fed is doing its job. The public simply watches the commodity ticker tape for the latest quotes.

While the Fed is busy assuring the stability of the value of money, the quantity of money takes care of itself. The amount of money people want to hold depends on how much the things they buy cost (the price level) and how many things they buy (real income). It also depends on how much holding on to dollars (versus something else) costs them. If the return on real assets falls, or if the dollar is expected to appreciate relative to other currencies, people will want to hold more money in dollars. The demand for dollars could therefore rise because prices rose, because income rose, because the dollar was again becoming a strong currency, or for whatever reason.

The important point is that, under the price rule, the Fed does not have to worry about whether or why money demand has risen or whether velocity is stable. If the private sector wants more money, for whatever reason, the Fed finds out soon enough. The dollar price of spot silver falls, as people try to become liquid, and the Fed must react. The Fed provides the market with dollars, in exchange for spot deliveries of silver, and the desired additional money becomes available. The Fed maintains the stable price between silver and the basic dollar unit, and the market tells the Fed when to adjust liquidity. The Fed need no longer concern itself with that imprecise, indirect policy barometer, the money supply. The private sector sees that the available money expands and contracts with its needs.

This "price rule," then, is straightforward and uncomplicated. All relevant information concerning the Fed's policy actions is available for both policy maker and money holder directly and continuously from a quote board. The probability of error is greatly reduced. Values, which people care about, are directly stabilized. The Fed must only decide precisely which prices to stabilize.

Life in the World of Unhinged Money

In contrast, in the current environment without a price rule the world is more complicated. Without a price rule, the basic dollar unit of account is unhinged. Without a price rule, the Federal Reserve foresakes its central role as an efficient channel of information concerning the dollar's value. The Fed no longer provides even the fuzzy outline of the basic unit of account. Without that information, the market must guess for itself. Financial uncertainties increase. The value of the dollar bounces up and down as financial markets continuously evaluate newly available information. The constant digging for and evaluating of new information adds to costs and reduces market efficiency. It becomes more difficult to conclude successful and profitable long-term contracts and other transactions.

The Fed faces a similar plight. Suppose the economy experiences a burst of growth. What policy does the Fed follow? With a growing level of commerce, people want more money. The money supply naturally tends to expand. If money is allowed to grow naturally and exceed the stated target, the Fed could appear to lose credibility. Yet if the Fed chooses not to accommodate the growing demand and takes steps to constrain arbitrary proxies for money like M1 or M2 within their arbitrary limits, credit markets can be disrupted. Like the public, the Fed faces increased uncertainty. What policy must be followed, "ease" or "tighten"? How much, and for how long? Unhinged money only creates more questions, not answers.

Why Unhinged Money Creates Uncertainty and Turmoil

A dollar bill is like a yardstick. It is a common guide for comparing the worth of different commodities today, and a single commodity over time. For example, the dollar unit is useful for comparing the worth of apples, oranges, strawberries, and light bulbs today, telling you in what proportions one commodity trades for another. Knowing the dollar price of these tomorrow tells you whether these proportions are changing over time.

Knowledge of future dollar prices also tells you what is happening to the yardstick. A light bulb may trade for a pint of strawberries both today and tomorrow. But the dollar price of each may rise from $1.00 to $1.15. While the supply and demand of the two commodities have not shifted enough to change their relative price, the yardstick has shrunk by 15 percent. The dollar buys less. The value of the basic unit of account has depreciated.

So the money yardstick is a system of conveying information about value. It is analogous to yardsticks used in specific industries. Take, for example, shoe sizes. Like the dollar, shoe sizes are a yardstick or information system; they provide a way to compare different pairs of shoes. All shoes in size 10C, for instance, should be almost precisely the same size, regardless of the style. A size 7B shoe will be shorter and narrower. As long as the local shoe sizes remain stable, they are profitably relied on and used by all.

But suppose the system were not stable. Suppose shoe sizes changed every month. The shoe industry would quickly fall on hard times if shoe sizes fluctuated from month to month, much less day to day. Each month a person wanting shoes would have to have his foot remeasured. Shoes marked as a certain size would also have to be dated. A 10C this month might be an 11D next month. With sizes changing every month, it would be hard for store owners and customers to order shoes. Ordering would require forecasting what sizes would be on the day the order is shipped. A spokesperson for the shoe manufacturers association might claim that shoe sizes are a stable function, which on average can be forecasted. But the necessity of forecasting repeatedly (not to mention occasionally forecasting incorrectly) raises the cost of using the system. Obviously the worth of such a yardstick declines. At some point people will resort to ignoring the yardsticks completely ("I'll just keep trying them on until one pair fits"), developing their own systems, or maybe using a more stable foreign system. The industry experiences a period of turmoil, uncertainty, and slow growth.

Money is like shoe sizes. The monetary system provides information that people use to make plans for today and for the future. It is only going to be used as long as it continues to provide reasonably accurate and dependable information. As the system becomes more volatile, people turn away from it, employing the best alternatives. As in the shoe-industry analogy, the economy experiences a period of turmoil, uncertainty, and slow growth.

How does the shoe industry avoid such turmoil? It sets up and maintains a basic unit of account, the standard shoe size. Shoe sizes are set in one of two ways. First, the government can set the standards and make sure that those standards are retained. Second, a group of people who are actively engaged in the shoe market (such as a trade group) can agree on an acceptable standard. In either case a system for transmitting information concerning sizes to those in the shoe market is created. With this information, shoe sellers and consumers adjust their behavior accordingly.

It is the same for money. The basic money yardstick is determined in one of two similar ways. First, the government can set the standard for what its monetary liabilities are worth and make sure the standard is retained. Second, where the government fails to set the standard, the private market can settle on what value the standard will be.

For much of the country's history, the U.S. government has defined the dollar unit of account. Defining the dollar began soon after the Revolutionary War. Even though trade with Spain was illegal under the British Navigation Acts, the Spanish Milled Dollar circulated in all thirteen colonies at the time of the Revolutionary War. Indeed, because it was the *only* coin that was the same in all thirteen colonies (the shillings of the different colonies being of various sizes), the dollar was adopted by the Continental Congress and later, in 1792, as the standard U.S. unit. A Congressional Committee was established to go around the states and measure the average size of the dollar. That average size became the dollar standard.[2]

Except for some slight adjustments in the 1830s, this dollar system remained intact (except for war-related periods) until 1933.[3] The system served to provide the private market (and the government) with exact information about the size of the dollar yardstick. Commerce could proceed without participants having to "guesstimate" first the yardstick on which to base their transactions. The precise form of national banking changed several times over this long period of time, but each banking system was based on this standardized dollar yardstick.

Compared with the early banking system, the present Federal Reserve System is a type of financial innovation. A government agency is now charged with providing information to the market about the value of the dollar yardstick. This was not always the case. At its inception, the Fed was only a loosely organized system of twelve regional banks. Each issued "dollars" with its own impression, but these dollars simply stood for the yardstick that had been already established in the eighteenth and nineteenth centuries.

In the 1930s, however, the role of the Federal Reserve changed. In that decade the traditional yardstick was abandoned. The dollar was redefined from $20.67 to $35 per ounce of gold, but it was not actually tied to a value until the late 1940s. The Board of Governors of the Federal Reserve was established, centralizing the Fed's powers. These powers were also extended to conducting open market operations and permitting variable bank deposit reserve requirements. The Fed was being handed more power and discretion for setting the value of the yardstick.

In the years since the Second World War, these discretionary powers of the Fed have been used in two quite different ways. During the Bretton Woods period, the Fed resumed the role of defining the yardstick as 1/35 of an ounce of gold. The Fed then used its discretionary powers to step into the market and stabilize the dollar yardstick whenever the value tended to fluctuate. The Fed again became a clearinghouse for information about the dollar. Its role was to assure the private market of the dependability of the value of money. Its commitment to the redemption of Federal Reserve liabilities was the most direct way of conveying that information about value.

In the post-1971 period, however, the Fed has failed to provide stable or consistent information about the standard. The Fed has increasingly abstained from its essential role of relaying information about the dollar's value to the market. It still continues to use its discretionary powers, but not to define continuously what the dollar yardstick is. Instead, it has increasingly tried to impress the financial markets by showing the approximate number of a certain subset (like M1) of yardsticks that exist.

To return to the shoe analogy, the current situation is a little like walking in to be fitted for a pair of shoes and instead being told the number of foot measures in the store. You wonder what the number of measures has to do with buying a pair of shoes. The financial markets face a similar quandary. They want information about the size of the yardstick. They are shown instead the approximate number of one type of measure sticks. How is this number to be interpreted? Is a certain number of this type of measure sticks directly associated with a specific size of yardstick? Few would claim it is. The Fed is no longer providing the information the market needs.

The Inadequacies of Current Economic Theory

So if there is a scarcity of anything in the money market today, it is a scarcity of relevant information about precisely what a dollar is. Just as with shoe sizes, in the absence of a definition provided by a central clearinghouse, the loosely organized market must find a definition for itself. How would the market determine a set of shoe sizes? We do not know for sure. It may even be that without a market coordinator (either the government or a private group such as a trade association), we may never get a stable set of shoe sizes.

In the case of money, the U.S. government currently has a monopoly on what is used as a monetary unit in the country. Legal tender is restricted to the U.S. dollar. There is no opportunity for a private group to develop an alternative legal monetary standard.[4] Yet the Fed refuses to provide a definition of the dollar unit of account. Without the government or a private group to guide it, how is the market to define or determine the standard dollar and the related dollar prices?

If you press economists for an answer to this question, you will find out they are not sure. Some may insist that it has to do with the supply and demand of money, generally some measure of domestic money supply and demand. We already know that such an approach is too narrow. A few may have some concept of world money supply and demand. Even here, however, new questions arise. If the analysis includes the relevant world supply of dollars, many of these dollars are created or extinguished at the discretion of the private sector. That supply of dollars is endogenous or very elastic. But if it is endogenous, so that the relevant world money supply always equals the world money demand, why should there ever be inflation? Conventional monetary theory does not seem able to answer that nagging, fundamental question.

What is becoming clear is that many questions concerning money and prices remain to be answered. We finally define the relevant money supply, only to run into new problems of explaining inflation under unhinged money. The problems encountered are reminiscent of problems with the Ptolemaic explanation of the universe. Ptolemy contended that the earth was the center of the universe, with all planets revolving around it. It was a simple, intuitively appealing, readily understood model. The only problem was that not all the observable data fit the theory. So those engaged in explaining the Ptolemaic system sought answers in a more complicated theory. They developed a system of circles within circles. With all the complications, more observed facts could be explained, but still not all. It remained for the radical departure of the Copernican system, with the sun at the center of the solar system, to provide a simple alternative theory that could bring together all the observed facts.

If you are sitting at the edge of your seat, anticipating a radical new revelation, you will be disappointed. We still await the economic Copernicus. An adequate alternative theory of prices and inflation with unhinged money has not yet been developed. All that can be described at present is the process by which prices seem to be determined in the marketplace with unhinged money. That process is very complex. It is constructive to continue the comparison of monetary systems by contrasting this complex market process with the simplicity of the marketplace in a world with price rules.

Converging to a Consensus Price Without a Price Rule

When the Federal Reserve or the Treasury fails to inform the market about the size of the dollar yardstick, the market must struggle to guess what its size actually is. In markets for all prices, the guessing becomes like betting on a horse race. Preparing for the horse race, the bettors in the market search for

information. The consensus constantly changes as new information is discovered and evaluated. One way to interpret the
current volatility in the dollar, therefore, is that it reflects
continued attempts by the private market to ferret out and
interpret information about the size and shape of the basic
dollar unit of account.

One source of information for the bettors is government
pronouncements. While the government is not currently re-
deeming its liabilities to set the standard, in theory it could
begin such a price rule at any time. The consensus value of the
dollar therefore reflects the market's best guess about the probability, the likely date, and the value at which such a redemption policy would occur. Statements by government officials
can alter that guess.

A good example of how such statements can affect this
market process was the foreign exchange market's reaction to
the Carter Administration's attempts in 1977 to "talk down"
the dollar. Prior to the summer of 1977, the U.S. government,
while not firmly pegging the value of the dollar to another
currency or commodity, was at least busy intervening to maintain "orderly markets." This intervention served to limit the
short-term fluctuations in the value of the dollar relative to
foreign currencies. While the market was unsure about the
dollar's foreign currency value one year later, it knew that
day-to-day fluctuations would be within limited values. The
Federal Reserve was effectively placing a floor and a ceiling on
the dollar's value in the near term. The market could argue
about the precise value of today's dollar, but that value would
always be within the "orderly market" range in the immediate
future.

Treasury Secretary Blumenthal's announcements, however,
yanked the floor out from under the dollar. The value of the
dollar today, tomorrow, and the next day was no longer limited

to this "orderly market" range, at least in the downward direction. The market no longer had the previous intervention actions of the Fed to provide even the fuzzy outline of the yardstick. The market now had to guess where within the broad range of possibilities the dollar's value would be each day.

The market did have some new information to go on, however. There was Secretary Blumenthal busy telling the world that the Carter Administration thought the dollar's value was too high. The market participants then laid out their bets on the size of the yardstick. The bets reflected not only what the Treasury Secretary said but also the market's estimate of how influential Blumenthal was in formulating policy. Needless to say, the first time Blumenthal made his comments there were not many takers of bets that the dollar's value would rise. Market consensus quickly formed that the U.S. government would not resume "orderly market" intervention until the dollar had dipped precipitously relative to other currencies. The dollar's value plunged, as the market began to grope for just how low the dollar would have to go before significant government intervention resumed.

Notice that the dollar's plunge did not revolve around the supply of and demand for the dollar, but rather around the market's evaluation of the dollar's likely value. It was not that the world market suddenly discovered it was holding more dollars than it wanted. It was instead that, with the new information, the market found that the best guess of the value of the dollars held was steadily falling. Buying and selling, borrowing and lending still occurred in dollars. It was just that the buyers and sellers, borrowers and lenders each agreed to appraise their transactions on a shorter dollar yardstick.

This process of shifting consensus value is quite similar to what happens in other financial markets such as the stock market. A share of stock also is a yardstick. A share of Ajax

Widget Company has no intrinsic value, as the shareholders of any bankrupt company can tell you. That share is just a yardstick of the value of a fraction of the company. The day-to-day price of Ajax Widget Company's stock is determined by the same kind of betting as on the horse race. Each participant places his wager (buys or sells) at prices that he or she believes the stock is worth. The prevailing price in the stock market is the one that dominates the betting. In a sense it is the "odds on" favorite price, the one where the most wagers are laid. It is not the only price in the race, however; other people still have their "long shots." Those who disagree with the consensus can still place bets by, say, taking positions in the options or futures markets.

Suddenly, a rumor begins sweeping the market. There is going to be a costly government-ordered recall of all Ajax widgets produced in the last three years. Does the betting change? You bet it does. The smart money now shifts to a lower value of Ajax stock. The lower stock price becomes the "odds on" favorite of people both buying and selling. The market price takes a plunge.

Notice that the plunge is not caused by an increase (or expected increase) in the supply of Ajax stock shares. Nor is it that people are holding fewer shares. All shares are held both before and after the rumor. Neither is it that more or less of the stock is traded. Trading could very well be the same, rise or fall. Rather, the price change occurs because both buyers and sellers recognize that the net worth of the company has declined. The yardstick of the company's value shrinks. This shrinkage can occur without one share of stock ever changing hands.

Another source of information for bettors is market leaders such as Henry Kaufman. Kaufman is well respected. His opinion is given high weight by people active in the market. Think of him as a respected handicapper or tout of market betting. If Kaufman predicts high interest rates, then the expectations of a significant chunk of the market shift towards higher interest rates. With this shift in opinion, the market reacts. With or without a significant change in the level of market transactions, prices now reflect expectations of higher interest rates.

Kaufman's effect on the market is larger at some times than at others. This variance of response is not surprising. With prices in spot and future markets unhinged from any stable value, participants are likely to drift from one opinion leader to another, sampling who is likely to provide the best guide. Without a working system of information about the size of the yardstick, the market gropes for information. It is in a kind of "free fall," participants clutching to whatever information they can find in an attempt to orient themselves with respect to the dollar's value. The market, always searching for bits of relevant information, samples trade balance statistics, money supply statistics, unemployment statistics, Kaufman's projections, Greenspan's projections. Prices drift as the market samples. The unhinged prices become more volatile.

The path of interest rates in 1982 certainly reflected such volatility. On a discount basis, three-month Treasury bill rates were 11.1 percent at the end of December 1981. By the end of January 1982 they were up to 12.5 percent. They were 13.3 percent by the end of March. By the end of May they had declined to 11.5 percent. Month-end rates were back to 12.8 percent in June. Then came July. On July 20th Paul Volcker told the Senate Banking Committee that he was "hopeful" interest rates would fall in coming months. The Treasury's huge borrowing needs to finance record federal deficits, he felt, did not present "an insuperable obstacle to lower interest rates during this period."[5] On this new information, bond prices rallied, and short-term rates fell.

Two days later word leaked out that Henry Kaufman had toned down his bearish outlook for interest rates. Mr. Kaufman confirmed that he expected further declines in short-term rates. Bond prices continued to surge. According to the *Wall Street Journal*, "Bond dealers said trading volume accelerated sharply as word spread of Mr. Kaufman's latest pronouncement."[6] Treasury-bill yields declined to 10.2 percent by the end of July.

Another big drop occurred in August. On August 17, both Kaufman and another well-respected handicapper, Albert Wojnilower, issued revised forecasts that long-term rates would be lower in 1983. These two forecasters had issued such gloomy forecasts in the past that they had been nicknamed "the bad news bears" of Wall Street. But now they both were painting rosier pictures of lower interest rates. The financial markets took off. The stock market bounded almost 39 points that day. Bond prices soared. By the end of the month, Treasury-bill rates had declined to almost 8 percent.

The Cost of Unhinged Money

Compare the process of finding out about prices with and without a price rule. With appropriate price rules, there is certainty about today's dollar yardstick. The Fed is telling the market what the dollar is worth, and the market decides the number of dollars it will use. A price rule in forward markets gives the market certainty about the size and shape of tomorrow's dollar unit as well. People can make long-term contracts without fear of being short-changed by inflation or other volatilities. There is no ferreting of information, no guessing, no continual reevaluation of information. The transactions costs of dealing in dollars is low. The system for conveying information is efficient.

Without a price rule, the story is quite different. Those using dollars must continually update their information. And such information is not inexpensive. Witness, for example, the tremendous growth in the economic staffs of corporations and banks. Or count the number of private consulting firms and newsletters that have appeared in the last ten years, promising to help forecast interest or exchange rates. If anything, the decision to unhinge money could be labelled a full-employment act for economists.

Even these expensive services provide the client with only a (perhaps educated) guess. As a guess it is subject to being wrong almost as often as it is right. Monetary uncertainty becomes a fact of life. Long-term contracts become more difficult to plan. Some may choose to reduce longer-run uncertainty through futures contracts or other innovations. Futures contracts, however, are an insurance policy. When the risk rises, the underwriters naturally want increased compensation. There is no escape from the rising cost of long-term contracts. In short, the uncertainty or lack of information with unhinged money produces an inefficient system of guessing about the basic dollar unit, greatly raising the private markets' transactions costs of using dollars.

Guessing on the Other Side of the Market— What Is Money?

The added costs and uncertainties of the private market under a quantity rule are matched by added problems for the policy maker as well. The policy maker is supposed to know what constitutes money, how to measure it, and how to control its quantity. As has been repeatedly pointed out, these requirements are an impossible task. So the central banker instead chooses a proxy (such as M1 or M2) for this elusive quantity and tries to measure and constrain its growth.

But the proxy for money is not very good, and it cannot be controlled anyway. The result is that the central banker's proxy can send him some very distorted signals about what he should do. For example, in a situation such as Secretary Blumenthal's trying to "talk down" the dollar, the money supply may appear to do some very funny things. If his statement is believed, it is likely to trigger a flight from the dollar by both borrowers and lenders, buyers and sellers. The uncertainty over what will be the new value of the dollar, and when it will finally be reached, raises the cost or risk of dollar transactions for any participant in an economic deal who retains an open position. Even for those seeking the safety of a transaction covered by a sale or purchase of dollar futures, costs still rise as underwriters demand increased risk compensation.

These higher costs drive some parts of portfolios and transactions out of dollars and into more stable currencies. American individuals and corporations retain some foreign money in their portfolios for future use instead of converting it to dollars. Thus Treasury Secretary Blumenthal's injection of uncertainty into the dollar market in late 1977 set off a stampede for the more stable deutsche marks and Swiss francs. In turn the money supplies of those countries responded to the increased demands for their money with peaked growth rates in 1978. Money growth in Germany was only about 3 percent in 1976 and 1979. In 1978, however, it topped 13 percent. The Swiss money supply grew at less than 1 percent in 1977 and 1979. Yet in 1978 it grew by about 18 percent!

A monetarist watching for central-bank adherence to a strict quantity rule would have been horrified by what he saw happening in Switzerland. Here was a country with virtual price stability suddenly allowing the supply of Swiss francs to expand enormously. Certainly the country was headed for trouble!

Yet price stability continued to prevail throughout 1978 despite the explosion of money. The measured Swiss wholesale price index *declined* about 2 percent in 1978. Had the monetarist policy indicator failed? Yes. That explosion was not the National Bank of Switzerland drowning the country in a sea of liquidity. It was simply the supply of francs growing stroke for stroke with the world demand for them.

Watching the money supply can therefore mean targeting the wrong variables. The supply target can give signals that produce counterproductive policies. Would the central bank of Switzerland have made the situation better by trying to keep the world from having the Swiss francs it wanted? Should the Bank have reduced the supply of francs by making the Swiss franc less desirable? Would shifting the demand from francs have raised or lowered franc inflation? Proper policies need proper (and preferably direct) indices that give correct signals.

A relevant domestic example of this point occurred at the beginning of 1980. Early that year the economy began to plummet. The NBER currently says that the economy peaked in about January of that year. The descent from that peak was very steep. The real economy in the second quarter of 1980 is recorded as declining at an annual rate of about 10 percent. Real income for the whole year fell by nearly 0.4 percent.

Guess what happened to the money supply. The growth rate of money (M1) between September 1979 and the January 1980 peak in the economy was an annualized 5.1 percent. In the next four months (to May, the middle month of the second quarter), the money supply growth rate was a *negative* 2.2 percent. This slowdown in money growth followed by only a few months the Federal Reserve's dramatic announcement of a shift in policy indicators to money aggregates. The slowdown was viewed as a sign that the Fed was finally getting tough in its fight against inflation, even though inflation rates in the spring of 1980 continued to hover around 14 percent, and the monetary base continued to grow at an annual rate of over 6 percent.

So the Fed worshippers had reason, they thought, to pat the Fed on the back. At long last the Fed was getting the situation under control. They had the tiger by the tail!

Indeed, they had just the tail. The money supply can be likened to the tail of the body economic. But remember, the body wags the tail, not the other way round. And when the body picks up steam, it gets up and begins scampering down the road to recovery, taking the tail and the Fed right along! That is what happened in mid-1980. As the real economy began to recover, so did the money growth rates. Money growth averaged an annualized 2.4 percent in the first six months of 1980, when real economic activity fell by 2.1 percent. In the final six months, the economy rebounded by 1.5 percent, and money grew by 10.3 percent. The result was that the Fed watchers patted the Fed on the back as the economy slumped, and panicked when it recovered. This puzzling behavior occurred because the money supply numbers led to misleading conclusions.

10

Beyond Monetarism:
Which Price Rules?

IN THE LAST CHAPTER we left the Fed, eyes fixed on the monetary kite, sailing in circles on a sea of liquidity. We saw how that adventure has exacerbated the uncertainties and difficulties of economic life. It is now time to make some specific suggestions for getting the Fed out of the water and on the road to redemption. The access to that road is price rules. But which price rules? Price stability is a nice general concept, but precisely which prices do we most want to stabilize? And which price rules are most likely to stabilize those prices successfully?

A general principle of economics states that the most efficient way to solve problems is to solve them most directly.[1] Solving a problem directly requires first a complete and precise understanding of the problem. Usually this step involves discriminating between symptom and cause. We would all like to see the pressing economic problems rectified. But the apparently calamitous situation crying out for change may just be the symptom of a more fundamental problem.

We have seen how treating symptoms has created problems

in the money markets. Quite a few people today are upset over the fluctuations in the money supply accompanying our general economic turmoil. Yet as we have surveyed the problem over the last few chapters, the ups and downs in money growth have hardly seemed worth all the fuss. The relevant quantity of money expands and contracts with the ups and downs in the economy and inflation. It only reflects economic illness or well-being. It is not the problem. Hence it should not be the target of government policy. And even if causality were to run from money to prices, targeting money would be a very indirect way of achieving our true objective. The problem is price stability, and the aim of an efficient economic policy should be to correct this problem directly.

What the Fed should be concerned with, then, is stabilizing a family's grocery bill from week to week, or striving to assure that a family saving for a new car can replace it at a price similar to what it paid for the last one. Or perhaps if the Fed worked directly to ease fears of future inflation, interest rates and housing prices might fall to where the mortgage of the average family buying the average home once again would consume only about 25 percent of its monthly income.

Obviously, even with price stability as a direct target, the Fed has some choices to make. There are a lot of prices out there in the economy. Which ones should be targeted? All? A few? Just one? There are also many alternative ways of trying to stabilize prices. For instance, are wage and price controls the answer?

There are still quite a number of pitfalls ready to trap the unwary policy maker. Before the Fed goes rushing into the marketplace with brand-new ideas of how to solve the underlying economic problems, it had better make sure it knows precisely where each of the policies will lead. In other words, the Fed needs some criteria for choosing among policies.

We have already suggested one criterion; chapter 9 described how an efficient price rule should involve market prices that are continuously quoted so that the government knows when and by how much to intervene and the public knows if the government is "playing by the rules." This chapter will suggest some further guiding principles. We will see that the three prices that most concern people are the price of goods today, the price of goods tomorrow or some other time in the future, and the rate of interest on borrowing or lending money. We will also see that these three prices are specifically interrelated, so that once two of the prices are set, the value of the third is also set.

The policy implications of these facts are extremely enlightening and important. One is that a policy of a single price rule is likely not to achieve the goal of stabilizing all three prices. A policy, for instance, of intervening to stabilize the spot price of gold can stabilize the price of goods today. But it does little to stabilize directly either the price of goods in the future or interest rates. Instead, to achieve stability of all three prices a *combination* of policies is required. Intervention in the spot gold market would have to be combined with intervention to stabilize interest rates or forward gold prices. Those who advocate a return to a gold or other commodity standard must therefore carefully and explicitly include two interventions in their proposals. The same warning is true for those who advocate targeting interest rates instead. In fact, as we will see, a superior policy proposal could be created if these two groups merely joined forces.

The chapter then concludes with a specific proposal describing how the government could combine a targeted financial futures contract with an interest rate target to produce complete price stability. One innovative aspect of this proposal is that the government would not have to worry about storing or running out of a reserve commodity. The goal of price stability could therefore be achieved efficiently and effectively.

Zeroing In on the Right Price Rules

Just picking any handy price rule will not necessarily solve the problems of monetary stability. The right rule or set of rules has to be chosen to get the desired results. As an example, suppose the Fed decides tomorrow that it will adopt a price rule, but it chooses the policy at random. The Board of Governors might say to themselves, "All we have to do is stabilize a market price" and, surveying the marketplace, see a nice price that probably had been the target of policy in years past, the exchange rate. They might decide that this is a price they can probably control and quickly draw up directives and operating instructions to put the central bank back in the fixed exchange rate business.

The Governors will think they have scored a coup. They have the central bank directly targeting a continuously quoted market price, just as the newly found policy suggests. They sit back to wait for inflation and high interest rates to disappear.

In all probability they will be terribly disappointed. Pegging the exchange rate does eliminate some uncertainties, so inflation and interest rates might possibly come down a bit. But it is unlikely that inflation and inflationary expectations would disappear completely. The reason? The policy has done nothing to define and stabilize the absolute size of the domestic yardstick now or in the future.

What *has* the fixed exchange rate done? It has simply tied the dollar yardstick either to one foreign yardstick or to a basket (weighted average) of foreign yardsticks. As the foreign yard-stick lengthens, so does the dollar one. If the foreign yardstick shrinks, however, the dollar is tied to the same fate. In other words, the fixed exchange rate is good for stabilizing relative purchasing power and inflation across countries. But by itself, it does little, if anything, to stabilize the absolute domestic purchasing power.[2]

On the surface the results are paradoxical and confusing. The policy makers have used the concept of a price rule, yet they have shot wide of their target. They have followed what they thought was the correct type of policy, but they have not achieved their desired results. The problem, however, is not price rules, but an imprecise application of the rules. The target is not just any prices in general, but domestic prices in particular. To get domestic prices stable requires a policy that deals with this problem directly.

Even knowing that domestic purchasing power is the target may not tell the policy makers all they needs to know. Again they are faced with several possible policies. They could, for example, choose to deal with the worries of the family budget. They could try to keep the average price of the family's grocery bill stable from day to day by targeting the dollar price of basic commodities people buy. Stability of daily prices would cer-tainly be appreciated by the Smiths of Main Street, USA. So the policy makers might target the spot price of gold, silver, wheat, or any other individual commodity traded in financial markets and stand ready to buy or sell these at some promised price. Alternatively, they could choose a combination (basket) of these commodities and aim to stabilize their combined price.

But the Smiths appreciate stable prices over longer horizons as well. Their family may be saving for a new van. They fear, however, that by the time they have saved enough to buy a van at today's price, tomorrow's price will be much higher. They worry not only about the cost of groceries today but about the cost of everything in the future as well. The policy makers might therefore choose to stabilize tomorrow's prices instead. They could do that by issuing government agreements to buy or sell the same gold, silver, wheat, corn, and so on (or a combination of commodities) at a specified price, but in this case at a later date—say, a year from now. Sufficient commitment to this forward price policy would remove the uncertainty about what the Smiths would have to pay for things next year.

The Smiths might also be complaining to their Congressman about the sting of high and volatile interest rates. Maybe the reason the family is saving for a van, instead of buying it on installment now, is that high interest rates make the monthly payments prohibitive. The policy makers might want to do something about that problem. Perhaps they will order the central bank to attack the interest rate problem directly by buying and selling bonds at a constant interest rate.

But why are interest rates high to begin with? Obviously the high rates reflect expected inflation. But what does the expected inflation in turn represent? It implies that the market expects the value of the basic dollar unit to depreciate over time. In other words, the market expects prices tomorrow to be higher than prices today. So the movement in interest rates reflects changing expectations about the relationship between the other two prices the policy makers might target.

In listing in this way the various possibilities for implementing price rules, the policy makers have begun to zero in on the most important price rules. They have also just discovered an important fact about the prices they want to see stabilized: they are interrelated. Today's prices, tomorrow's prices, and the interest rate do not diverge in three separate directions. There is an overall relationship among the three that keeps them moving together. As tomorrow's prices rise, for example, chances are either today's prices or the interest rate also rise.

The Relationship Among Prices

Understanding better the relationship among these three prices is the key for choosing the appropriate combination of price rules. Spot prices reflect what the market thinks the basic dollar unit buys today. Stable spot prices reflect expected stability in the amount of corn, wheat, strawberries, or light bulbs a dollar will buy. Rising prices, however, mean that the market thinks the dollar yardstick is shrinking at this time. Each dollar buys less than before. The market believes that the dollar is depreciating in the spot market.

Prices in the forward market reflect the market's best guess about what the yardstick will be in the future. These prices are, of course, free to move independently of spot prices. Spot prices could be stable or falling (a larger spot yardstick) while forward prices reflect the belief that the future dollar is likely to be worth much less than today.

The interest rate reflects the market's best guess of the rate of shrinkage between the spot and forward yardsticks. More precisely, the higher the interest rate, the more the forward yardstick is expected to shrink relative to the spot yardstick. If the dollar unit is expected to be stable in value over time, the average forward price will be the same as the spot. Interest rates will be low, reflecting only the "real" (marginal time preference) cost of borrowing and lending. High interest rates, on the other hand, reflect the market's belief that bonds (forward yardsticks) are expected to be worth fewer commodities when they mature.

As the description suggests, the simultaneous relationship among these three relevant market prices means that only two can move independently at once. The three prices can be visualized as three sides of a triangle.[3] If the length and position of any two sides are known, the connecting third side can be immediately drawn. If the market expects today's yardstick to be longer (spot deflation), but tomorrow's yardstick to be shorter (inflation), the connecting third price must behave consistently. Interest rates (along with forward market prices) must rise. Alternatively, if both spot and forward dollars are expected to depreciate to the same degree, spot and forward commodity prices should rise by the same percentage. But since spot prices have not changed relative to forward prices, interest rates should be unchanged.[4]

The policy makers could choose to focus on any of these three prices. If the policy makers target today's prices and stabilize them, the spot price level becomes a constant. Expected inflation then varies positively with the expected level of future prices. The higher prices are expected to be tomorrow, the more the yardstick is expected to decline over time and the higher expected inflation. In turn, lenders will want to be compensated for this expected depreciation, so market interest rates also rise.[5]

Alternatively, if the policy makers target and stabilize tomorrow's prices, then the forward price level becomes a constant. Regardless of prices today, we know what prices will be tomorrow. Expected inflation under this scenario is inversely related to today's price level. If prices today rise above the stabilized forward prices, prices will have to fall over time. If today's prices are below tomorrow's, prices will be rising. The necessary rate of change in prices to the fixed forward level in turn dictates what must happen to market interest rates in the interim.

The third possibility is for the policy makers to target market interest rates. Stable interest rates, given any real interest rate, imply a certain expected rate of inflation. In other words, this policy defines a specific relationship between today's prices and tomorrow's. For example, if long-term interest rates are pegged at historical levels of real rates, there should be no inflation over time. The forward price level should be exactly the same as today's. If today's price level should rise in a sudden burst of spot inflation, the forward price level will move right along. Alternatively, if the government should suddenly announce its intention of pegging the spot value of money at a higher value, both today's and tomorrow's price levels should fall in unison.

So the three relevant prices are interrelated and determined simultaneously. That relationship also means that in order for all three prices to be stabilized, only two have to be targeted. For instance, if the government were to undertake policies to stabilize simultaneously the spot and future value of money at the same level, inflationary expectations would disappear. In turn this implies that inflationary premiums in interest rates would disappear, and market rates would return to their traditionally lower levels. Or if the government chose to stabilize today's value of money and simultaneously target interest rates at low levels, expectations of a forward value of money close to today's would be generated simultaneously.

Investigating the relationship among the government's three possible policies has provided an important new insight. A policy limited to targeting only one price is probably not optimal. Target one price, and you get one stable price. Target the right two prices, however, and you get complete price stability.

This insight illustrates why a return to a simple spot gold standard is not likely by itself to be the panacea some proponents claim. A simple gold standard is a spot price rule. It attempts to stabilize today's price level in terms of gold. Without an additional price rule, however, it does little, if anything, to stabilize either the forward price level or interest rates. Inflation in the near term may fall, but we have no guarantee of what the price level or inflation will be in the longer run. Interest rates are likely to remain high.

Not only is it important to pick the proper price rule, therefore; it is also important to pick the proper *combination* of price rules. Stability of all three prices requires at least two rules. We will now turn our attention to details of how the Fed might carry out each of the three possible price rules.

Option One: A Spot Price Rule

One part of the solution to today's monetary problems could be a spot price rule. This policy aims to do something about the rate at which today's prices are rising. Its goal is to stop the immediate shrinkage in the value of money: make sure that the Smiths' paychecks go as far in the grocery store this week as last. Make this week's increase in the wage bill of small businesses tied to productivity, not simply to inflation.

With the obvious political advantages in these goals, it is not surprising that two competing proposals for stabilizing spot prices have received extensive attention in recent years. One is wage-and-price controls, and the other is the gold standard. In principle these two options are designed to do the same thing, though they go about it in very different ways. Both are intended to eliminate the horrendous symptoms of inflation. Wage-and-price controls are attempts to accomplish this goal by administrative fiat. The gold standard, on the other hand, works to stabilize the basic dollar unit through government intervention in an organized commodity market.

On the surface, wage-and-price controls appear to be a legitimate weapon in the policy makers' arsenal. After all, if we have identified rising prices as the problem with which we must deal directly, price controls appear to do that. Price controls, however, have problems of their own. In fact, they point out an important corollary to the principle of dealing with the underlying problem directly. When faced with more than one apparent direct solution to the problem, one of the solutions is likely to be more efficient than the others.

A major problem with wage-and-price controls is the absence of a market mechanism through which to apply them. The policy therefore runs into the same kind of information problems as the quantity rule. If prices are to be administered, on the one hand the market must know what each administered price is going to be, and on the other hand the government must know whether the administered prices are being adhered to. Both sides of the policy need extensive information. Yet there is no convenient market mechanism through which these streams of information can flow. The government is forced into the business of creating channels for this information. In most cases the government simply issues a dictum declaring what prices will be and hopes that the information in the dictum will reach all the participants in the marketplace. The government is often forced to create a new bureaucracy and hire an army of monitors to gather information about how well market participants are complying with the dictum and to punish the miscreants.

However noble the aims of this army of monitors, the chances are that it cannot keep tabs on each and every transaction. Experience tells us that the inability to police each transaction efficiently creates many incentives and opportunities to cheat. Buyers and sellers work out private deals, outside the view of the monitors, that effectively allow prices to rise. The more easily these transactions can slip by the monitors, the more transactions escape controls. Shelves in the marketplace may become barren, while nonmarket activity flourishes. The policy to control prices eventually becomes too ineffective and/or too costly to monitor. In either case, the policy is eventually abandoned.

The tendency for wage-and-price controls to fail highlights a second, and related, problem. Although wage-and-price controls are targeted towards rising prices, they are dealing with symptoms rather than curing problems. They are an administrative attempt to prevent the value of money from depreciating, but they fail to deal with the causes of that depreciation. As we saw in chapter 9, the depreciation of money reflects the market's belief that the government will not stand by the current yardstick. The government is willing to allow that yardstick to shrink.

What do wage-and-price controls do to alleviate this fear of the marketplace? Nothing. The controls do nothing to indicate an increased government commitment to the yardstick. Rather, the government's new commitment is more perverse. Despite the fact that the market believes the size of the dollar yardstick is shrinking, the government is trying to force the market to continue to use an old yardstick. The effect is as though the government were trying to delude the market. Unless the yardstick is stabilized, the desired behavior will not appear to be in the interests of most people.

A workable policy must use market mechanisms to try to stabilize the domestic yardstick of value. Hence the support for a gold standard. The gold standard is designed to stabilize the current value of the dollar in terms of the commodity gold. If the government's policy defines a dollar unit as 1/35 of an ounce of gold ($35 per ounce), then as long as the policy is effective, the market knows that the yardstick today is stable. Simultaneously, the gold standard uses the marketplace to stabilize the value of money. The Fed's charge is to step into the market whenever the value of Fed liabilities deviates from 1/35 ounce of gold per dollar. The government then buys or sells gold in exchange for dollars until the 1/35 ounce value is restored.

Because the government uses the marketplace, there is a direct channel through which information flows from one side of the market to the other. The channel is the financial market for gold. Both the government and the private sector watch the financial ticker tape or quote screen for quotes from the gold market. By watching the screen, the government knows whether market consensus about the dollar's gold value is changing. If it does change, the government knows to intervene. By watching the screen, the private sector knows if the government is standing behind its commitment. If the dollar price of gold changes, is the government there in the market to bring the price back? If so, the yardstick is stable.

The gold standard therefore fulfills the criterion of stabilizing the yardstick directly through the marketplace. The dollar price of gold should be stable. The remaining question, however, is, does a stable gold price imply in turn price stability for the other things people buy? Should the dollar be stabilized in terms of just one commodity, or should the government's target instead be some combination or basket of commodities?

Spot Gold Versus a Spot Commodity Basket

Ideally the government should set its monetary sights on a representative basket of things that people buy. The basket should reflect the price of houses, automobiles, tomatoes, cucumbers, meats, haircuts, vacations, and so on that the "average" consumer purchases. Stabilizing the value of this basket should presumably stabilize prices that the average consumer faces. Such a policy should produce behavior very close to ideal price stability.

So why not adopt this policy tomorrow? The first problem is to identify the representative basket. Theoretically the consumer price index reflects what the average consumer purchases. It is a weighted average of goods purchased by the "typical" family, as determined by consumer surveys. One possible policy might be to try to stabilize this index. Yet this index produces a second problem, time delay. The consumer price index reflects data collected by monitors during one month, then computed and reported the following month. In other words, the numbers reported today reflect what was happening last month. The government would be acting on very stale information if it formulated its latest monetary policy based on the most recent CPI.[6]

The problem here, as with wage and price controls, is a lack of a market for channeling information. Again the data are gathered by a bureaucracy. Both sides of the policy are therefore left guessing for some time about what the other is doing. The government does not know how the market is thinking or acting about prices in general until the monitors collect the data. The market has no formal information about government policy until the data are reported. There is room for distrust and guessing on both sides. Effectively stabilizing prices is made very difficult.

We return to the conclusion that whatever policy is chosen should involve information readily available through well-organized markets. Such markets tend to be markets for basic commodities—gold, silver, corn, wheat, oil, and so on. The question then comes back to whether just one commodity or a group of these commodities should be stabilized.

Which Price Rules?

Historically governments have tended to stabilize their yardsticks in terms of one or two commodities, usually gold or silver. Stabilizing money in terms of one commodity is an easier policy to follow than trying to target a basket. The government has to keep track of the market price of just one thing. Similarly the private market need watch only one price on the ticker tape. The government need only intervene to keep that one price stable. The private market need only be assured that the government is intervening to stabilize that one price. Implementation and verification of the policy are nice and easy.

The drawback is that stabilizing the dollar price of one commodity may not effectively stabilize prices in general. Certainly if the price of, say, gold is constant in terms of the prices of other commodities like oil, vegetables, and housing, then stabilizing the dollar price of gold stabilizes the dollar price of other commodities as well. But the relative prices between gold and other commodities (the terms of trade) are not always constant. They often fluctuate from day to day. Attempts to stabilize the dollar price of gold may therefore be associated with rising or falling dollar prices of other commodities. The policy unfortunately cannot guarantee to keep the dollar price of corn or aluminum from changing. While fluctuations in overall prices are quite likely to be significantly less than they are today, a gold standard cannot therefore guarantee overall price stability.

In contrast, the broader the range of commodities targeted for price stability, the more stable the overall or average prices will be. Choosing the alternative of a basket of commodities brings monetary policy closer to the goal of stabilizing the purchasing power of the average individual.

Yet problems again crop up concerning the relative price of the commodities, or terms of trade. The broad range of commodities would have to be defined. It would involve, for example, so many bushels of corn and wheat, ounces of gold and silver, board feet of plywood, and so on. The precise relationship implies a certain relative price among these commodities. If, say, the relative price of wheat and plywood changes because of market supply and demand conditions, the relationship among the commodities in the basket is upset. Dollar prices of some commodities fall, while others rise. A stable basket price does not mean that the dollar price of each individual commodity is stable.[7]

The terms-of-trade problem also points out a potential political drawback of a commodity basket. Such an index would be constructed by giving each commodity a weight towards the value of the overall basket. What would happen if there were significant pressure for the dollar price of the index to rise, or if demand suddenly shifted towards a few of the commodities, significantly altering their relative price? Quite likely, political pressure would build to change the construct of the index. Politicians would want to lower the weights or exclude commodities whose relative prices were rising most. On the surface, this alteration would make government policy appear more successful. To the market, however, it would make government policy less dependable and believable. The greater the chance that such a shift in weights could occur, the more difficult it would be to gain price stability.

In sum, spot price stability means minimizing the variation of consumer prices. A one-commodity target such as gold is not ideal because it does not minimize variation of all prices. Hence, the policy should ideally target all commodities people consume. However, constructing such an index encounters problems like the weighting scheme, terms-of-trade changes, and political tampering. The decision of gold versus an index therefore involves a trade-off between assuring minimum price variation and the problems of computing the index.

The Limitations of a Spot Price Rule

Whether a single commodity standard such as gold or a commodity index approach is used, it is still important to recognize that this policy is not sufficient by itself to produce complete price stability. Two prices must be stabilized, either today's and tomorrow's prices, or one price level and the market interest rate. Any commodity standard is only one price rule and at most can stabilize only one price. So while a gold standard might reduce inflation or bring down interest rates, it cannot do both simultaneously. The simple spot gold standard by itself is not the panacea for all monetary ills. Claims that the spot gold standard is a magical cure-all are likely to lead to dashed expectations and to increase the probability that policy makers will turn away from price rules rather than pursue a complete price-rule package that could yield more complete monetary stability.

Some policy makers might counter that, while a spot gold standard is not enough, all that is needed is a gold standard plus government credibility. If the private market knows that the Fed is not only committed to pegging the dollar price of gold today but is determined to do anything necessary to maintain that relationship thirty years from now, both spot and forward prices will be stabilized and interest rates will fall. In a sense this argument is correct. But remember the adage about not watching the mouths of policy makers, but their feet instead. It is one thing for the Fed to *say* it will maintain the spot price of gold over time. It is quite another thing for the Fed to intervene actively in both the spot *and* the forward markets to maintain the targeted price. In the first case we have to take the Fed's word. In the second case we actually observe the Fed backing its future commitment. In a sense the second (forward) price rule provides a mechanism for creating the desired government credibility.

The historical experience of the links between the dollar and gold certainly supports this important point. A formal link between the dollar and gold has been associated with stable average prices, but it has had no discernable pattern of effects on dollar interest rates. The U.S. dollar was tied to gold from April 1792, when a bimetallic standard was adopted, until March 1933, when an embargo was imposed on gold and convertibility was suspended permanently. There were, of course, periodic interruptions in convertibility associated with wars. Redemption of the dollar in gold was suspended from 1861 to 1879, the famous "greenback" period, when the U.S. government first paid its Civil War debts in paper currency and later retired those notes. Convertibility was also suspended from September 1917 to June 1919, when the United States incurred large debts associated with its involvement in the First World War. Yet despite these temporary interruptions in convertibility, the official dollar price of gold was constant during much of the period. In 1792 the official price was $19.39. It rose to $20.69 in 1834 and then declined marginally to $20.67 in 1837, remaining at $20.67 until 1933.

Inflation was quite moderate during these 140 years (figure 10–1). Naturally, the war years (War of 1812, Civil War, First World War) were associated with high rates of inflation. Typically, however, wars were followed by periods of negative inflation as convertibility was restored. During the nonwar years, inflation did not occur in sustained spurts. It is difficult to find three consecutive years in which inflation exceeded five percent. Such a record would be welcomed by today's inflation-weary consumers and policy makers. Furthermore, the years of inflation were offset by years when prices fell. The 140-year period as a whole was one of virtual price stability. The pro-

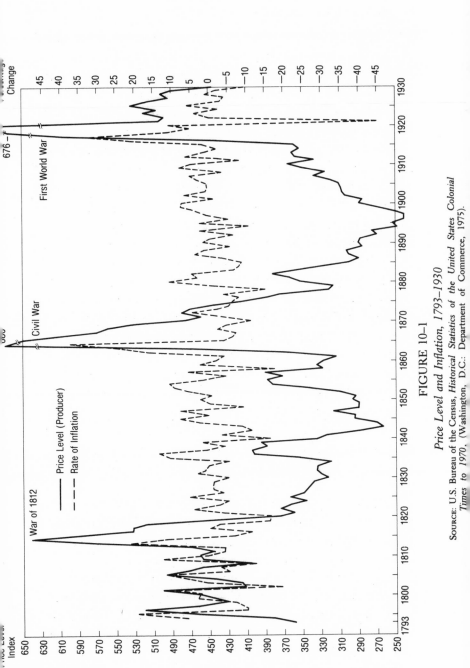

FIGURE 10–1

Price Level and Inflation, 1793–1930

Source: U.S. Bureau of the Census, *Historical Statistics of the United States Colonial Times to 1970*, (Washington, D.C.: Department of Commerce, 1975).

ducer price index in 1933 was 5.4 percent less than it had been in 1793. That represents an average annual price change of less than four one-hundreds of one percent.[8]

While the gold standard, as expected, produced relative stability in the spot price level, its record on interest rates was quite different. There is no discernable relationship between convertibility and the interest rate for either short-term commercial paper (figure 10–2) or long-term bonds (figure 10–3). The only long-term trend is a decline in interest rates until the 1950s, probably as capital markets became more developed. In fact, of the four occasions when the United States returned to convertibility (figure 10–4), long-term interest rates went up during one and interest rates went down during another. Overall, however, interest rates changed very little.[9]

The option of stabilizing the spot price level is therefore a useful one. History shows that it can lead to low, stable rates of inflation. It is a policy designed to moderate gyrations in the spot price market, and it can achieve that goal. It is of questionable use by itself, however, for attaining other price goals.

Option Two: A Future Price Rule

The alternative to worrying about the spot price level is to worry about prices in the future. How much will the van cost when the Smiths have finally saved at least enough for a sizable down payment? The policy's goal is to target prices that will exist some time in the future, say a year from now. Bring stability back into consumers' decision making by letting them know what they should expect to pay for items they want a year from now.

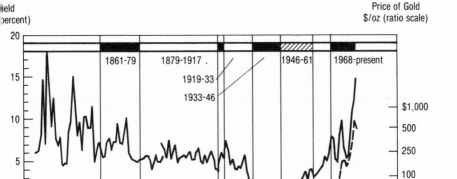

FIGURE 10–2

U.S. Interest Rates and the Gold Standard: Commercial Paper

NOTE: Printed with permission from an unpublished presentation of H. C. Wainwright & Co., Economics.

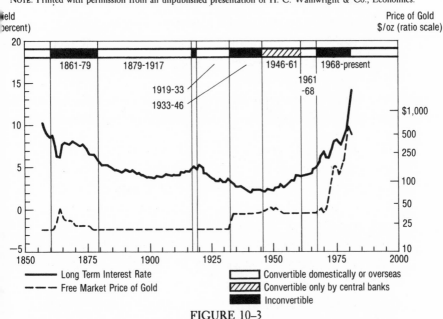

FIGURE 10–3

U.S. Interest Rates and the Gold Standard: Yields on Railroad and Treasury Bonds

NOTE: Printed with permission from an unpublished presentation of H. C. Wainwright & Co., Economics.

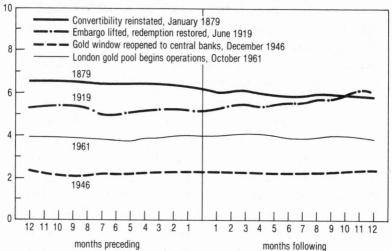

FIGURE 10–4

U.S. Interest Rates and the Restoration of Convertibility: Bond Yields

SOURCES: 1879 and 1919, U.S. Railroad Bonds (Macaulay, 1938); for 1946 and 1961, U.S. Government Long-Term Bonds (Washington, D.C.: Federal Reserve Board).

NOTE: Printed with permission from an unpublished presentation of H. C. Wainwright & Co., Economics.

Notice that this future price policy is not necessarily tied to a spot price policy. The government could, for example, undertake a policy of promising what the price of oil will be in a year. The government simply buys or sells commitments to supply oil at a specified price one year from the date of transaction. If these commitments are freely traded on commodity markets, the government's policy is quite clear. Simply keep the price at which these commitments change hands constant. If the market thinks that oil is worth more dollars than the government is selling it for, the market price of the contracts will rise. The government policy makers, noting this price rise on the ticker tape or quote screen, step in and sell more contracts at the stated price. Alternatively, if the contract price should dip below the commitment level, the policy makers know to buy back enough contracts to return the price to the desired level.

The policy makers do not watch the spot price. It may be

above, below, or equal to the commitment price one year ahead. The spot price is free to vary as the market wishes. Naturally, however, the year-ahead commitment price, minus carrying costs (interest rate), will equal the spot price. But since only the year-ahead price is stabilized by the policy, this relationship simply means that the spot price and interest rate will fluctuate inversely with each other. The policy only stabilizes one price. To stabilize more prices requires more price rules.

This future price level policy, then, is very similar to a spot price level policy. The only major difference is the precise temporal market stabilized. This policy therefore is subject to the same questions and options as the spot policy. Should the price of one commodity alone be stabilized, or should the government target the price of a weighted basket of commodities? If a basket is used, which commodities are included, and what should be their individual weights in the basket? Again, the government is faced with the problem that it is easier to target only one price, but targeting a basket produces something closer to the desired overall price stability.

Option Three: An Interest-Rate Rule

The third possibility is not to stabilize either the spot or the future price level, but rather the expected changes between the two. This relationship, of course, is reflected in the interest rate. Changes in the market interest rate reflect changes in the market's expectations about how much forward prices will rise (how much the dollar will depreciate in value) relative to the spot prices. Higher interest rates reflect a bearish outlook about the forward prices relative to today's. Low interest rates reflect a market belief that the prices will be relatively stable over time.

How does the government influence the level of interest rates? By buying and selling bonds through open market operations. It is a well-known fact that bond prices and interest rates move inversely. High interest rates can therefore be alternatively described as low bond prices. The government can raise the price of bonds and lower interest rates by simply agreeing to redeem bonds at a higher price.

The mechanism for such redemption is already well established. The Federal Reserve is currently engaged in open market purchases and sales of bonds in an attempt to control money growth. Under an interest-rate rule, the Fed would continue to engage in these open market activities, but instead of trying to stabilize the quantity of money, the policy would be geared towards a stable interest rate. The Fed would agree to buy or sell as many bonds as the public wanted at the stabilized rate of interest.

If the Fed is following such a policy, and interest rates suddenly begin to rise, the Fed must immediately step into the bond market. Higher interest rates reflect an increased gloom about the the value of future dollars (bonds) relative to today's dollars. The Fed reacts by buying back some of the future dollars outstanding (open market purchase). Bond prices rise again, interest rates fall. The tendency for bond prices to deviate from the established price is eliminated. Interest rates return to the target level.

Of course, in performing this stabilization policy, the government has changed the composition of its debt. The quantity of bonds has been decreased, and the quantity of short-term, liquid debt (money) has increased. Thus, while the policy may stabilize spot relative to forward prices, the increased short-term debt may reduce the probability that the government can redeem its short-term debt at the prevailing price. Increased spot inflation may ensue. Stabilizing interest rates only evens out the value of the dollar (and inflation) over time; it does not stabilize the absolute value of either the spot or the forward dollar.

Two Congressional Proposals

Having listed the policies required for complete price stability, it is interesting to use them to evaluate two monetary proposals introduced in Congress in 1982. One, the Balanced Monetary Policy Act of 1982, was introduced by Senate Minority Leader Robert Byrd and a number of his Democratic colleagues. The second, the Balanced Monetary Policy and Price Stability Act, was introduced in the House of Representatives by Republicans Jack Kemp and Trent Lott. The two bills appeared to have one thing in common: both would direct the Federal Reserve to stop targeting monetary aggregates alone and instead to use interest rates or other prices as a target.

The Democratic Proposal

The Democratic proposal wanted Fed policy to aim at keeping market interest rates one to four percentage points above the rate of inflation. The proposal targeted interest rates, but it was not really a price rule. It did not attempt to keep market interest rates stable. The plan did nothing to guarantee an end to double-digit interest rates. Interest rates are tied to the rate of inflation, yet there was no policy to keep inflation rates down. As inflation moved beyond 6 percent, market interest rates, under this proposal, would again break through the double-digit level. No aspect of this proposal was designed to ensure a more stable price level. The proposal simply tied the market rate of interest to another volatile number, leaving interest rates free to fluctuate widely.

What the proposal really intended to target was the *real* rate of interest. The real rate is theoretically equal to the market rate minus the *expected* rate of inflation. In fact, no one can say that they have ever accurately measured the real interest rate, since there are no accurate measures of the inflation rate that people expect over the maturity of the credit agreement. What is often substituted for expected inflation by those who claim to estimate the real rate is some measure of the current inflation rate. From the perspective of economic theory, such an estimate makes little sense.

Furthermore, the measure of current inflation to which interest rates would be tied was derived from an index, not a market price. Presumably the Fed's hand would be forced by the monthly producers' price index. As mentioned earlier, this index is known to have seasonality problems and statistical limitations, making the precise market rate-of-interest target difficult to determine. In addition, since the index is monitored only once a month, neither the government nor the public has up-to-date information on what the inflation rate is, or what interest rate policy should be. Presumably this policy would change suddenly each month as the inflation rate for the *previous* month was announced. The suddenness of change would create volatility as well as new profit opportunities for those with advance information about the index.

Perhaps even more fundamentally, this proposal missed the whole meaning of Federal Reserve policy. The Fed is a monetary institution, employing monetary instruments and generating monetary effects such as a high expected rate of inflation. It is therefore the inflation premium in the market rate, not the real rate, which should be part of the Fed's target.

In sum, this plan suffered from the same shortcomings as

wage-and-price controls. On the surface it appeared to stabilize prices, but it did nothing to solve the rumblings just below. In this case, since the interest rate was tied to the mercurial price level, the two would likely erupt together.

The Kemp-Lott Proposal

The Kemp-Lott proposal also retained the ill-defined target of maintaining real interest rates at "historical levels." Where this proposal surpassed its Democratic counterpart, however, was by subordinating the interest-rate target to the overriding objective of achieving price stability. Price stability would be measured by an index of current market commodity prices, either the Bureau of Labor Statistics' spot commodity index or the Commodity Research Bureau's wholesale price index. If the interest rate and price stability targets ever conflicted, price stability would take precedence.

The commitment to target price stability was a clear departure from prevailing policies. This emphasis on price stability was also clearly consistent with Representative Kemp's previous widely known support of a gold standard. In addition, the proposal broke new ground by suggesting that price stability and interest-rate stability are linked. Unfortunately, the proposal was not designed to achieve stability in both.

The triangle analogy suggests that stability of spot prices, forward prices, and interest rates requires two price rule policies. The Kemp-Lott proposal really only had one, to stabilize commodity prices. Having the Fed perform open market sales of bonds when spot commodity prices rise, and purchase bonds as prices fall, could certainly help to stabilize spot prices in the economy. But that policy by itself could not guard against jumps in forward prices and market interest rates. A second side of the policy triangle had to be introduced before the complete object could take form.

The Kemp-Lott bill therefore correctly worried about what to do if its targets of price and interest-rate stability conflicted. With only one policy instrument, the two targets could conflict. The important message to Kemp, Lott, and the entire Congress, however, is that the two policies do not *have* to conflict. Those who want stable prices do not have to be at odds with those who want stable interest rates. To the contrary, these are two compatible policies that dovetail into a superior policy. One price rule could keep spot prices constant. A second price rule could target the market rate of interest. Together they would simultaneously stabilize forward prices as well.

For example, suppose that in addition to buying or selling bonds to stabilize market interest rates, the Fed chose to buy or sell either a basket of commodities or gold to stabilize spot prices. Some worry that exchanging money for bonds, in order to bid up bond prices and make interest rates fall, could make inflation worse. If the interest rate policy were carried out in isolation, such fears could be justified. But where the interest rate price rule is accompanied by a spot price rule, there is no need to worry. The second policy keeps the value of money stable. The government is simultaneously acting to keep money's value anchored to gold or other commodities. In fact, by simultaneously stabilizing the commodity value of money and stabilizing claims to future dollars, the government in effect is also stabilizing the commodity value of bonds.

Designing a Workable Policy for Full Price Stability

The various options for attaining price stability create a Chinese restaurant menu of policy alternatives. There are three columns of policies to choose from: spot prices, future prices, and interest rates. In each column are numerous alternatives, such as a gold standard, a silver standard, various combinations of tradable commodities, short-term interest rates, or long-term rates. Successful price stability requires picking one alternative from each of two different columns. Which ones should be chosen?

There seems to be a natural inclination to pick one of the alternatives for spot prices. People tend to be concerned foremost with what goods cost today. They would like to see those costs come down, or at least stabilize, so discussions quickly migrate to a policy which can assure such stability most directly. The policy may involve the government stabilizing the value of money in terms of gold or some basket of commodities. Whichever is chosen, it is usually agreed that the government must hold some stocks of the target commodities to buy and sell them as the market dictates.

Holding stocks of commodities immediately presents two problems. First, these commodities must be stored somewhere safe. In the case of gold, Fort Knox or the vaults of the Federal Reserve Bank of New York will do quite well. In the case of commodities, some place must be found that minimizes not only the chance of theft but also the amount of corrosion or rotting. Plans must also be made for getting the commodity to and from its storage location. Storage and transportation costs are involved.

Second, with the government holding limited stocks of the target commodity or commodities, there is always the chance that the government reserves may become depleted. Certainly, as the fact that supplies are running low becomes known to the public through the required published reserve figures, people in the market will sense that the government's ability to maintain the value of money is faltering. Pressure will build on the dollar's value, increasing the chances supplies will run out.

Certainly any proposal for a spot price rule will have to detail what the central bank must do as reserves are diminished or increased.[10]

Critics often seize upon these problems as evidence that a spot commodity standard cannot work. They claim, for example, that a basket target is unmanageable, and when reserves of a single target commodity become low, central banks will simply walk away from their commitment. Would it not be nice, therefore, to come up with an alternative proposal that is largely immune to these criticisms?

A Proposal

The following proposal describes a price rule policy that is not only immune to such criticisms but fulfills the criteria for stable prices now and in the future. In this proposal, the central bank stays completely out of the spot market in attaining its two price rules. Instead, it concentrates its efforts on interest rates and forward prices.

In the bond market, the Fed works to stabilize the yield on long-term (twenty-to thirty-year) bonds. The Fed picks an appropriate long-term rate, say 3.5 or 4 percent, and intervenes to prevent interest rates from deviating more than, say, 25 basis points on either side of the target. If the rate of interest should start to rise, the Fed instructs its bond traders to buy up supplies of these bonds. If rates fall, the Fed must be there with more bonds for the market. The amount bought or sold is not predetermined. The Fed just continues its actions until interest rates are again within the target band.

In the futures market, the Fed agrees to keep the value of

the dollar one year out (or two years, or both) stable. The dollar's value should therefore be pegged to commodities deliverable in one year. If, for instance, the Fed wanted to peg the dollar to the future price of gold at, say, $400 per ounce, it could buy and sell forward contracts to assure that gold one year from now will be delivered at $400 per ounce.[11] If the forward price of gold begins to rise, the Fed steps in to sell forward contracts for delivery. If the price starts to fall, it buys back forward contracts instead. Just as the Fed can establish a price rule in the spot market by buying and selling gold, it can establish a price rule in the forward market by buying and selling promises of future gold deliveries.

The Fed, of course, does not have to choose gold as the target commodity. It could choose any commodity traded in forward markets. It could also choose to target some combination of these commodities. It would then buy and sell contracts for these commodities in order to keep the price of the weighted average or basket stable.

As described so far, the Fed's commodity intervention does not really differ from more conventional schemes. The timing of the intervention differs, involving forward instead of spot delivery, but little else does. As in the conventional spot intervention, the government is still theoretically holding stocks of the commodities used in the intervention. The proposal, therefore, is still subject to the same criticisms concerning storage costs and the possibility of running out of reserves.

One way to get around the reserve problems is to depart from traditional price-rule systems by incorporating a recent financial market innovation, the index futures contract. In this form of trading, traders buy and sell contracts promising to deliver the value of an index on a certain date, say the following September 30. Trading in index futures began in March, 1982, with stock market indices. The first trading was on the

Kansas City Exchange, involving the Value Line index of stocks. Similar trading began later that year on the Chicago Mercantile Exchange and on the New York Futures Exchange, involving the Standard and Poor's, the New York Stock Exchange, and other indices.

The truly innovative part of this new contract is the method of payment. In the past, if you held a futures contract of a commodity—say, potatoes—until it became due, you could end up with a car load of potatoes on your front lawn. A delivery contract meant just that. You got physical delivery of whatever commodity you bought.[12] But when the Value Line index contract becomes due, you do not physically receive shares of all the stocks in the index. Instead you receive the cash equivalent of the index on the settlement day. At that point you have the alternative of either buying all those shares of stock or keeping the cash.

This concept of futures contracts payable in cash has spread to other financial markets. Eurodollar contracts on the International Monetary Market in Chicago are also payable in cash.[13] The Treasury-bill contracts on the Mid-American Exchange are, too. Additional contracts are likely to appear.

One potential new contract could be used by the Fed to stabilize forward prices. This contract would involve a composite price of a basket of traded commodities. As do all other futures contracts, this one would promise to deliver a certain standardized item at a certain place at a certain time. The standardized item would be the cash equivalent of a predetermined weighted average of commodity prices. If a contract fell due for delivery on September 30, the settlement price would be the weighted average of the settlement prices of the individual commodities that day. Trading would therefore consist of the price individuals are willing to pay to have the cash equivalent index delivered on the specified day.

These individuals always have the choice of trading in the individual commodities or trading in the index. Arbitrage assures, of course, that prices of commodities deliverable on the same day move in concert with the index. If the price of commodities rises, but the index does not, investors have an incentive now to put more of their money in the commodity index. The price of the index rises and keeps rising until it is in line with actual commodity prices.

If the government adopts a price-rule policy of keeping the value of the dollar in terms of the index constant, it is therefore implicitly tying the value of the dollar to the actual commodities as well. The impact of this policy is the same as direct intervention into the commodities futures market. The superiority of this new proposal, however, is that the Fed does not have to retain stocks of the various commodities. The commodity basket futures contracts are all payable in cash, just like the stock market index futures contracts.[14] If government intervention requires the sale of more index contracts, the government just creates new ones and offers them on the market at the target price. If intervention requires buying up contracts, the government does that at the target price, in the process either retiring contracts it had issued earlier or buying up those offered by the market. There is no requirement that the government tend to be either long or short in these contracts. The quantity of contracts outstanding is not important, only the stability of the price at which they settle.

So under this proposal the government is pegging both forward prices and the interest rate through purchases and sales of financial instruments that are in abundant supply. The Fed should be empowered to make as many forward contracts as are required to keep forward prices stable. In keeping down interest rates, the Fed can buy back as many U.S. Treasury bonds as necessary. After all, under current procedures the interest and principal received by the Fed in excess of its expenses are simply turned back over to the U.S. Treasury. The only potential problem is that as interest rates tend to fall, the Fed might conceivably run out of bonds as it attempts to keep interest rates from falling. Perhaps a behavior rule is needed for the Fed when its bond supplies begin to run low. Or, since falling market interest rates are a signal that the market wants to hold relatively more bonds, perhaps the Treasury should be empowered to supply the Fed with additional bonds. But notice that the potential problem only arises as interest rates start to fall —hardly an incident of great concern to most people. Choosing the right target interest rate can help alleviate this potential problem.

Setting Up the System

The proposed system immediately raises questions of how the commodity basket may be selected and target prices chosen. There are no completely objective criteria for picking which commodities to include in the forward contract. Ideally, as many internationally traded commodities as possible should be included. The more commodities included, the fewer problems caused by changes in relative commodity prices. With a sufficient number of commodities, any rise in the relative price of one commodity is essentially offset by the fall in the prices of the others. The absolute price of the basket therefore remains unaffected, and the target price remains operational.

Part of the decision about how many commodities to include in the contract is the trade-off between completeness of coverage and the costs of computing additional commodities in a contract price. The contract would be of little value, for example, if traders found its extensive coverage cumbersome. Whatever the ultimate extent of its coverage, the contract should probably include items from the basic groups of traded commodities such as metals (gold, silver, copper, tin), grains (corn, soybeans, oats and so on), other foods (sugar, coffee, frozen orange juice and so on), fibers (cotton, wool, plywood, and so on), and maybe others such as tobacco, palm oil, or live beef cattle.

To work as a vehicle for a futures contract, the market must find the index chosen to be a relevant measure of the purchasing power of the dollar. In other words, the market must trust the index. The market is likely to have the most confidence in an index it chose itself. Unfortunately there is no obvious method of allowing the market to decide on the composition of the commodity basket, but in the absence of such a mechanism the next best alternative is to choose an index with which the market is already familiar. This problem of choosing the appropriate index is similar to the problem faced in setting up a stock market futures contract. In that case, the problem was solved by employing indices the market already knew and followed—the Standard and Poor's, the Value Line, and the New York Stock Exchange indices. In the case of a commodity index, the problem could be solved by using existing indices such as the Commodity Research Bureau futures, the Bureau of Labor Statistics spot, or the Dow Jones commodity indices.[15]

Once the precise composition of the contract is selected, the target price must be chosen. The commodity markets will adjust to whatever price is chosen. But too high a price leads to inflation, and too low a price to deflation. How can we be most confident of choosing a contract price that will produce price stability? Clearly we do not want to choose a contract price at random. The contract price should reflect the weighted average of market prices of each commodity. But which market prices? The ones prevailing today?

BEYOND MONETARISM

Today's market prices reflect information available today. Prices therefore reflect expectations of inflation under current monetary policy. Those expectations are likely to be different (significantly lower, it is hoped) under this proposed scheme of price rules than under current policy. The targeted basket contract price chosen should be consistent with the new set of expectations.

In other words, today's prices will not do. The commodity market must be informed of the proposed new monetary procedures and given time to sort out its reaction to them. So the new system would not be implemented overnight. Rather, once the details of the basic forward contract were decided, the Fed would announce its plans to the public. The Fed would declare that it was going to begin targeting the forward contract at a later date (say, thirty days later). It would also reveal all other aspects of its new policy. The Fed would then refrain from any intervention in the thirty-day interim. During that period, the market could sort out its expectations.

On the closing day of the waiting period, the Fed would calculate the value of the previously specified forward contract and would begin intervening to stabilize that value on the next trading day. Instead of some ad hoc contract price, the Fed would be targeting the closest thing available to the correct market price.

The initial announcement of the program would also include details of the interest-rate target as well. The Fed might choose for the interest-rate target the historical (say, the average over the 1947–67 period) yield on U.S. government twenty-year bonds. Alternatively, the Fed could use the same procedure as employed for picking the forward commodity basket price target. The Fed could announce that twenty-year bond yields are to be stabilized and again allow the market thirty days to decide what that twenty-year yield should be.

Intervention Under the Proposal

The Fed, of course, pays for any bonds it buys, or any contracts it delivers, with dollars. Some may fear that such payments are themselves a source of inflation. For example, as interest rates tend to rise, the Fed buys bonds in exchange for dollars. The additional dollars appear inflationary from a quantity theory perspective. For the moment, assume that additional dollars did produce pressure for prices to rise. Certainly inflationary pressures would be associated with a rise in forward prices. But as the price of the forward index rises, the Fed sells more futures contracts for delivery of the index at the targeted price. That action promises a reduction in the outstanding money supply, reducing the apparent inflationary pressure.

The actual change in money does not occur until the settlement date. For example, suppose the Fed is targeting the contract price at $100. The market price, however, rises to $101. Under the proposal, the Fed reacts by selling more contracts for delivery. If the Fed has maintained its commitment, when settlement day rolls around, the value of the contract is $100. But the person who bought the contract pays $101 to get $100. In other words, the supply of outstanding Federal Reserve liabilities is reduced by one dollar.

What happened in this example is that when the contract price was $101, the private market was sending a signal to the Fed that there was too much money relative to commodities in the marketplace. The $101 price represented a dollar premium people would pay to get commodities. By selling the futures contract at $101, the Fed accommodates the market's wishes. The Fed promises to reduce the money outstanding when the contract is settled for $100. Conversely, if the contract price were $99, the Fed would buy contracts.

Even more importantly, this focus on the precise *quantity* of money per se is not important. Under price rules, the government stabilizes prices. Under the proposal outlined, the government is setting long-term interest rates and forward prices. The private sector then chooses how much it wishes to hold in money, bonds, or commodities at these prices. As long as market prices remain at the targeted levels, the private sector has these three items in the desired proportions. A deviation from the targeted price, however, is a signal that there is too much of one item and not enough of another. A rise in interest rates, for example, tells the Fed that at prevailing prices the private sector wishes to hold fewer bonds and more dollars. The Fed's open market operation merely accommodates that desire. A rise in the forward index price means that the private sector wishes to hold less money and the equivalent of more commodities. Again the Fed's actions accommodate the private sector. An increase in money is therefore not inflationary, because it can occur only in response to an increased market *demand* for money. Money supply and money demand move stride for stride.

What the Fed is doing here instead is stabilizing *value*. The forward index price rule tells the market what the dollar yardstick will be in the future. A spectrum of forward indices, maturing at different dates, but pegged to the same value, assures the stability of the standard over time. The interest-rate price rule defines what the dollar yardstick must be today relative to tomorrow. In other words, how much must that yardstick change? With a stable forward yardstick, and a stable interest rate, the rate of spot inflation is determined. The lower the interest rate, the lower spot inflation. With a properly chosen interest rate, even stable spot prices can be achieved.

II

Summing Up

WHAT LESSONS have we learned? First, we have learned that monetarism can never work to achieve price stability. Monetarism rests on myopic theories of domestic and world money markets. The U.S. money market cannot be separated from the global market. Domestic substitutes, Eurodollars, and foreign money present abundant opportunities for the public to create or extinguish money independently of Federal Reserve policy. M1 or M2 is therefore only a fraction of the relevant supply of money. The Federal Reserve can potentially control only a part of even that fraction. In other words, the truly relevant money supply is endogenously controlled by the public, rising and falling with the needs of the economy. Even if the Fed could define or measure this supply of money, it cannot adequately control it. It certainly cannot control, as price stability would demand, the quantity of that money relative to its demand.

Second, we have learned that to achieve price stability, monetary policy should instead focus on price rules. The Fed must resume its more traditional role of providing up-to-date and precise information about the size of the dollar yardstick. Historically, policies focusing on the value of money have been associated with lower, more stable prices. That desirable result can be achieved again if only the Fed will adopt the proper combination of two price rules.

Third, we have been given additional insight into the misconception that recent monetarist policy has worked. True, the measured rate of inflation was lower in May 1983 than in May 1980. But that measure only reflects what is happening to the spot price level. What about price levels and inflation in the future? Will inflation remain as low? The continued high interest rates indicate it will probably not. In other words, concentrating solely on current inflation gives a misleading impression. Somehow policies have made the present look better. But at what price? The future continues to look bleak. More price stability in the present may have come at the expense of more future inflation. Spot inflation has been like a roller coaster over the last decade, and what we experienced in 1982–83 may turn out just to be another periodic low.

Fourth, we have been alerted to the extremely important point that a single price rule like the spot gold standard is not enough. A spot gold standard needs another price rule to go with it. Some advocates of the gold standard ask us to think what would happen to interest rates if we knew our dollars would be worth the same thirty years from now. These advocates are correct that interest rates would fall. The only problem is that a spot gold standard alone does not give us that security. There is no mechanism to assure that the dollar will be worth the same in thirty years. We have to rely on just the promises from the lips of policy makers, not the actual movements of their feet. To force them into action, there must be another price rule. The spot price rule must be accompanied by an explicit price rule in the forward markets or a commitment to stabilize long-term interest rates.

Fifth, there are some objections to a price rule that must be addressed. The Fed could run out of reserves. There are costs of storing reserves. While a basket may be better than one commodity for a target, there is the problem of picking the right combination of commodities. There is also the problem of picking the right price level to target. There are other problems or costs related to the transition period.

But if we put our minds on the problem, we can find practical ways to overcome these objections. If we really want price stability, we know we must adopt price rules. We know now what types of prices must be targeted. We also know that in the adjustment from an economy where inflation is the rule to one where it is the exception, there will be some winners and some losers. Change always creates groups of people who anticipate incorrectly. Yet the same groups who supported the headlong plunge into unhinged money in the early seventies, with the resulting swings in grain prices, oil prices, housing prices, and so on—not to mention the entire last decade of volatile markets—are now cautioning those who want to return to price stability about the potential costs or disruptions of the transition!

Answers come from focusing on the objectives and the objections. The example in chapter 10 of a two-price-rule policy, targeting long-term interest rates and the price of a financial futures contract for a basket of commodities, is designed to illustrate how, by putting our minds to the allegedly insurmountable problems, we can find solutions. We can find the way to low and steady rates of interest and inflation. We can find a way around the problems of finite reserves and the costs of storage. We can find or create a useful market basket of goods whose price is quoted continuously. We can find a way to come as close as possible to the right prices to target. We can, in other words, design a logical, workable system.

That is what today's monetary policy debate should be about. We should forget, once and for all, about slapping more bandaids on the system of controlling the quantity of money. If we are going to have a rational monetary policy with price stability, we must recognize that monetarism has had its day. The monetary system is in need of a major operation. Prayers and wishful thinking will not pull it through. We must focus our energies instead on which operation has the greatest chance of restoring the U.S. and world monetary systems to health. Should the United States go it alone, or should another Bretton Woods–like international monetary conference be convened? Is gold the answer? Are interest rate targets? Are commodity baskets? The Treasury and the Federal Reserve should be actively discussing the details right now. We must act fast. The longer we wait, the longer we will experience the painful side effects of uncertain money—high and volatile interest rates and inflation, high unemployment, and continued slow economic growth. While we debate the costs of the imagined transition, the costs of the unhinged money reality continue to mount. It is a price we can no longer, nor must we, pay. The time has come for the monetary reform that can truly promise us decades of stable money.

Notes

Chapter 1

1. "Wide Swings in Important Currencies Vex Businessmen, Bankers, Government Aides," *Wall Street Journal*, 29 December, 1981.

2. Milton Friedman, "The Federal Reserve and Monetary Instability," *Wall Street Journal*, 1 February, 1982.

3. Allan H. Meltzer, "The Results of the Fed's Failed Experiment," *Wall Street Journal*, 29 July, 1982.

Chapter 2

1. Even though Texas and Rhode Island are expected to have the same inflation, price indices in these two regions are observed to deviate. Part of the problem is data collection, as listed prices may change at different rates across regions, even if actual transaction price changes are more aligned. Another prominent problem is the weights given each good in constructing the regional price index. Even if prices rose at precisely the same rate across regions, since heating oil, cold soda, and other items are different fractions of the average consumer budget in Texas and Rhode Island, measured price indices would diverge. There are additional problems in constructing comparable indices, and these problems only compound as we compare prices across countries. But as Hans Genberg has shown in "Aspects of the Monetary Approach to Balance-of-Payments Theory: An Empirical Study of Sweden," in Jacob A. Frenkel and Harry G. Johnson, eds., *The Monetary Approach to the Balance of Payments* (Toronto: University of Toronto Press, 1976), inflation rates among countries are as closely related as rates among cities in the United States. He writes, "It is evident . . . that differences between OECD countries are no greater on the average than those between cities within the United States. Thus, if we believe that the whole of the U.S. can be treated as a single market in a macroeconomic context, then the area composed of the above countries can be treated likewise." (p. 302)

2. Ronald I. McKinnon, "Currency Substitution and Instability in the World Dollar Standard," *American Economic Review* 72 (June 1982), 324.

Notes

3. In recent years there have been attempts to develop statistical models of causality. These techniques strive to delineate empirically the temporal sequence of events. Did the money supply grow and then prices, or vice versa? However, no such causality technique passes the critical stock market test. Stock prices rise in response to higher earnings. Yet stocks rise first, in anticipation of higher earnings, and then the higher earnings are reported. Current causality tests would still imply that higher stock prices "caused" higher earnings. More on this point in chapter 5.

4. For a more complete explanation of this relationship, and the statistical results for many countries, see Marc A. Miles, *Devaluation, the Trade Balance and the Balance of Payments* (New York: Marcel Dekker, 1978).

5. There is an ongoing debate in the economics profession over precisely how closely aligned prices are across countries, and how one can measure the "closeness." As pointed out above, Hans Genberg provided one benchmark. An excellent review of this debate and explanation of the problems is contained in Donald McCloskey and J. Richard Zecher, "The Success of Purchasing Power Parity," in Michael Bordo and Anna J. Schwartz. eds., *A Retrospective on the Classical Gold Standard,* (Chicago: University of Chicago Press for NBER, forthcoming).

Chapter 3

1. "Fed Cuts Money-Supply Growth Targets, Stressing Commitment to Battle Inflation," *Wall Street Journal,* 22 July, 1981.

2. "Taxes and 'Real' Interest Rates," *Wall Street Journal,* 22 July, 1981.

3. *Wall Street Journal,* 16 March, 1981. For a more detailed version, see "The Real Rate of Interest," *Economic and Investment Observations,* H. C. Wainwright & Co., Economics, 3 March, 1981.

4. For future reference, M1 and M2 are defined by the Federal Reserve as: M1—Currency, checkable deposits at banks and credit unions, and travelers checks; M2—M1 plus money market mutual fund shares, savings deposits, small time deposits, overnight repurchase agreements, retail repurchase agreements of less than $100,000, and overnight Eurodollar deposits by Caribbean branches of member banks.

5. A more precise statement would be that monetary policy would eventually be dictated by the market participants. To the extent that the United States had gold reserves, it could adopt a short-run policy which was inconsistent with the $35-per-ounce rule. The result, however, would be an outflow of gold reserves. If the United States were determined to maintain the $35 price of gold, eventually this policy would have to be brought into line with the market's wishes.

6. These countries could use their foreign exchange reserves to deviate temporarily from the required monetary policy. The consequent reduction in foreign exchange reserves would eventually force policy back into line.

7. Special Drawing Rights are a paper international reserve created by the International Monetary Fund and used only by central banks for discharging debt among themselves.

Chapter 4

1. This policy of constant money growth is usually associated with conservative economists like Friedman. See for example his presidential address to the American Economic Association, "The Role of Monetary Policy," *American Economic Review* 58 (March 1968): 1–17. This and other classic essays can be found in Milton Fried-

man, *The Optimum Quantity of Money and Other Essays* (Chicago: Aldine, 1969). But Alan Reynolds, in his "The Trouble with Monetarism," *Policy Review* 21 (Summer 1982): 19–42, claims the origin is quite different.

> The idea of a fixed rate of growth of the money supply originated in 1927 with the even more interventionist left wing of the "Chicago School," namely Paul Douglas. Douglas (later a Senator) was then quite excited about a "planned economy" and "public ownership," and even called himself a socialist.

Reynolds further suggests that Friedman's suggestion of raising M2 3–5 percent every year "was a return to Paul Douglas, neglecting the doubts of Henry Simons and Frank Knight."

2. Friedman, "The Role of Monetary Policy," in *Optimum Quantity of Money,* 108.

3. Ibid., 109.

4. This example is not precisely correct. With n countries there are only n–1 exchange rates, leaving the nth country (the United States under Bretton Woods) as the reserve currency country. The binding constraint on the United States was the price rule between the dollar and gold, while the fixed exchange rate was a constraint on the other n–1 countries' monetary policies. For a further discussion, see Arthur B. Laffer and Marc A. Miles, *International Economics in an Integrated World* (Glenview, Ill.: Scott, Foresman & Co., 1982), chap. 18.

5. Again, subject to the caveat that short-run discretion could be purchased temporarily with foreign exchange or gold reserves.

6. Milton Friedman, "The Case For Flexible Exchange Rates," in *Essays in Positive Economics* (Chicago: University of Chicago Press, 1953), 200.

7. In September 1968 the Federal Reserve gave member banks greater flexibility in calculating and fulfilling their reserve requirements. Reserve accounting was shifted from contemporaneous (effectively a one-day lag) to a two-week lagged reserve accounting. Vault cash was also lagged two weeks, so that reserve requirements in the current maintenance period could be satisfied by vault cash held two weeks earlier. In addition, carry-forward privileges were liberalized. Previously, reserve deficiencies of up to 2 percent of required reserves could be made up in the next maintenance period. After September 1968, in addition to being able to make up deficiencies, banks could carry forward any surplus reserves (not exceeding 2 percent of required reserves) to be applied against the next maintenance period's requirements.

8. Statement of Board of Governors of the Federal Reserve System, October 6, 1979, as reported in the *Federal Reserve Bulletin* (October 1979): 830.

9. Milton Friedman, "Defining Monetarism," *Newsweek,* 12 July, 1982, 64.

Chapter 5

1. Milton Friedman and Anna Schwartz, *A Monetary History of the United States, 1867–1960,* (Princeton, N. J.: Princeton University Press, for the NBER, 1963). A summary of Friedman and Schwartz's findings relating to the business cycle can be found in their "Money and Business Cycles," *Review of Economics and Statistics* 45 (February 1963), reprinted in Milton Friedman, *The Optimum Quantity of Money and Other Essays* (Chicago: Aldine, 1969). Friedman and Schwartz did their research under the auspices of the National Bureau of Economic Research, an organization whose studies have historically been concerned with business-cycle theory.

2. For a description of how regular and distinct business cycles may exist more in the mind than in reality, see for example R. David Ranson, "Money, Capital, and the Stochastic Nature of Business Fluctuation" (Ph.D. diss., University of Chicago, 1974).

Notes

Ranson demonstrates that business cycles do not exist in the sense that future GNP behavior can be forecast by past behavior:

> Most of the results reported are quite consistent with the random walk model and quite inconsistent with models in which the economy reapproaches equilibrium slowly following a disturbance, or displays a "cyclical" equilibrium path. That is not to say that departures from a pure random walk . . . cannot be detected. Certain departures are clearly identifiable in the data, but their nature and magnitude lend little support to conventional models of business fluctuations. (pp. 167–68)

The idea that movements in GNP are a random walk is not new. Ranson points out that his approach "conforms closely to the thinking of Irving Fisher, Evgeny Slutsky and others in the 1920s." He also demonstrates that random data undergoing the official X-11 seasonal adjustment method used by the U.S. Department of Commerce develop a strong first-order serial dependence. Further, he shows that the two-quarter rule-of-thumb about how to identify a downturn in a cycle "will detect cycles of apparently quite constant periodicity in data which are known to follow a random walk."

3. See Robert E. Weintraub, "Three Large Scale Model Simulations of Four Money Growth Scenarios" (Joint Economic Committee, 97th Cong. September 1, 1982). The precise relationships estimated were:

1. $\% \, \Delta \, \text{GNP} = 3.31 + 1.02\% \Delta M_1 \quad R^2 = 0.73$
   $\qquad\quad (5.22) \quad (8.32) \qquad\qquad DW = 2.35$

2. $\% \, \Delta \, \text{real GNP} = 2.17 + 0.24\% \Delta M_1 \quad R^2 = 0.02$
   $\qquad\qquad\quad (2.21) \quad (1.27) \qquad\qquad DW = 1.49$

3. $\% \, \Delta \, \text{GNP deflator} = .34 + .996\% \Delta M_1(t-2) \quad R^2 = 0.81$
   $\qquad\qquad\qquad (.73)(10.32) \qquad\qquad\qquad DW = 1.65$

4. $\% \, \Delta \, \text{Velocity} = 3.32 - 0.16\% \Delta M_1 \quad R^2 = -0.04$
   $\qquad\qquad\quad (5.38) \quad (0.13) \qquad DW = 2.39$

4. See Keith M. Carlson, "Does the St. Louis Equation Now Believe in Fiscal Policy?" Federal Reserve Bank of St. Louis *Review* 60, no. 2 (February 1978): 13–19. The equation Carlson reported for the sample period 1953/I–1976/IV was:

$\% \, \Delta Y = 2.69 + .40\% \Delta M_1 + .41\% \Delta M_1(t-1) + .25\% \Delta M_1(t-2)$
$\qquad\quad (3.23) \, (2.96) \qquad (5.26) \qquad\qquad (2.14)$

$+ .06\% \Delta M_1(t-3) - .05\% \Delta M(t-4) + .08\% \Delta G + .06\% \Delta G(t-1)$
$\quad (.71) \qquad\qquad (.37) \qquad\qquad (2.26) \qquad (2.52)$

$+ .00\% \Delta G(t-2) - .06\% \Delta G(t-3)$
$\quad (.02) \qquad\qquad (2.20)$

$\quad - .07\% \Delta G(t-4) \quad R^2 = .40$
$\quad (1.83) \qquad\qquad DW = 1.78$

High employment government expenditures (G) are estimates of what government expenditures would be if the economy had been at some measure of "full employment." In the original article Andersen and Jordon claimed that using the more conventional national income account measure of government expenditures did not qualitatively change the results.

5. Milton Friedman, "Defining Monetarism," *Newsweek*, 12 July, 1982.

6. Milton Friedman, "The Lag in Effect of Monetary Policy," *Journal of Political Economy* 69, no. 5 (October 1961): 447–66.

7. Certainly if there were a precise, known time lag, the time lag would quickly disappear. If people knew that whenever the money supply grew more rapidly, nominal income increased more rapidly nine months later, people would act on that information. They would buy now in anticipation of higher prices, businesses would accelerate production in anticipation of higher sales, and so on. The result would be that nominal income would spurt long before nine months elapsed. The implication of this "rational expectations" or "efficient markets" argument is that it is unlikely that the money supply could ever be used repeatedly for anticipating future economic activity in the way the monetarists are suggesting. Any observed, repeated lags between changes in money and changes in income therefore proba-bly reflect either the way data are collected and reported or the fact that the pub-lic is adjusting its money balances to anticipated changes in income. These points are discussed below.

8. In a well-known article, "Money, Income, and Causality," *American Economic Review* 62 (September 1972): 540–52, Christopher Sims provided evidence of a unidirectional causal relationship running from the money supply to nominal income, using a statistical test now called Sims's test. In a later article, "The Casual Causal Relationship Between Money and Income: Some Caveats for Time Series Analysis," *The Review of Economics and Statistics* 61 (November 1979): 521–33, Edgar L. Feige and Douglas K. Pearce provide evidence that such a unidirectional causal relationship is by no means certain. They find, for example, that the results are sensitive to the method used to prefilter the data. Feige and Pearce evaluate three different empirical procedures for evaluating causality. They conclude that "a major substantive hypothe-sis, albeit boldly formulated, is by and large not substantiated by our empirical findings. . . . What is even more disturbing is the finding that the three alternative methods for detecting causal relationships do not necessarily yield unambiguously compatible economic conclusions, even when the data base is uniform across test procedures." (p. 531)

9. The potential fallibility of these statistical tests can be shown in another way. Two sets of numbers may be correlated without there being any causality. Recently two researchers used these causality tests to demonstrate (tongue in cheek) that "Jevons' argument that a relationship exists between sunspots and economic activity was right but for the wrong reason." According to the causality tests, U.S. GNP has a significant impact on sunspots, but sunspots do not influence GNP. See Richard G. Sheehand and Robin Grieves, "Sunspots and Cycles: A Test of Causation," *Southern Economic Journal* 48, no. 3 (January 1982): 775–77.

10. In fact there are two problems. First, information relevant to the month is transferred to other months' data. Second, the seasonal pattern among months is not completely eliminated. For a discussion of these problems, see Arthur B. Laffer and Marc A. Miles, "Distortions In the Seasonal Adjustments of the Official Money Supply Data," *Economic Study*, H. C. Wainwright & Co., Economics, 20 September, 1978.

11. The problem, of course, is further complicated by what happens when industrial production is also seasonally adjusted. The opportunity arises for all kinds of spurious correlations.

12. Arthur B. Laffer and R. David Ranson, "A Formal Model of the Economy," *Journal of Business* 44 (July 1971): 247–70.

13. Unlike the later version of the Andersen-Jordan equation, the initial version examined the relationships among absolute changes, not percentage changes, in the variables.

14. Interestingly, Feige and Pearce ("The Casual Causal Relationship,") found that

Notes

when Sims's causality test is applied to seasonally unadjusted data for money and income, in almost all cases there is an absence of causality. Since Sims's test relies on estimating lagged relationships, this result reinforces Laffer and Ranson's point. This observation was also consistent with the results of the other two test procedures Feige and Pearce examined. Feige and Pearce comment, "We are thus led to the conclusion that the empirical results are highly sensitive to the use of seasonally adjusted data. . . ." (p. 530)

15. R. David Ranson and Arthur B. Laffer, "The Laffer-Ranson Model of the Economy After Four Years: Extensions and Further Results," *Simulation and Modeling* 6, part 2, 1975.

16. M3 adds to M2 large-denomination time deposits, term repurchase agreements, and institutional money market mutual funds. L is the next and broadest official money supply measure. In addition to term Eurodollars, it adds other liquid assets such as bankers acceptances, commercial paper, Treasury bills and other liquid Treasury securities, and U.S. savings bonds.

17. The repo also provides the bank with a domestic monetary instrument that circumvents the Federal Reserve Act's prohibition of interest payments on deposits with maturities of less than fourteen days. Since the repo is not defined as a deposit, it can have a maturity as short as one day and still pay a market rate of interest.

18. More precisely, for the period 1960–81 the equations for GNP and money are:

$$\%\Delta GNP = .03 + 1.05\%\Delta M1 \quad R^2 = 0.79$$
$$(4.28) \quad (8.61) \qquad DW = 1.83$$

$$\%\Delta GNP = .01 + .88\%\Delta L \quad R^2 = 0.81$$
$$(.66) \quad (9.27) \qquad DW = 1.86$$

Similar results hold for Weintraub's other three estimated relationships.

19. Betsey Buttrill White, "Monetary Policy Without Regulation Q," *Quarterly Review* 6 (Winter 1981–82): 7.

20. Bank for International Settlements, *Fifty-Second Annual Report*, Basle, Switzerland (June 1982): 87.

21. Frank E. Morris, "A Fed President Views the Money Supply," *Wall Street Journal*, 22 June, 1982.

22. Phillip Cagan, *Determinants and Effects of Changes in the Money Stock, 1875–1960* (New York: National Bureau of Economic Research, 1965).

23. Ibid., 287.

24. Ibid., 43.

25. Arthur B. Laffer and Marc A. Miles, "Factors Influencing Changes in the Money Supply Over the Short Term," *Economic Study*, H. C. Wainwright & Co., Economics, 18 August, 1977.

26. See Appendix A, "Evidence of Money Demand Instability in 1982," in "The Economic and Budget Outlook: An Update," 97th Cong. Congressional Budget Office, September 1982.

27. Arthur B. Laffer and Marc A. Miles, "Constraints on the Usefulness of Just-Released Money Supply Figures," *Economic Study*, H. C. Wainwright & Co., Economics, 13 December 1977, and Laffer and Miles, "Distortions in the Seasonal Adjustments."

28. Alan Reynolds, "The Trouble with Monetarism," *Policy Review* 21 (Summer 1982): 24.

29. For a discussion of the monetary system during the Irish Bank Strike, see Antoin

Notes

F. Murphy, "Money in an Economy Without Banks: The Case of Ireland," *The Manchester School* 46 (March 1978): 41–50.

Chapter 6

1. These figures exclude the fiduciary liabilities of Swiss banks. This number was $38 billion (Sfr. 68 billion) at the end of 1981. The figure is courtesy of Bruce Brittain of Salomon Brothers.

2. Some of these Eurodollar accounts are already captured in M2 and M3. Subtracting those deposits from the total, the uncaptured Eurodollar deposits as percentages of M2 and M3 are 14 percent and 11 percent. Of course, adding in the item in footnote 1 raises these back to about 16 percent and 13 percent.

3. In the monetarist framework, the velocity of money is the V in $MV = Py$. By definition, velocity equals the ratio of nominal income to the supply of money, that is, $V = Py/M$. It represents roughly how many times the stock of money has to change hands to facilitate all the transactions in the economy.

4. Bruce Brittain and Henri Bernard, "The Relevance of EuroCurrency Claims for Domestic Financial Aggregates," (Basle, Switzerland: Bank for International Settlements, November 1980, Mimeographed). They also found that a measure of dollars held in the U.S. and Eurodollar markets by both U.S. residents and foreigners yields an even more stable measure of velocity. This result reinforces the concept that the relevant dollar market is global.

5. Loophole Is Found in Federal Reserve's Tight-Credit Policy," *Wall Street Journal*, 26 October, 1979.

Chapter 7

1. This analogy suffers from the drawback that monies are not only close substitutes in demand, but also in supply. Not only is the private sector indifferent as to which type of dollar is used in a transaction, but the Federal Reserve Banks stand ready to convert one type of dollar into another on demand. The analogy is still useful, however, for illustrating why an independent monetary policy is impossible.

2. For a description of how markets circumvent capital controls, see Arthur B. Laffer and Marc A. Miles, *International Economics in an Integrated World* (Glenview, Ill.: Scott, Foresman & Co., 1982), chap. 15.

3. Haim Levy and Marshall Sarnat, "Exchange Rate Risk and the Optimal Diversification of Foreign Currency Holdings," *Journal of Money, Credit, and Banking* 10 (November 1978): 453–63.

4. Marc A. Miles, "Currency Substitution, Flexible Exchange Rates, and Monetary Independence," *The American Economic Review* 68 (June 1978): 428–36, and "Currency Substitution: Some Further Results and Conclusions," *Southern Economic Journal* 48 (July 1981): 78–86.

5. Foreign currency in the United States and Germany is measured by the foreign currency–denominated short-term assets of the nonbank private sector. In Canada, foreign currency is measured by the short-term U.S. dollar assets of nonbank, nonofficial Canadians.

6. Bluford H. Putnam and D. Sykes Wilford, "How Diversification Makes the Dollar Weaker," *Euromoney* (October 1978): 201–4.

Notes

7. Marc A. Miles and Marion B. Stewart, "The Effects of Risk and Return on the Currency Composition of Money Demand," *Weltwirtschaftliches Archiv* 116, no. 4 (December 1980): 613–26.

8. Short-term claims on foreigners by non-bank U.S. enterprises, as measured by the U.S. Treasury Department.

9. Bruce Brittain, "International Currency Substitution and the Apparent Instability of Velocity in Some Western European Economies and in the United States," *Journal of Money, Credit, and Banking* 13, no. 2 (May 1981): 135–55.

10. Leroy O. Laney, "Currency Substitution: The Mexican Case," Federal Reserve Bank of Dallas *Voice* (January 1981): 6.

11. This rapid diversification was again visible following the 1982 devaluation, as the peso traded at a huge discount to the dollar, and the Mexican Government moved to eliminate the use of the dollar in Mexico.

Chapter 8

1. This and subsequent sections are drawn from Marc A. Miles, "The Monetary Control Act of 1980," *Economic Study*, H. C. Wainwright & Co., Economics, 18 March, 1981.

2. See R. Alton Gilbert, "Utilization of Federal Reserve Bank Services by Member Banks: Implications for the Costs and Benefits of Membership," Federal Reserve Bank of St. Louis *Review* 59, no. 8 (August 1977): 10.

3. See R. Alton Gilbert and Jean M. Lovati, "Bank Reserve Requirements and Their Enforcement: A Comparison Across States," Federal Reserve Bank of St. Louis *Review* 60, no. 3 (March 1978): 23.

4. This experience was the only time the Credit Control Act was ever used. Congress allowed the Act to expire on June 30, 1982.

5. This schedule was speeded up. Fierce competition from money market mutual funds forced the DIDC to allow banks to offer "Super NOW" accounts effective January 5, 1983. These accounts have no interest rate ceiling and effectively deregulate short-term accounts. As a result, other accounts such as the thirteen- or twenty-six-week certificates become less attractive, and pressure builds to deregulate their returns. In fact on June 30th, 1983, the DIDC voted to remove ceilings on all accounts (except passbook, NOW accounts, and savings deposits with maturities of seven to thirty-one days) opened after October 1, 1983.

6. The Fed has been exempting the first $2 million of deposits at all depository institutions from reserves, thus exempting about 17,755 of about 19,882 institutions. So the very smallest are avoiding this tax. Also, the reserve requirement on less than $25 million of deposits is only 3 percent.

7. The full difference between previously existing reserve requirements and those under the Monetary Control Act did not become effective immediately. For member banks the phase-down was scheduled to take 3 1/2 years. Requirements were reduced by 1/4 of the difference on November 13, 1980 and by steps of 1/8 every six months beginning September 1, 1981. Nonmember banks were scheduled to be phased in over seven years. Reserve requirements were raised by 1/8 of the difference November 13, 1980 and by steps of 1/8 annually starting September 1, 1981. Branches and agencies of foreign banks were phased in on a quarterly basis over a two-year period beginning November 13, 1980.

8. This example is taken from "New Rules For Reserves," *Business In Brief* (Economics Group, Chase-Manhattan Bank, September/October 1980).

Notes

9. Both quotes from "Fed Adopts Rule to Ease Swings in Money Supply," *Wall Street Journal*, 29 June, 1982, p. 7.

10. Ibid.

Chapter 9

1. Or to put it in terms of a "long and variable lag," do you decide to buy a stereo on the basis of how much money you had in your checking account months ago?

2. My thanks to Joe Cobb for this example. The Spanish Milled Dollar was a silver coin. The dollar had a bimetallic definition, with a ratio initially of 15:1 and an official price of gold of $19.39.

3. The bimetallic standard was adjusted in 1834 and again in 1837, when the ratio of silver to gold became 16:1. The official price of gold became $20.67 in 1837. This official price remained until 1933. The major periods of suspended specie payments were 1861–79 and 1917–19.

4. Presumably other things can serve as money in black markets. But contracts denominated in anything but dollars are not likely to stand up in U.S. courts. Notice, however, that a monopoly on defining what is legal tender is not the same as a monopoly on the number of units of legal tender in circulation.

5. "Short-Term Interest Rates Fall Further," *Wall Street Journal*, 21 July, 1982. The experience of the summer of 1982 is also an excellent refutation of the belief that large government borrowing, brought about by large government deficits, causes interest rates to rise. Interest rates were falling just as the government was doing some of its heaviest borrowing.

6. "Bond Prices Surge and Rally Generates Sellout of Several New Corporate Issues," *Wall Street Journal*, 23 July, 1982.

Chapter 10

1. For a more detailed discussion of this principle, see Arthur B. Laffer and Marc A. Miles, *International Economics in an Integrated World* (Glenview, Ill.: Scott, Foresman & Co., 1982), chap. 6.

2. In some small countries it is sometimes argued that the relevant yardstick is a foreign one. Perhaps because of the smallness of the economy or because of the lack of complete domestic financial markets, the money of some major country is the yardstick by which residents measure value. An example might be the U.S. dollar in Mexico. It is then often argued that monetary policy in the small country should target the relative values of the two monies. Tying monetary policy to the foreign yardstick is the best the small country can hope to achieve. This assertion has some validity, but at best it means that domestic purchasing power is stabilized relative to that of foreign money. This policy may increase the perceived value of domestic money and reduce inflation. Unless the foreign country is engaged in policies to stabilize the value of its basic money unit, however, inflation will not clear up completely.

3. The separation of the relationships into three prices, and the triangle analogy, were first suggested by David Ranson.

4. This overall relationship can be seen more clearly in two simple equations. If

Notes

today's prices are symbolized by P_t, and P^e_{t+1} symbolizes what tomorrow's prices are expected to be, then the expected rate of inflation is

$$\%\Delta P^e = \log P^e_{t+1} - \log P_t.$$

This expected inflation is also the difference between the nominal or market rate of interest i and the real rate r:

$$\%\Delta P^e = i - r.$$

5. That is, assuming that the real or commodity rate of interest remains constant. Inflation, however, may cause the real rate to change. For example, with a progressive income tax system, inflation produces "bracket creep," pushing individuals into higher tax brackets. Thus, in order to get the same after-tax real return, a larger pre-tax return is needed. Hence, gross of tax market real rates might rise. Simultaneously, net of tax real rates may fall.

6. The lag in measurement of some items can be more than a month. In addition there are such problems as selecting weights for the goods in the index, seasonal adjustment, price discounts, and changes in the quality of goods with no corresponding price changes.

7. Theoretically, if *all* commodities are included in the basket, there is no terms-of-trade problem. For each commodity whose relative price rises, there is an equivalent fall in other commodity prices.

8. Comparing the price index of 1793 to that of 1933 may not be entirely valid. The index of the earlier period was probably constructed from quotes of prices of only internationally traded agricultural products. The index of the later period involved a more diversified set of items.

9. My thanks to David Ranson for these examples.

10. See, for example, Arthur B. Laffer, "Reinstatement of the Dollar: The Blueprint," (Rolling Hills Estates, Calif.: A. B. Laffer Associates, 29 February, 1980).

11. As with the interest-rate target, the Fed would actually attempt to keep prices within a narrow band around the target price—say, plus or minus $4. Without some small band, professional dealers would be unwilling to make a private market in the commodity.

12. It is said that only a small amount of commodity futures contracts (under 5 percent) actually result in physical delivery of the commodity. The reason for this phenomenon, however, is not that the commodity is not delivered. Instead, most people on the receiving end of a futures contract turn around and sell the delivery rights in the spot or cash market.

13. In fact, the Eurodollar contract began trading before the stock index contract, on December 9, 1981.

14. The government could conceivably deal in a similar basket of commodities in the spot market, buying and selling units of the spot index in exchange for cash. The government would then be stabilizing the spot market and interest rates instead of the forward market and interest rates. Theoretically the two policies should have the same effect. However, the forward market policy may be superior to a spot policy because it stabilizes values over the contract period.

15. The composition of these indices is as follows:

CRB futures price index, 27 commodities: barley (Wpg), broilers (Chi), cattle "live" (Chi), cocoa (NY), coffee "C" (NY), copper (NY), corn (Chi), cotton "2" (NY), eggs (Chi), flaxseed (Wpg), grease wool (NY), hogs (Chi), oats (Chi), orange juice (NY), platinum (NY), plywood (Chi), pork bellies (Chi), potatoes (NY), rapeseed (Wpg), rye

Notes

(Wpg), silver (NY), soybean méal (Chi), soybean oil (Chi), soybeans (Chi), sugar "11" (NY), wheat (Chi), wheat (Mpls).

BLS spot (now computed by CRB), 22 commodities: hogs (Omaha), steers, choice (Omaha), butter, AA, 93 (Chi), soybean oil, crude (Decatur), lard (Chi), cocoa beans, Accra (NY), corn, no. 2 yellow (Chi), sugar, raw (NY), wheat, no. 1 hard winter (KC), wheat, No. 1 spring (Mpls), copper, scrap no. 2 (NY), lead, scrap, heavy soft, Steel scrap, no. 1 heavy melt (Chi), tin, grade A (NY), zinc, prime western (NY delivered), burlap, 10 oz. 40" (NY), cotton, 1 1/16" (9-market average), print cloth, 48", 78 × 78 (NY), wool tops - nominal (Boston), hides, cow, lt. native (Chi), rosin, window glass (NY), rubber, no. 1, ribbed smoked sheets, (NY), tallow, prime (Chi).

Dow Jones spot and future indices, 12 commodities: cattle, coffee, copper, corn, cotton, gold, hogs, lumber, silver, soybeans, sugar, wheat.

Index

Index

Index

Index

Index

Index

Index

Dear Parent:
Your child's love of reading starts here!

Every child learns to read in a different way and at his or her own speed. Some go back and forth between reading levels and read favorite books again and again. Others read through each level in order. You can help your young reader improve and become more confident by encouraging his or her own interests and abilities. From books your child reads with you to the first books he or she reads alone, there are I Can Read Books for every stage of reading:

SHARED READING
Basic language, word repetition, and whimsical illustrations, ideal for sharing with your emergent reader

BEGINNING READING
Short sentences, familiar words, and simple concepts for children eager to read on their own

READING WITH HELP
Engaging stories, longer sentences, and language play for developing readers

READING ALONE
Complex plots, challenging vocabulary, and high-interest topics for the independent reader

ADVANCED READING
Short paragraphs, chapters, and exciting themes for the perfect bridge to chapter books

I Can Read Books have introduced children to the joy of reading since 1957. Featuring award-winning authors and illustrators and a fabulous cast of beloved characters, I Can Read Books set the standard for beginning readers.

A lifetime of discovery begins with the magical words **"I Can Read!"**

Visit www.icanread.com for information
on enriching your child's reading experience.

WALT DISNEY PICTURES AND WALDEN MEDIA PRESENT "THE CHRONICLES OF NARNIA: THE LION, THE WITCH AND THE WARDROBE" BASED ON THE BOOK BY C.S. LEWIS
A MARK JOHNSON PRODUCTION AN ANDREW ADAMSON FILM MUSIC COMPOSED BY HARRY GREGSON-WILLIAMS COSTUME DESIGNER ISIS MUSSENDEN EDITED BY SIM EVAN-JONES PRODUCTION DESIGNER ROGER FORD
DIRECTOR OF PHOTOGRAPHY DONALD M. McALPINE ASC, ACS CO-PRODUCER DOUGLAS GRESHAM EXECUTIVE PRODUCERS ANDREW ADAMSON PERRY MOORE
WALDEN MEDIA SCREENPLAY BY ANN PEACOCK AND ANDREW ADAMSON AND CHRISTOPHER MARKUS & STEPHEN McFEELY PRODUCED BY MARK JOHNSON PHILIP STEUER DIRECTED BY ANDREW ADAMSON Walt Disney Pictures

Distributed by BUENA VISTA PICTURES DISTRIBUTION THE CHRONICLES OF NARNIA, NARNIA, and all book titles, characters and locales original thereto are trademarks of C.S. Lewis Pte. Ltd. and are used with permission. ©Disney Enterprises, Inc. and Walden Media, LLC. All rights reserved.

Narnia.com

❖

THE CHRONICLES OF NARNIA

THE LION, THE WITCH AND THE WARDROBE

WELCOME TO NARNIA

Adapted by Jennifer Frantz

Based on the screenplay by
Ann Peacock and Andrew Adamson and
Christopher Markus & Stephen McFeely

Based on the book by C. S. Lewis

Directed by Andrew Adamson

HarperCollinsPublishers

The Pevensie family never dreamed
that a magic wardrobe would change
their lives!

Lucy was the first Pevensie to find out the secret inside the wardrobe.

She and her brothers and sister were
playing hide-and-seek.
Lucy needed a place to hide!
She dashed inside a wardrobe in an
otherwise empty room.

As Lucy moved toward the back of the wardrobe, she felt a cold wind. What was going on?

That was when Lucy discovered Narnia—a magical land full of snow and different, wonderful creatures!

Later, Lucy shared her discovery.
At first no one believed Lucy's story
about Narnia.

Peter, Susan and Edmund thought she
was just playing a game.
How could there be another whole world
in the back of a wardrobe?
But soon the other Pevensie children would
visit Narnia, too.

Lucy was the youngest in the family.
She loved to read and have adventures.
Lucy also liked to make new friends . . .

. . . like Mr. Tumnus, the Faun.
She met him on her first trip to Narnia.

Edmund was the second of the Pevensie
children to visit Narnia.
At first he teased his sister Lucy.
Then he found out her story was true.
But while Lucy made nice friends
when she went to Narnia,
Edmund did not.

You see, Edmund had a way of finding trouble wherever he went.

And that was what he found in Narnia! Just after entering the land beyond the wardrobe, Edmund met the White Witch. She was the evil Queen of Narnia.

The White Witch gave Edmund
some enchanted candy called Turkish Delight.
He quickly fell under her spell.

Peter and Susan, the oldest children,
were the last to visit Narnia.

They could not believe their eyes!

At first Susan was worried that her
family might be in danger in Narnia.
She thought it would be safer to go home.

But as time went by,
Susan grew to love Narnia.
She was a fierce protector of Narnia
and its creatures.

Peter, the oldest, always tried to protect his family and keep them together.

Peter tried to protect his family
in Narnia, too.
It was a lot of responsibility,
but as the oldest,
Peter knew it was his job.

The great Aslan saw how Peter took care
of his brother and sisters.
Aslan saw the bravery inside Peter.

He asked Peter to help him lead the creatures
of Narnia against the White Witch.
They worked together and freed Narnia.

The Pevensie family never dreamed
of the adventures they would have . . .

. . and the many creatures they would meet.

Or that they would later become
Kings and Queens of the magical place
called Narnia!

Peter the Magnificent
Susan the Gentle
Edmund the Just
Lucy the Valiant

Though they returned to their home eventually, Peter, Edmund, Susan and Lucy always kept Narnia in their hearts!